ACROSS THE AISLE

ACROSS THE AISLE

Why Bipartisanship Works for America

—ᵐ—

EDITED BY JILL LONG THOMPSON

INDIANA UNIVERSITY PRESS

This book is a publication of

Indiana University Press
Office of Scholarly Publishing
Herman B Wells Library 350
1320 East 10th Street
Bloomington, Indiana 47405 USA

iupress.org

Manufactured in the United States of America

First Printing 2024

Cataloging information is available from the Library of Congress.

978-0-253-07070-8 (hdbk)
978-0-253-07071-5 (pbk)
978-0-253-07072-2 (web PDF)

CONTENTS

PREFACE

Achieving Progress through Bipartisanship

THE HONORABLE MARCY KAPTUR,
OHIO DISTRICT 9

"LET US DEVELOPE THE RESOURCES of our land, call forth its powers, build up its institutions, promote all its great interests and see whether we also in our day and generation may not perform something worthy to be remembered."

This quotation by Daniel Webster—carved high above the Speaker's rostrum in the US House of Representatives—is a daily reminder of our solemn duty as sworn representatives of the American people.

Article I of the US Constitution created the legislative branch designating two coequal bodies—the House and the Senate, each being half of the Congress. It is to the Constitution that representatives, upon their swearing-in, pledge their allegiance. Serving in the military also requires it, as does serving in the US Senate, as president of our nation, as justices of the US Supreme Court, and as a high-ranking US government official. Other professions do not require such an oath.

None of us pledges fealty to any one person, potentate, ruler, band of rebels, tyrant, or sovereign. We pledge our service to the rule of law as spelled out in the US Constitution. Millions of our fellow citizens have fought and died in wars defending our liberty—pledging allegiance to the "rule of law"—over lawless mobs, would-be dictators, and selfish prognosticators, who care only for their selfish, narrow pursuits.

Governing well requires bipartisanship. It requires listening to people, articulating their interests, creating solutions to real problems, negotiating with colleagues on both sides of the aisle, all toward the mission of advancing American progress. It is tedious, hard work because we are a giant nation now approaching 350 million people with fifty states as well as the District of Columbia and five permanently inhabited territories.

As a very junior member of Congress, I was chief sponsor of legislation to build the World War II Memorial in our nation's capital, Washington, DC. When I arrived in the capital, I could not believe that such a tribute to this most unselfish generation had never been built. They bequeathed liberty to us. Thus, in 1987, I introduced the first legislation to build the memorial. It was dedicated in 2004.

The effort took seventeen years. Today, more than ninety-five million people have visited this memorial. I would venture to say not a single visitor is cognizant of how long it took, the many legislative hurdles we faced, and the financial challenges that confronted us. But fervent supporters in both political parties pulled together to achieve this lasting tribute to the twentieth century's greatest achievement—the victory of liberty over tyranny.

As one member quipped while the memorial was being built, "It took longer to build the memorial than fight the war."

That painstaking legislative experience stuck with me, in terms of understanding what it takes, and how hard one must work, to move legislation through Congress. While a deliberative process is to ensure we consider the needs of all who could be impacted by the laws we adopt, equally important are collaboration and compromise. By definition, democratically representative government requires we respect the interests and knowledge of everyone, even those with whom we disagree.

Let me illustrate further how essential determination is to achieving progress for our nation, one region and community at a time.

The decades-long, dogged, bipartisan, bicameral leadership of Congress's Great Lakes Task Force champions the enormous task of restoring Great Lakes freshwater quality. After nearly two decades, our pleas were embraced by the Biden administration. In 2022, President Biden became the first American president to travel to Lorain, Ohio, where he announced an additional $1 billion dollars to hasten clean-up of heavily polluted sites across the Great Lakes. Further, he signed bipartisan legislation passed by Congress that I led along with Congressman David Joyce as cochairs of the House task force to rebuild the Soo Lock, a vital transportation node critical to seaborne commerce across the entirety of the Great Lakes system. This project had been delayed for a quarter century.

Yes, there are many more towns and rivers across our great nation needing attention. But we are achieving progress, and know it is possible, with an engaged and enlightened citizenry. The essays in this book reflect what we can accomplish for the greater good when we work together in a bipartisan way to find solutions that address real challenges to America today and prepare us for the tomorrows to come. Onward Liberty!

MARCY KAPTUR *is a Democratic member of the US House of Representatives from Ohio.*

ACKNOWLEDGMENTS

WHAT A PLEASURE AND PRIVILEGE it has been to work with people and institutions I respect to produce this book on the importance of bipartisanship to democracy. I thank Gary Dunham and Indiana University Press for suggesting and supporting this book project and am honored by the trust you have placed in me.

The support of Steve Scully and the Bipartisan Policy Center, and Grayson Moore and the Association of Former Members of Congress is very appreciated. Their engagement and guidance have been critical to the number and quality of essays submitted for publication.

And I thank all those who wrote and submitted the essays: Marcy Kaptur, Tom Daschle, Trent Lott, Jason Altmire, Don Bonker, André Carson, Dan Glickman, John Harwood, Paul Helmke, Marjorie Hershey, Charlene Mac-Donald, Richard Painter, Allyson Schwartz, Olympia Snowe, Curt Weldon, and Todd Young. More significant than their contributions to the book are the contributions they make to strengthen our democracy. The leadership they provide every day in their respective roles is invaluable.

Finally, I thank my family for supporting me and my work on this project. Most significantly, I appreciate the support and encouragement my late husband, Don Thompson, always provided for every one of my professional and personal goals.

It is my hope that this book will lead to a better understanding of the role of bipartisanship in our democracy, and that will lead to a stronger America.

ACROSS THE AISLE

INTRODUCTION

America Is Facing a Crisis Point

TRENT LOTT AND TOM DASCHLE

AFTER PEARL HARBOR AND AMERICA'S entry into World War II, British Prime Minister Winston Churchill (quoting former Foreign Secretary Sir Edward Grey) mused that the United States was like "a gigantic boiler. Once the fire is lighted under it there is no limit to the power it can generate." And Grey was right: not just militarily, but across the board, our nation awoke to the challenge and rallied to surmount it.

In their book *That Used to Be Us: How America Fell Behind in the World It Invented and How We Can Come Back*, authors Thomas L. Friedman and Michael Mandelbaum look beyond our country's documents and laws to a set of practices that are unique to our nation: *those*, they argue, are what made the American Experiment a continued success. They call it the "American formula" and argue that the Constitution was "necessary but not sufficient" for our grand experiment to endure. The formula still works: we have to maintain faith in its durability and be strong enough to adapt it to changing times and circumstances.

Risk-taking is in America's DNA. It ran through the blood of those who came and built their lives here. Risk-taking has been handed down for generations, lodging itself in our collective consciousness. It continues to be a rich and healthy part of the American psyche and American idea. The worst bet anyone could ever make is against American ingenuity. Misconceptions abound that we as a country have lost this important trait, but they're unfounded, premature, and false.

Nevertheless, we need to ask ourselves: Are we still supporting the ideas that give Americans the opportunity to rise and prosper? If not, how do we

1

start doing that again? We cannot forget how we got here or what enables this great Republic to remain great—the blood, sacrifice, and hard work of others.

—⚏—

The term *melting pot*, a common description of the United States, is a misnomer, because Americans haven't really melted together. Our country is more like borscht: we keep our unique identities and cultures and toss them into the mix of American experience. That's part of the American formula. Our country welcomes opportunity and innovation because we remain open to the new—in people and in ideas.

America's strength has always come from its unique diversity—its willingness to not just permit but encourage competing viewpoints in order to strengthen the whole. Checks and balances, which the Founding Fathers embedded in our system of government, were meant to spur debate, challenge complacency, and drive progress. They have sustained our Republic for more than 225 years.

Now, however, we have to face a sad truth: *checks and balances have stopped working.* In fact, they have begun to work against us. Checks and balances were not designed to encourage the kind of inertia plaguing our current leaders in Washington, DC. Our Congress—and, by extension, America's government— is growing increasingly dysfunctional.

We—the authors of this introduction—are not just former lawmakers but also fathers and grandfathers, and we recognize how critical it is that we serve as stewards for the next generation of Americans. In some respects, we don't have the confidence that we're leaving them a better country.

We served in Congress a combined fifty-nine years, with more than sixteen as Senate majority and minority leaders, so we know of what we speak. The center can no longer hold under today's mindless and unprecedented partisanship; the state of our democracy is as bad as we've ever seen it.

The two of us led our parties during extremely partisan times—for example, President Clinton's 1999 impeachment vote, with the Senate split 50–50 between the parties on the obstruction-of-justice article—so we are not naive about how combative Washington can get. Nevertheless, though we have philosophical differences about the role of government, as well as divergent views on many important issues, we agree that it is time to sound the alarm.

—⚏—

We've traveled around the world and attended the inaugurations of other leaders, and our system stands out in a remarkable way: almost without exception, foreign leaders take an oath of office to the people. In America, leaders take an oath of office to support and defend the Constitution. They take an oath not to the masses but to an idea and a set of principles. That's magical.

The Constitution was not written to be a precise set of instructions; it was to serve as a blueprint for how the young Republic would sustain itself and grow for the future. The generation of Jefferson and Madison had enormous faith in generations to come, including ours—enough to trust our judgment. At the very least, they'd be confused by what has happened. More likely, they'd be devastated. Partisan rancor has overtaken reasoned debate so completely that today's generation wonders what Congress does all day. And we'd be hard-pressed to answer.

The two of us entered politics at different times, under different conditions, and from far different perspectives, but our respective stories help tell the larger story of this great nation. Our careers, battles, and accomplishments flow into the larger river of the American story.

Although we don't claim to have a panacea for all the problems, we know the ingredients needed to get us moving forward again. We know that communication within and between the parties—and the relationships that result—creates chemistry, an absolute necessity to the functioning of good government. Along with chemistry, we need compromise, leadership, courage, and vision.

—〰—

During the historic 50–50 Senate of 2001, the chamber was deadlocked numerically but not operationally.

As the leaders of our parties, we came together to formulate a historic power-sharing agreement, attracting the vitriol of some members of our respective caucuses in the process. Trent nearly received a vote of no confidence from the Republican caucus for even negotiating with Tom and the Democrats. But we managed to line up our colleagues behind us—through leadership, compromise, and a good dose of chemistry—and got to work conducting the country's business.

Believing in the need for direct communication amid the noise, we installed phones on our respective desks that each rang directly through to the other. The phones were practical, but they were also symbolic of the open line of communication we maintained while in our leadership positions. Considering what the country endured in 2001 alone, direct communication could not have been more necessary.

—〰—

Bipartisanship is not a tactic to be used only in times of crisis. Nor is it an ideal to be mocked. It is, instead, the life force that keeps our government running.

"The best way to persuade," former Secretary of State Dean Rusk once said, "is with your ears." Bipartisan negotiation, however, has run dry in today's Washington, DC. Without it, the government amounts to little more than voices shouting—with no one listening.

Today, leaders in Washington don't practice bipartisanship and the governing environment doesn't encourage it. Planes and telecommunication have made it feasible for lawmakers to work in Washington without living there, which leaves fewer opportunities to nourish the chemistry that encourages bipartisan cooperation. (In fact, elected officials who live in Washington, DC, are often attacked by their opponents as "Washington insiders" at election time.)

The media is a convenient filter through which both sides can launch partisan assaults against each other without having to face each other. Meanwhile, party primaries increasingly reward candidates of the extremes—because the most extreme elements of both parties tend to be the most active and engaged in primaries—chasing away moderate candidates and turning off middle-of-the-road voters through an increasing arms race of outside money and negative messages.

—∞—

But there is hope. And it begins with the strength that exists within this great nation and its people. It begins with each of us. The future is not preordained.

During our extensive congressional careers, we each drove hard to push divergent agendas—under presidents from opposing parties—but we recognized the need for bipartisan cooperation as well. We have dedicated our lives to serving our country, and we are deeply committed to its bright future. We sincerely believe that the tide can be turned. Nothing less than the country's future is at stake.

We have joined together for a common cause because we know that when we reconcile our opposing voices and come together, we create a force stronger than what we can do on our own. We can serve as a useful metaphor for the country. We've worked together, remained friends, and we share a vision for how we can get moving again.

Facing mounting challenges at home and abroad, the nation no longer has the luxury of petulance. We need to change course. America has the tools, the resilience, and the motivation to do so. The future is in our hands.

TRENT LOTT *(Republican-MS) is a Senior Fellow at the Bipartisan Policy Center and former Majority Leader of the United States Senate.*

TOM DASCHLE *(Democrat-SD) is a Co-Founder of the Bipartisan Policy Center and former Majority Leader of the United States Senate.*

PART I

BIPARTISANSHIP AND AMERICA

ONE

BIPARTISANSHIP AND A STRONGER DEMOCRACY IN AMERICAN HISTORY

JOHN HARWOOD

OPEN

On August 9, 1974, following two years of escalating scandal, Richard M. Nixon etched his ignominious place in history. He became the first American president to resign in disgrace.

The Watergate saga of law-breaking and cover-up only deepened the loathing that Democrats had felt for Nixon over decades. The Republican president reciprocated with enmity so fierce that, by his own accounting, it triggered his downfall.

"Always remember," he told aides assembled in the White House, "others may hate you, but those who hate you don't win unless you hate them. And then you destroy yourself."

That searing lament, expressed minutes before the nation's thirty-seventh chief executive headed toward exile in California, helps explain why so few associate that bitter political era with bipartisan comity.

An adolescent in the Washington, DC, suburbs then, I can recall that bitterness vividly today. But I also recall something else: I attended school with children of Nixon's aides, as well as those of his partisan adversaries.

My classmates included the kids of members of Congress from both parties, White House economic and national security aides, and even Nixon's 1972 Democratic opponent for reelection, Senator George McGovern of South Dakota. As an editor at the *Washington Post*, my father helped oversee coverage of Nixon's Watergate downward spiral.

Those personal details reflect something of national significance: the conditions for personal relationships that oil the gears of government, fostering the bipartisan cooperation that helps Washington serve Americans better.

Those relationships across party lines came more easily then. They mattered. In fact, they were among many reasons that Nixon's foreshortened presidency—vitriol notwithstanding—produced significant bipartisan achievements together with a Democratic-controlled Congress.

The list runs surprisingly long.

In 1969, the Tax Reform Act established the "alternative minimum tax" to ensure that wealthy Americans couldn't avoid federal levies altogether.

In 1970, the Clean Air Act expanded the federal government's role in limiting pollution. To enforce it, Nixon created the Environmental Protection Agency.

In 1972, Nixon signed into law new benefit payments for the disabled and poor elderly through the Social Security system.

That same year, he signed Title IX barring discrimination on the basis of sex at schools receiving federal aid. The result was creation of robust athletic programs for girls that Americans have since come to take for granted.

In 1973, he signed the Endangered Species Act protecting the animal world against the impact of human encroachment.

Cooperation across party lines produced all those Nixon administration achievements. In one of history's poignant ironies, it also forced his political demise.

In 1974, when Democrats on the House Judiciary Committee passed articles of impeachment, seven of Nixon's fellow Republicans joined them in voting yes. (One of them, first-term Rep. William Cohen of Maine, would later serve as secretary of defense in the Democratic administration of President Bill Clinton.)

While Nixon still mulled trying to hang on, three leading members of Congress went to the Oval Office on August 7, 1974, to advise him. They were the House and Senate Republican leaders, John J. Rhodes of Arizona and Hugh Scott of Pennsylvania, and the 1964 Republican presidential nominee, Sen. Barry M. Goldwater of Arizona. They told their party's president that his support had collapsed.

The next day, Nixon told the nation in a televised address that he would resign. The day after that, he lifted off on Marine One from the South Lawn of the White House for a final time.

—⁂—

PART ONE

As the means of apportioning society's burdens and benefits, government in a democracy is inescapably contentious. At America's dawning, James Madison in the Federalist Papers No. 10 called factional conflict "sown in the nature of man." Political parties, the Founding Fathers worried, would make it worse.

Writing as "Publius," Madison explained:

> A zeal for different opinions concerning religion, concerning government, and many other points, as well of speculation as of practice; an attachment to different leaders ambitiously contending for pre-eminence and power; or to persons of other descriptions whose fortunes have been interesting to the human passions have, in turn, divided mankind into parties, inflamed them with mutual animosities, and rendered them much more disposed to vex and oppress each other than to co-operate for their common good.
>
> So strong is this propensity of mankind to fall into mutual animosity, that where no substantial occasion presents itself, the most frivolous and fanciful distinctions have been sufficient to kindle their unfriendly passions and excite their most violent conflicts.

The constitutional system that Madison and his colleagues in Philadelphia devised in 1787 made no provision for parties. Fearing tyranny, they did create a system of "checks and balances" to limit the powers of each of the three branches of government—executive, legislative, and judicial. Those constraints in practice mediated conflict between the rival parties that inexorably became permanent features of the new nation's political landscape.

The balance proved stable enough until an irreconcilable divide over slavery ignited the "most violent conflicts" the Founders had feared. The Civil War that set North against South also pitted the new antislavery Republican Party of Abraham Lincoln and the Democratic Party that spoke for the Confederacy.

The bloody war left the union intact. However, the political alignments it burned into the American psyche would underpin partisan competition for generations afterward.

Over time, those "mutual animosities" between Republicans and Democrats have waxed and waned in their intensity. Cross-party cooperation comes more easily in some historical eras than others.

The era I grew up in during the second half of the twentieth century proved more accommodating than most. Among multiple reasons, most important was the heterogeneous composition of both dominant parties.

Long after Robert E. Lee surrendered to Ulysses S. Grant at Appomattox, Democrats relied on the segregated "Solid South" in presidential elections. But by the 1950s their national majority coalition had grown to embrace Northern intellectuals, blue-collar immigrants from Europe, and Black people drawn by Franklin D. Roosevelt's New Deal response to the Great Depression. Having produced the first Catholic nominated for the presidency—Al Smith of New York, in 1928—Democrats then produced the first Catholic to win it, John F. Kennedy of Massachusetts, in 1960.

That variegated stew created awkward alliances. The 1952 Democratic ticket, for instance, paired presidential nominee Adlai Stevenson and running-mate John Sparkman. The former was an erudite Illinois governor running on a pro-civil rights platform, the latter an Alabama senator staunchly opposed to racial integration.

The party of Lincoln had also diversified. It linked pious Main Street conservatives like Senator Robert Taft of Ohio, a former president's son known as "Mr. Republican," with more affluent pro-business liberals like Senator Prescott Bush of Connecticut, father and grandfather to two future presidents. The GOP had also gained an edge in Nixon's California and other western states.

The disparate interests and ideologies contained within each party made the boundary between them permeable. So did the practical considerations of everyday political life.

Today, with air travel cheap and ubiquitous, members of Congress generally drop into Washington, DC, mid-week while keeping their families and residences back in their home states. But back then, they largely lived in Washington as neighbors. That's why I attended school with so many lawmakers' children.

Moreover, those political neighbors had just emerged from a shared experience with immense unifying power. The service and sacrifice World War II required cut across every segment of society—rich and poor, Black and White, immigrant and native-born. It produced a core layer of mutual understanding that later generations would struggle to grasp.

Indeed, an emerging sense of common purpose in the run-up to war contributed to its successful outcome. Even in the heat of the 1940 presidential campaign, Republican nominee Wendell Willkie lowered the partisan temperature enough to smooth FDR's path toward helping Great Britain withstand Germany's onslaught. That helped the Allies ultimately defeat the Axis powers.

"The good side of the American character was in the ascendancy," wrote Charles Peters in *Five Days in Philadelphia*, a historical account of the 1940 Republican Party convention. "Simply put, Roosevelt couldn't have done it without Willkie."

In victory, the Army's Supreme Allied Commander in Europe personified the fluidity of political attachments. General Dwight "Ike" D. Eisenhower emerged from the conflict as a hero without partisan identification. Democrats and Republicans each courted him to run for president under their banner.

In 1952, Ike won as a Republican. But he governed in a practical style. Instead of demolishing achievements of Democratic predecessors, he sought to build on them.

The new president explained his temperate approach in a private letter to his brother. It acknowledged the durability of Roosevelt's social reforms and rejected demands from a "stupid ... splinter group" of GOP extremists to roll them back.

"The federal government cannot avoid or escape responsibilities which the mass of the people firmly believe should be undertaken by it," Eisenhower wrote his brother Edgar. "This is what I mean by my constant insistence upon 'moderation' in government. Should any political party attempt to abolish Social Security, unemployment insurance, and eliminate labor laws and farm programs, you would not hear of that party again in our political history."

At the outset of Eisenhower's term, the Chief Justice of the US Supreme Court died suddenly of a heart attack. The chief justice, Fred Vinson, was a Democrat who had been appointed by President Harry Truman.

To replace him, Eisenhower nominated a Republican, Governor Earl Warren of California. A Republican-controlled Senate confirmed him.

But because partisanship proved less divisive then, the shift did not fracture the court on its most momentous work. The following year, in the case of *Brown vs. Board of Education*, Warren joined his eight Democratic-appointed fellow justices in the unanimous decision that ended legal segregation in American public schools.

Three years later, Ike safeguarded that landmark civil rights achievement by sending one thousand federal troops to Arkansas to protect Black schoolchildren integrating Central High School in Little Rock. He signed the Civil Rights Act of 1957 that passed Congress with bipartisan support.

National security initiatives commanded broad consensus. In Eisenhower's first term, a Democratic-controlled Congress created the interstate highway system by acclamation in the House and 89–1 in the Senate. In his second term, jolted by the Soviet Union's launch of Sputnik, the first satellite to orbit Earth, Congress united with the White House to create the National Aeronautics and Space Administration.

Under Eisenhower's Democratic successors, bipartisan accomplishments continued across social, economic and defense fronts. In 1963, the Senate approved President Kennedy's Nuclear Test Ban Treaty on an 80–19 vote. After

Kennedy's assassination, large majorities of Democrats and Republicans passed his tax cut plan at the behest of successor Lyndon B. Johnson.

Johnson's Great Society agenda won critically-needed Republican support for creating the Medicare and Medicaid health care programs for the aged and poor, which decades later would spark intense partisan fights. Senate Republican leader Everett Dirksen of Illinois helped shepherd passage of the Civil Rights Act of 1964 and the Voting Rights Act of 1965.

Dirksen's assistance allowed LBJ to overcome fierce intraparty opposition from Southern Democrats. Among those opponents: Senator John Sparkman of Alabama, the Democratic vice-presidential nominee from a decade earlier.

—⚊—

PART TWO

Those achievements hardly signaled an absence of political disputes. As always, liberals and conservatives fought over the size and role of government, the contours of the federal budget, the direction of national security policy, and the pace of social change.

But neither those disagreements nor the quarrels between Democrats and Republicans determined the outcome of every political debate. Ideological conflict and partisan conflict were different things. And because they were different, politicians did not divide neatly into warring tribes.

Those blurry cross-cutting alignments made bipartisan compromise easier. But they didn't last.

Over decades, the political legacy of the Civil War faded. Partisan identification shifted.

Increasingly, the lines separating liberals from conservatives and Democrats from Republicans came to track the same path. The double-layered barrier that produced became harder and harder to cross.

Paradoxically, the bipartisan civil rights triumphs of the 1960s dramatically accelerated that process. After LBJ and other national Democratic leaders broke with the South on segregation, white Southern conservatives broke with them.

Eventually nearly all white Southern conservatives flocked to the GOP, whose 1964 presidential candidate Barry Goldwater opposed Johnson on civil rights. Blacks and liberal Republicans migrated in reverse. Realignment happened first at the presidential level, later in state and local contests where familiar, long-standing allegiances proved stickier.

The result was two parties with ever more homogeneous views—and ever greater distance from each other.

The political system retained some bipartisan muscle memory. Crossing the reinforcing barriers of partisanship and ideology grew harder, but not impossible.

Ronald Reagan's bold-color conservatism accelerated realignment. Yet during his presidency, Republicans and Democrats joined hands to shore up the finances of Social Security, reform the tax system, and overhaul immigration laws.

Reagan's Republican successor, George H. W. Bush, compromised with a Democratic Congress to reduce the federal budget deficit, update the Clean Air Act to reduce acid rain, and enact historic protections for disabled Americans. The Democrat who followed Bush, Bill Clinton, worked with Republican lawmakers to expand trade, deregulate the financial system, and balance the federal budget—even as they impeached him over the Monica Lewinsky scandal.

Following the bitterly contested 2000 presidential election, George W. Bush cooperated with Democrats to revamp federal education policy and add prescription drug benefits to Medicare. After the unprecedented shock of the 9/11 attacks, House Democratic Leader Richard Gephardt and future presidential nominees John Kerry and Hillary Clinton backed his successful request for authorization of war with Iraq.

That unity faded. The Iraq War went south and became a new engine for polarization. So did the subsequent "Wall Street Bailout," though it kept the financial crisis of 2007–2008 from turning into a second Great Depression.

Eisenhower-style acceptance of the governing status quo became a memory. A new generation of Republicans and Democrats aimed to reverse the opposing tribe's achievements as soon as they got the chance. That dramatically raised the stakes of electoral competition.

The all-or-nothing zeitgeist spurred more ambitious state-level attempts to gerrymander election districts to help whichever party controlled a state's legislature. Party leaders in Washington sought lockstep discipline, with rebels facing the risk of intraparty primary challenges.

Breaking old taboos, congressional leaders visited the home states of partisan counterparts to campaign against them. Committee chairs lost autonomy in shaping legislation in their areas of expertise while gaining new responsibility for helping their own party's candidates raise campaign funds.

The old personal solvents didn't disappear altogether.

In 2004, Republican Representative Jim McCrery of Louisiana, preparing to become chairman of the tax-writing Ways and Means Committee, moved his family from Baton Rouge to the Washington, DC, suburbs to diminish the constant travel that would impinge on the new job. Among his new neighbors there: Democratic Representative Chet Edwards of Texas.

The two lawmakers had served together in Congress for ten years but remained mostly strangers. Then their sons joined the same Boy Scout troop. They began to view one another other differently. The Louisianan's attempts to defeat the Texan in previous elections no longer felt right.

"When you get to know somebody as a neighbor, or your kids play together on the soccer team, it's harder for you to go on the floor and call them names," McCrery reflected later (John Harwood and Gerald F. Seib, *Pennsylvania Avenue: Profiles in Backroom Power*, Random House, 2008). "I told the leadership, I'm not contributing to Chet's opponent this time."

As it happened, Republicans lost their House and Senate majorities in 2006. McCrery never attained his ambition for the chairmanship.

Yet such examples had become exceptions proving the rule.

During that same election season, a young Democratic representative from Florida named Debbie Wasserman-Schultz neared the finish line for a top priority: legislation to enhance the safety of swimming pools. In a GOP-controlled Congress, she found a prominent Republican ally in Senator George Allen of Virginia.

Senate Democratic leaders blocked her effort for a nakedly partisan reason. The election would determine control of the Senate and her partner's seat was a top campaign target.

Democrats "didn't want to give Allen a victory before the election," she explained later (Harwood and Seib, *Pennsylvania Avenue*).

The political trajectory of Barack Obama illustrated the challenge of bipartisanship. In 2004, as an obscure Illinois state senator, Obama burst onto the national scene with an ode to unity. Obama told the Democratic National Convention in Boston:

> There are those who are preparing to divide us—the spin masters and negative ad peddlers who embrace the politics of anything goes. Well, I say to them tonight, there's not a liberal America and a conservative America—there's the United States of America.
>
> There's not a black America and white America and Latino America and Asian America—there's the United States of America. The pundits like to slice and dice our country into red states and blue states, red states for Republicans, blue states for Democrats. But I've got news for them too. We worship an awesome God in the blue states, and we don't like federal

agents poking around our libraries in the red states. We coach Little League in the blue states, and have gay friends in the red states.

There are patriots who opposed the war in Iraq, and patriots who supported it. We are one people, all of us pledging allegiance to the Stars and Stripes, all of us defending the United States of America.

Obama won the presidency four years later. But the nation he governed grew more divided along partisan lines, not less.

Republicans threw up a wall of resistance to the new president's stimulus plans to revive an economy in free fall. They did the same on his health care plan, even though Obama had modeled it on an old conservative proposal that GOP Governor Mitt Romney had implemented in Massachusetts.

As America's first African American president, Obama triggered visceral opposition that overpowered details of policy. He personified the twenty-first century social and cultural changes that left millions of conservative white Republicans feeling aggrieved, frightened, and angry.

The resulting backlash spurred the rise of Donald Trump and his pledge to roll back change and "Make America Great Again." Trump then provoked an even more ferocious backlash, leading to his defeat for reelection in November 2020.

On January 6, 2021, Trump allies staged a violent insurrection at the US Capitol. Their attempt to stop the peaceful transfer of power, which has made American democracy a model for the world, became the ultimate symbol of a polarized polity.

Joe Biden entered the White House two weeks later against that smoldering backdrop. An avuncular seventy-eight-year-old, he brought five decades of experience as senator and vice president spanning the Republican and Democratic configurations before and after realignment.

Biden disproved predictions that his efforts at bipartisan consensus would go nowhere. He drew enough Republican support to enact the major infrastructure investments that had eluded Obama and Trump. He repeated that formula on a massive program to boost domestic production of semiconductors, capitalizing on broadly shared angst about the rise of China. Even on the supremely fractious issue of gun safety, he goaded Congress to enact modest bipartisan steps in response to mass shootings.

Yet signs of comity had vanished by the time Biden announced his reelection bid in early 2023. The first major initiative of the new House Republican majority elected in 2022 was investigating members of Biden's family. The second was threatening a catastrophic default on the government's obligations by resisting an increase in the federal debt limit. (Biden and congressional Republicans ultimately struck a bipartisan compromise to defuse the threat.)

Responsibility for the toxic climate extends far beyond Republican and Democratic politicians. The news media has become its own driver of discord.

In the hopeful decades after World War II, news organizations buttressed the country's cohesion. A rising generation of journalists discarded the open partisanship of their forebears and elevated an ethic of objectivity. Mass media with vast reach imparted common pictures of America and its challenges through national television and radio networks, major magazines, and local newspapers.

Now the "mass" has melted. The digital revolution of the late twentieth century shattered the industry's business model.

Audiences for news, on-air and in print, fragmented.

Journalistic employment shrank. The atomized media that resulted was left to cultivate smaller, niche customer bases by appealing to specific points of view.

Social media firms have exacerbated conflict with algorithms that send users content designed to outrage them. Exploiting the vulnerability of an open society, foreign adversaries have piled on to weaken America by amplifying division.

If Fox News and MSNBC swapped channel numbers for a day, viewers would not recognize the worlds they'd see. That's no accident; holding dwindling viewerships requires repeated provocation.

For Fox News, the distortions imposed by business strategy became unmistakable in a voting machine company's defamation lawsuit over false allegations of 2020 election fraud. Internal communications disclosed in the case showed that leading network figures cared more about comforting Fox's audience than providing accurate information.

—m—

PART THREE

The portrait of Washington, DC, engulfed in partisan warfare, however, shows only part of how government actually works. Senate Majority Leader Charles Schumer of New York likens the reality to that of an iceberg: a smaller sphere of conflict visible above the ocean's surface, a larger block of cooperation concealed underneath.

That concealment can be a critical ingredient for compromise. Media attention mobilizes rival armies of activists, interest groups, financial supporters, and campaign strategists. The more obscure an issue, the easier to preserve space for negotiation.

"When we do things together, it almost never makes any news," Senate Republican Leader Mitch McConnell once observed (*Roll Call*, Nov. 7, 2018) of his relationship with House Speaker Nancy Pelosi. "There are plenty of things we work together on, and I always have to tell constituents, who think we all hate each other, that the Senate's a pretty collegial place."

By definition, the bipartisan boost provided by obscurity applies mainly to incremental advances; transformative change can't escape the spotlight. Many of those incremental advances occur in the annual congressional appropriations process.

On appropriations committees, Republican and Democratic colleagues spend years quietly pursuing shared priorities through the tedious labor of funding government programs. That's where McConnell and Pelosi first developed their working relationship.

"Members of the Appropriations Committee work closely together to produce bills in a bipartisan way," explained Pelosi (Pelosi press release, July 30, 2015). As her colleague Nita Lowey of New York, who rose to chair the House spending panel, once boasted: "We're adults" (*Roll Call*, May 2, 2019).

One of those adults was Senator Lamar Alexander of Tennessee. As the parties drifted further apart nationally during the 1980s, Alexander had built a moderate record as his state's Republican governor with a special focus on economic development.

Alexander later served as Education Secretary for President George H. W. Bush. He twice sought his party's presidential nomination before winning a Senate seat in 2002.

With his penchant for serious political work, Alexander accumulated seniority on the Appropriations and Health committees while rising to the third-ranking post in the Senate's Republican leadership. But he bumped into conflict between his legislative goals and party leadership.

So in 2011, Alexander stunned colleagues by quitting his leadership job to pursue bipartisan problem-solving.

"Stepping down from leadership will liberate me to spend more time working for results on the issues I care most about," Alexander explained at the time in a letter to colleagues (Sept. 20, 2011). "I want to do more to make the Senate a more effective institution so that it can deal better with serious issues.

"There are different ways to provide leadership within the Senate. After nine years here, this is how I believe I can now make my greatest contribution."

The move helped shield Alexander from partisan clamor. As one of "The Cardinals" chairing powerful appropriations subcommittees—specifically the panel handling labor, health, and education spending—he felt free to shrug off inflammatory proposals from his own party's president.

"We've increased spending for biomedical research, for the National Institutes of Health, more than any other Congress in many, many years," Alexander remarked in 2017 (Nov. 20, 2017, interview with the author). "Now, the (Trump) budget didn't. But we don't pay attention to presidents' budgets, whether they're President Trump or President Obama."

That same year, Alexander went to work on the era's biggest partisan flashpoint. The Affordable Care Act (ACA), also called Obamacare, had been enacted with only Democratic votes. The Tennessee Republican found a Democratic partner to help him.

Patty Murray of Washington won her Senate seat a decade before Alexander did. Casting herself as a "mom in tennis shoes," she joined a cadre of female Democrats who triumphed in 1992 in what was dubbed "The Year of the Woman."

Like Alexander, Murray served on the Appropriations and Health committees while rising within her party's leadership. Like Alexander, she preferred low-key work over partisan flame throwing. In congressional parlance, each was a workhorse rather a show horse.

They disagreed fundamentally on Obamacare, voting in opposite directions for its creation in 2010 and its repeal in 2017. Once repeal failed, however, Alexander and Murray accepted shared responsibility for improving it.

"It is clearer than ever that the path to continue making health care work better for patients and families isn't through partisanship or back room deals," Murray said in announcing their partnership (Murray press release, Aug. 22, 2017). "It is through working together across the aisle, transparency and coming together to find common ground where we can."

It was an obvious priority for Murray; fellow Democrats had spent decades pursuing expanded access to affordable care. Alexander found the needs of his red state's country music industry as a reason to move beyond rigid ideological opposition.

"(Political) rewards today are for people who do stand up, and stand on their principles, and don't work together to get a result," Alexander lamented (Nov. 20, 2017, interview with the author). "But I think the satisfaction of public service is getting a result, is lowering the songwriter's health care premium."

Their initial efforts highlighted a specific category of ACA subsidies that helped financially squeezed customers with out-of-pocket costs. Amid a legal challenge from House Republicans, the Trump administration announced it would no longer pay the subsidies. That decision triggered a complex chain of consequences that only serious legislators like Murray and Alexander were inclined to deal with.

The Congressional Budget Office estimated that would increase premiums for the most popular ACA plans by 20 percent. That's because insurance companies, under an ACA requirement to keep out-of-pocket costs lower, would raise premiums to cover the lost subsidies. And those higher premiums, in turn, would cost the government money by triggering a different category of subsidies for a larger group of beneficiaries.

So Alexander and Murray negotiated a remedy that met objectives of both parties. It would have pleased Democrats by restoring the subsidies and gratified Republicans by granting states more flexibility under Obamacare regulations.

Their compromise attracted twenty-four Senate cosponsors—a dozen from each party. One of them, Senator Susan Collins of Maine, made it such a high priority that she conditioned her vote for Trump's tax-cut bill on McConnell's pledge to support the Alexander-Murray deal later (Collins press release, Dec. 1, 2017).

McConnell's pledge proved unavailing. The deal continued to languish when the 116th Congress expired in January 2019. But the Senate partners kept trying in the 117th Congress.

They resumed work with a new proposal that tackled an additional priority: the mammoth bills that often surprised patients after they received hospital care. The problem typically stemmed from episodes of care in which either a doctor or hospital was outside their insurance plan's lower-cost "network" of providers.

Alexander and Murray proposed an "in-network guarantee." It required that if a hospital was in the network of a patient's insurance plan, all doctors treating patients there could only bill the patient at in-network rates. To settle disputes between insurance plans and providers, they proposed independent arbitration using standard benchmarks for charges.

"These are common sense steps we can take, and every single one of them has the objective of reducing the health care costs that you pay for out of your own pocket," Alexander explained.

Health care providers, and the private equity firms that owned many of their practices, hated the idea. They fought the compromise with lobbyists and millions of dollars of television ads.

As 2019 turned into 2020, the coronavirus crisis shoved other priorities aside. Democratic Representative Richard Neal of Massachusetts, chair of the powerful House Ways and Means Committee, suggested once again deferring action on an Alexander-Murray proposal until a subsequent Congress.

That couldn't work for Alexander. The eighty-year-old Tennessean had declined to seek reelection and was retiring at year end. So he and Murray didn't give up.

Opponents weakened, but did not eviscerate, their proposal. It required more transparency in billing. Under its rules for arbitration between health providers and insurance companies, mediators couldn't use the lower rates paid by Medicare as a benchmark. But nor could they use the sky-high rates providers often sent other patients.

After years of political warfare over Obamacare, "the idea that there was an effort at bipartisan progress was pretty remarkable," said Larry Levitt, executive vice president for health policy at the Kaiser Family Foundation. "There was a bipartisan compromise that truly helped patients."

As is typical on Capitol Hill, the merits of their compromise hardly assured that the House and Senate would both approve it. As every Congress nears its end, the funnel through which legislation must pass grows ever narrower.

Fittingly, Alexander and Murray found their opening with fellow Senate appropriators. The two congenial octogenarians atop the process—chairman Richard Shelby, Republican of Alabama, and ranking Democrat Patrick Leahy of Vermont—were negotiating a year-end, $1.4-trillion government spending bill.

What dominated public and press attention was the bill's $900 billion in relief for households and businesses staggered by the coronavirus pandemic. That money allowed for checks of $600 apiece for every adult and child in most households.

The Alexander-Murray compromise on restoring the lost Obamacare subsidies had fallen by the wayside again. But not their deal on surprise medical bills; it survived, winning a place in the final spending bill.

Four days before Christmas, the bill passed both the Republican-controlled House and Democrat-controlled Senate by overwhelming margins. After years of toil, part of the Alexander-Murray team's handiwork was headed to the White House for President Trump's signature.

But the story still wasn't over.

Through a flurry of legal challenges, Trump continued to contest his November loss to Biden. Sounding a populist trumpet, he shocked lawmakers by blasting the bill as "a disgrace." Instead of $600 checks, he declared, Congress should deliver $2,000 checks.

Rattled lawmakers worried that the embattled chief executive might throw everything into chaos with a veto. Under the brightest of klieg lights, legislation that had enjoyed broad support suddenly acquired a partisan tinge.

Senate Leader McConnell opposed the idea of larger relief checks. House Speaker Pelosi embraced it. So did Democratic candidates in two Georgia run-off elections that, within two weeks, would decide control of the Senate.

Then, almost as suddenly as it had arisen, the threat passed. Two days after Christmas, Trump reluctantly signed the bill.

"As president of the United States, it is my responsibility to protect the people of our country from economic devastation and hardship that was caused by the China virus," he said (White House press release, Dec. 27, 2020).

Consider the irony: the last major legislative act of the most divisive president in modern history made a bipartisan improvement of the most divisive government program in a generation. It was tucked inside a bipartisan spending bill.

JOHN HARWOOD *is a veteran Washington, DC, correspondent.*

TWO

—ϖ—

REFLECTIONS ON BIPARTISANSHIP

TODD YOUNG

ON THE EVENING OF NOVEMBER 11, 1940, Wendell Willkie addressed Americans over the radio. Days before, the Hoosier businessman had lost his bid for the presidency to Franklin D. Roosevelt. The incumbent won 60 percent of the vote earning an unprecedented third term in the White House.

Americans went to the polls that autumn with war spreading on the other side of the Atlantic Ocean and the fate of democracy in Europe very much in doubt. The stakes at the ballot were high. Close to fifty million Americans—the highest number ever at that point—voted in the election. It had been a bitter and divisive one.

Willkie was an often harsh critic of Roosevelt's New Deal. The former executive and corporate lawyer viewed some of its initiatives as encroachments by the federal government into American industry. But when it came to events abroad, Willkie struck a different note. "We here are not Republicans alone, but Americans," he reminded the Republican convention the previous summer.

During the campaign Willkie had agreed, at Roosevelt's request, not to make a political issue out of the president's controversial plan to send destroyer ships to Britain, in an effort to solidify Europe's remaining free nation in its fight against Germany. In the thick of the 1940 election, Willkie warned voters that Roosevelt would send America's sons to war, while he would keep them home. Still, he endorsed the president's peacetime draft. After the election Willkie supported the Lend-Lease Act, another Roosevelt program providing much needed aid to Winston Churchill and cash-strapped Britain in its desperate fight against the Nazis.

Willkie's statesmanship afforded Roosevelt the opportunity to fortify America's allies, build its "Arsenal of Democracy," and eventually save Western civilization. And he did this at a cost, angering the isolationist wing of his own party. When he sought the Republican presidential nomination again in 1944, Willkie was an also-ran.

In his 1940 postelection address to the nation, Willkie waived away any bitterness he felt over the election and urged his followers to do the same. While he was no doubt disappointed by defeat, Willkie was also worried about the future of his country, even if he would not be its president. And indeed, he pledged his support for Roosevelt—"He is my president"—but also, when their objectives diverged, he promised to provide faithful opposition and thoughtful criticism.

"National unity," he cautioned, "can only be achieved by recognizing and giving serious weight to the viewpoint of the opposition."

Willkie's warning was right then and still relevant today.

In the early decades of the twenty-first century, America is once again facing significant national security challenges. Not in the form of a world war but in a global power competition with China. At its heart is a race to develop the technologies that will ensure economic and military superiority. But it is also an ideological contest that will determine whether America's faith in liberty and dedication to human rights or China's disregard for both will govern the future and define the decades to come.

The truth is that the Chinese Communist Party (CCP) has a head start in this race and America is in danger of falling further behind. The CCP has invested $14 trillion in the frontier technologies that will shape our modern economy and decide winners of future wars—quantum computing, robotics, and artificial intelligence (AI). It has also made advances in hypersonic technology, which allows missiles carrying nuclear projectiles to travel at five times the speed of sound while evading our current defense systems. And while China accounted for less than 4 percent of microchip production half a decade ago, it is now on pace to control roughly 20 percent of the market in 2024.

When Chinese President Xi Jinping told an audience that "time and momentum are on our side," he was not entirely incorrect. How then does America make up for lost time and reverse China's momentum?

It will take a collective effort across government, industry, and academia to outcompete and out-innovate Beijing. It will require an updated Arsenal of Democracy. Building it, though, is complicated by the fact that our contest with China coincides with a period of intense polarization at home.

According to the Pew Research Center, rising numbers of both Democrats and Republicans view the opposing party not as citizens with differing beliefs who want what's best for the country but rather as a threat to its well-being.[1] If we view those who disagree with us politically as enemies, why would we seek to find common ground with them?

This attitude reverberates through our politics. As the nation becomes more tribal, as entire regions become monolithically Democratic or Republican, there is little incentive for lawmakers to collaborate with colleagues outside of their party. Indeed, doing so in deeply blue or red states or districts, where elected officials face the toughest challenges not from the other party but from within their own, risks that your intentions will be misrepresented and used against you come primary season.

There are a number of complicated factors driving this discord. Some are inevitable byproducts of larger, positive changes. The information age has ushered in a Fourth Industrial Revolution, changing the way we work and live. The democratization of media has created a welcome proliferation of news outlets, but also has resulted in a self-sorting of news consumption where we read coverage that confirms our own biases and pulls us further from those who do not share them.

Automation is creating efficiencies in our economy, but also is displacing workers, creating gaps between rural and urban areas, and leaving many Americans and their communities out of a rapidly evolving twenty-first century economy. Since 2000, 94 percent of the nation's job growth has been in urban areas. Just thirty-one counties out of more than three thousand nationwide account for a third of the nation's gross domestic product. And only five cities—Boston, San Diego, San Francisco, San Jose, and Seattle—enjoyed more than 90 percent of the job growth in advanced sectors such as tech, computer manufacturing, biotech, and telecom between 2005 and 2017. This disparity of opportunity has led to a gap between our citizens that is reflected in our current political divisions.

And make no mistake, China is wagering that these divisions are too great and our political system too dysfunctional to meet its challenge to our global leadership. The Chinese government even sponsors online disinformation campaigns designed to further divide Americans.

That is the bad news. Here is the good: by retrofitting America's economy, providing more pathways for our citizens to participate in it at all levels, we can at once address the inequality of opportunity in part responsible for our increasingly toxic politics and create the technologies necessary to best the CCP and win the twenty-first century. But it will take a conciliatory spirit—among our leaders, among our people—and a recognition that whatever the future holds for America, it holds for us all, regardless of politics.

Should the Chinese, or some other nation, develop the decryption technologies to unlock America's most closely guarded secrets or the autonomous weapons systems that give our military the ability to disable America's nuclear submarines, the safety of all Americans, no matter their political persuasion, will be endangered. In, God forbid, another war, our would-be enemies would not discriminate along party lines.

Should the CCP dominate the world's production of semiconductors, the tiny chips that bring life to our cellphones, cars, appliances, and almost anything with a motor or a plug, including our military platforms, our supply chain would be tied in a knot. Factory floors across the country would sit idle. Farmers would be unable to get their combines fixed or access the GPS technology used to determine yields. America's economy would grind to a halt and Democrats and Republicans alike would suffer.

And here is where Wendell Willkie's voice, beaming over the radio, speaks to us once again. Politics are important. But the endurance of our republic is more important. Willkie's example shows us that we can prioritize the latter over the former. It reminds us that even amid our most impassioned arguments, we can step back and see shared interests so much greater than our disagreements and resolve to work together to advance those interests.

Doing so, it is important to note, should not require the abandonment of principles. It does not mean we can expect our politics to cease revolving around parties. That would not only be impractical, it would be unwise. Political parties imperfectly but effectively give expression to our citizens' demands—the essential ingredient in a representative democracy such as ours. And that our two major parties are often in conflict regarding policy is not unhealthy: the vigorous debate it produces can be beneficial for the country, both in arriving at workable ideas and also encouraging our leaders to move away from the extreme edges of their parties and meet on common ground in between.

And bipartisanship is certainly no guarantee of success. Our history is full of unsuccessful laws supported by both Democrats and Republicans, or their predecessors. The Fugitive Slave Act hastened the Civil War. The Smoot-Hawley Tariff Act accelerated the Great Depression. These laws are certainly not viewed any more favorably by history because they had some degree of bipartisan support.

As much as addressing our greatest national challenges requires bipartisanship, it really calls for a revival of the virtues that make it even possible in the first place. Empathy for life experiences other than our own. Forbearance for and a willingness to hear out opinions and expressions we disagree with. The humility to concede the possibility that we are capable of mistakes as well as the strength to admit when we make them. And the basic civility to treat those who we disagree with not as enemies, but as fellow patriots with a different means of achieving a common goal: helping this country and its people flourish.

Starting from there, we can work through differences, identify commonalities, build a reservoir of trust, and tackle America's most pressing challenges together.

Sound overly idealistic? I do not believe it is.

Several years ago, I struck up a conversation with Senator Chuck Schumer in the Senate gym. Schumer is a liberal New Yorker. I am a conservative Hoosier. On paper, we don't agree on much. But we were both concerned that our nation was falling behind in the technological race with China. What began that morning ultimately resulted in the CHIPS and Science Act (CHIPS stands for Creating Helpful Incentives to Produce Semiconductors).

The bill went through numerous iterations and revisions during the three years between that initial conversation and the bill's enactment in 2022. The legislation President Joe Biden signed into law was the result of years of collaboration, disagreement, and compromise with one goal in mind: giving the American people the means to outcompete and out-innovate the CCP and win the current global power competition.

The CHIPS and Science Act provided $52.7 billion to jumpstart semiconductor production here in the United States, putting America on the offensive against China. No wonder the CCP actively lobbied against the law. It knew the law was bad for China and good for the United States.

The CHIPS and Science Act is both a national security and economic development investment in our people and communities. Much of the funding goes toward ensuring that more Americans have the requisite skills to work in the industries of the future. That of course includes semiconductors, but also includes biotechnology, AI, and advanced manufacturing.

A thriving domestic microchip industry will prevent future supply chain stoppages and protect our military readiness. And what benefits our economic security also benefits the industrial Midwest, where we pride ourselves on making things—including microchips.

A corridor of the semiconductor industry will run through the American heartland, benefiting people not just in Indiana but all over the Midwest. The regional "Tech Hubs" funded by the act will launch innovative companies, help revive American manufacturing, and lay the foundation for new jobs to jumpstart our local communities.

The law enhances our ability to research and develop and ultimately commercialize the trailblazing technology essential to our national power. It is also creating economic opportunity for many Americans who have been overlooked in recent decades. And this will not only give us a competitive edge, but I believe address the disparity of opportunities that is driving part of our national discord.

The process that led to passage of the CHIPS and Science Act involved considerable negotiation and debate, a great deal of give and take, and no small amount of frustration for and patience from Democrats and Republicans alike. In the end, though, we took a significant step in outpacing China and ensuring more Americans are connected to the workforce of the future.

There are more steps to take in constructing a broader "innovation agenda" to beat China. Those steps include establishing rules of the road for digital trade and artificial intelligence so that these new frontiers of global commerce are not dictated by the values of the CCP but reflect the values of our Declaration of Independence. America also needs to keep pace with China's state-sponsored entrepreneurs by encouraging our own innovators through competitive research and development incentives. Accomplishing these goals will once again require cross-party cooperation and collaboration.

Of course, a revival of the civility and openheartedness that animates bipartisanship cannot be the responsibility of elected officials or leaders alone. I believe it has to rise up in and spread from our communities, neighborhoods, and homes. The responsibility of national reconciliation and the work of reaching a better understanding of one another comes down to us—we can't outsource that to politicians or presidents. It is not going to happen if we do.

We all have the means at our disposal. We can mentor. Advice and guidance are among the greatest gifts we can give our fellow Americans—and among the most in demand. We can mix with our neighbors. This is a low-risk, high-reward proposition to engage with and learn from those around us. We can help recreate community living rooms, the voluntary associations and public spaces that have historically brought Americans of different backgrounds together for conversation, recreation, and fellowship.

We can let media inform us rather than agitate us and enrage us. It is not easy, but a broader array of information will help us better understand one another.

We can mend. We all have the means at our disposal to fill the little gaps in our civic society close to home with acts of simple service to others.

And last, we can mobilize. No, not in service of political cause—though of course there is a time for that—but to see each other as friends and countrymen, and to enrich the lives of others and provide greater meaning to our own.

It occurred to me while writing these pages that they form a time capsule of sorts. Decades from now, a future American might possibly read them and the other chapters in this book knowing the eventual outcome of our current national trials. Did America and the cause of freedom and human dignity once again hold the day against autocracy? And did we, along the way, repair our fractured republic?

I conclude with confidence that a future reader will understand the talk of civil strife and international threats here as relics of an earlier, happily ended period of turmoil in our history. Though only, to borrow Wendell Willkie's words, if we can work "shoulder to shoulder . . . for the defense of our free way of life . . . and for the development of that new America whose vision lies within every one of us."

We have before and I believe we will once again.

NOTE

1. Pew Research Center, "Political Polarization in the American Public," June 12, 2014, https://www.pewresearch.org/politics/2014/06/12/political -polarization-in-the-american-public/.

TODD YOUNG *is a Republican member of the US Senate from Indiana.*

THREE

—◈—

COLLABORATION, COMPROMISE, AND BIPARTISANSHIP

DAN GLICKMAN

AFTER MY SIX YEARS WITH the Motion Picture Association of America (MPAA), and after a brief time at Refugees International, a global policy refugee organization, I joined the Aspen Institute Congressional Program as well as the Bipartisan Policy Center, the latter a Washington, DC, think tank promoting constructive partisanship, founded by four recent Senate majority leaders. Throughout my political career, I have come to believe that we have an excellent system of government, but it can only function well if it has a crucial ingredient: *moderate* politicians who are willing to compromise.

The Founding Fathers essentially institutionalized gridlock by creating a separation of powers, ensuring checks and balances so that no one branch of government can control the others. They wanted one foot on the brake and one foot on the gas, even in the days of horses and buggies. However, a system where power is not centralized requires consensus and compromise to get anything done.

Compromise—that is a word relevant to democracy.

Our government, as envisioned and drafted by the First Continental Congress in Philadelphia, relies on collaboration and empathy as a template for how one party views the other when it comes to moving the country forward. Unless actors within the system—voters and politicians—seek to build coalitions, especially on challenging issues, you will be left with benign neglect or, in some cases, harmful inaction.

Today, most of the incentives in our political system do not favor consensus or—God forbid—compromise. Notice how that word keeps coming up, as if it's important or even essential, like oxygen?

Party loyalty trumps devotion to country, and an excess of money in the system discourages political risk-taking and leadership. Our conflict-driven media encourages Americans to fear and loathe those who hold political views different from their own and to celebrate conflict and division, further exacerbating a lack of risk-taking and leadership.

This is not a prescription for a thriving country, let alone one that functions well for everyone.

My political life has taught me many invaluable lessons, which can all be summarized by one guiding principle: life is about building bridges between rivals, not making permanent enemies. This principle must exist if we are ever going to achieve fairness and equality.

To build bridges with genuine intention, several fundamental truths need to be accepted. First and foremost, be guided by integrity so that your peers respect and trust you. Be a man or woman of your word. To build the bridges needed to help you achieve your goals, find ways to connect on a personal level, which for me means using humor. Don't take yourself too seriously but also be known as a person of substance and intellect. Come to a discussion committed to civility and empathy but ready to defend your views. In a political context, this means you are willing to hear dissenting opinions and recognize that the person across the table is as convinced about their beliefs as you are about yours.

For this formula to ultimately succeed, it relies on one central factor: personal character. The bottom line is, if you don't make people with whom you disagree your enemy, you can find the space to work together. Plenty of politicians today perceive the risk of doing something, anything, beyond what is dogmatically party doctrine as a political risk that could lead them to lose their seat. They believe they could be defeated in a primary or a general election if they stray too far off the predetermined path set forth by activists within their party coalitions. But members of Congress, keep it firmly in your minds that losing your seat is not the end of the world. It certainly wasn't for me. So please, dear elected officials, live a little and vote what you think is right for your district and the country, not just for your party. Don't be a fool about it, but pick your moments to be a leader and make those moments the ones that really matter.

Shortly after I was sworn into my first term in Congress, I experienced an extraordinary event that has stayed with me ever since. Former vice president Hubert Humphrey, who had returned to the Senate after losing his bid for the White House in 1968, addressed the entire House of Representatives. Humphrey was still a sitting senator but was extremely frail because he was dying of cancer. Most of the current House members, Republicans as well as Democrats, came knowing that this was a historic occasion and probably one of the last times this highly respected public servant was going to speak in public. Few moments in my life have been as moving as listening to this speech. He stood (clearly with heroic effort) in the well of the House, with Daniel Webster's quote, "Do Something Worthy to Be Remembered" visible behind him.

His message to us was so simple, yet remarkably crucial: "Fight every legislative battle with vigor, passion, and the belief that it is the most critical issue of your life. When that fight is over, no matter what the outcome, cross to the other side and shake your opponent's hand, because he or she could easily become your ally in a future fight. There will be future fights, and you will need allies. Never burn that bridge that is so flammable in the heat of battle."

Then he said what I believe every voter, candidate, and elected official needs to hear: "Respect for your opponent and your opponent's opinion does not weaken your integrity or your position—quite the opposite."

Hubert Humphrey died two months later, on January 13, 1978. I wish every sitting member of Congress today would read his remarks and take them to heart. To be fair and transparent, did Humphrey's voting record prove his point? I'm not too sure about that.

I served as an elected or appointed official during four presidencies: Jimmy Carter, Ronald Reagan, George H. W. Bush, and Bill Clinton. I campaigned as a Democrat during a Republican administration, and while in Congress, I opposed a specific policy promulgated by my own party's president. It never occurred to me, nor to many of my fellow members of Congress, that the president was my enemy or that the other party had set out to destroy our nation. All of our presidents in my tenure as elected officials were true patriots, a fact I never doubted as they each presented their vision for America to the voters. I may have strongly disagreed with their views on how to move the country forward, but I never assigned them any motive other than a love of our country. Even those who followed Clinton, especially George W. Bush and Barack Obama, are men of honor and decency. I have great hope in our president, Joe Biden; certainly, his years as a senator and vice president have exemplified excellent character.

Nothing is a clearer example of the intrusion of vicious and small-minded partisanship into our government than the presidency of Donald Trump. In my opinion, he changed the country in a raw and vulgar way, feeding off the dysfunction that enabled his rise to power in the first place. He embraced the role of a great divider, understanding the deep-seated tribal nature of our current politics, and he played the political system to keep himself and his party in power.

Our biggest challenge in this era is to ensure the continuation of America as a nation based on sound values and good character. We cannot allow the institutionalization of the dark tendencies that Trump's election legitimized. Even those presidents with whom I disagreed, like George W. Bush in his decision to take us into Iraq, deserve my congratulations for the display of transformational leadership in the fight against AIDS and malaria in Africa.

I refuse to believe that our current division is permanent and that what ails us cannot be overcome. We have surely descended into tribal politics that stifle our success rather than nurture it. But the "better angels of our nature" described by Abraham Lincoln, are still, deep down, part of America's DNA. Where we are today is a reflection of uncertainty, economic inequality, fear, and insecurity. Our nation's psyche is fragile, much like the America we witnessed during the Vietnam era. We have been struggling for America's soul for almost an entire generation, and as our society is changing from a white majority to a minority majority, we need to understand and appreciate that the change is challenging for many Americans. At the same time, we need to remember that one of this country's greatest strengths is our diversity.

That said, even though Trump is not currently in office, his voters still live among us, so what do we do about them and their belief system?

What can see us through to a more civil era is for voters who believe we are on the wrong path to commit to supporting moderate political candidates. And for those candidates, once elected, to stand firm in the belief that pragmatism and civility must be the guiding principles of government.

In 2007, I watched a town hall with then GOP presidential candidate, John McCain, where he argued with a voter who made outrageous claims about then Senator Obama's citizenship and religious affiliation. McCain was booed by some people in that audience for simply saying, "Barack Obama is a citizen and a family man, but I disagree with him about many things and that is why I want to be president."

Senator McCain's response was a class act by a man who held deeply conservative views but embodied the principles of pragmatism and civility. It was the same commitment to working together for the common good that made John McCain one of the leading Republican voices against the divisive tactics employed by Donald Trump and his minions.

Having now observed candidate after candidate succeeding by using messages of fear, anger, and even outright hatred for their political opponents, I wonder if common manners, decency, and civility are values no longer taken seriously in politics or society itself. Seeing people respond to brash self-promotion, or regarding schoolyard bullying and direct ad hominem attacks as qualities of leadership, is deeply disturbing to me, not just as a former politician, but as an American and a citizen of the world.

The bottom line, which deserves repeating, is that political leadership, like any type of leadership, relies on character. The foundation of democratic politics requires leaders of deep integrity and good character who are committed to the ideals of democracy as well as to working within the system to advance the interests of their constituents.

We have arrived at this challenging crossroads for several reasons, which must be addressed and resolved. This should begin with vastly improving how we elect our officials, who we elect, and to what standards we hold them. This means focusing on money in politics, gerrymandering, and divisive hyperpartisanship. Grassroots efforts to address these ills are springing up all over the country. I am involved in several of them through my work with the Aspen Institute, the Bipartisan Policy Center, and the Former Members of Congress Association.

No issue is more vital than addressing money in politics. Everybody talks about the corrosive role permanent fundraising plays in our representative government, but no one from either party really wants to do anything about it.

Jesse Unruh, former speaker of the California State Assembly, said in 1966 that "money is the mother's milk of politics." By now, it has become the cottage cheese, yogurt, and pretty much the entire meal of politics.

What we used to call *payola* is suffocating our political system.

With rare exception, the ability to raise money has become the primary criterion to judge a candidate's political worthiness. Consider how the political world judges the success of presidential candidates. If they don't meet an extraordinary threshold of fundraising, they are deemed not viable, regardless of their leadership qualities, policy positions, experience, or charm. Proposals to help the country are an afterthought to a candidate's fundraising prowess.

Although politicians of all colors, stripes, and backgrounds claim to hate what is happening to the system, when push comes to shove, few are serious about changing the corrosive influence of money. This is because gaining exclusive access to the sources of funding gives them a competitive edge over would-be political challengers.

This is disgraceful. It is ridiculous to believe that money, especially large sums from individual donors and corporations, comes with no strings attached. As Adolf Rupp, former basketball coach at the University of Kentucky, used to say, "If it doesn't matter whether we win or lose, why do we keep score?" If it doesn't matter where the money comes from, why do people give it, and why do candidates obsess over raising it?

My first run for Congress in 1976 was a door-to-door operation where money was a nonissue. My seat was not gerrymandered for or against me, even though I was from a Republican-dominated state. I unseated an incumbent because I outworked him and connected with voters. My election would not be possible in today's money-driven campaign environments. I would need $3 million to $5 million simply to be competitive. There would be no time for direct voter contact because fundraising and schmoozing with deep-pocketed donors from out of state would occupy most of my calendar. What a screwed up sense of priorities!

Though money was not a factor in winning my first election, I am convinced it was a factor in losing my last campaign. By 1993, Koch Industries, headquartered in my hometown of Wichita, Kansas, had decided that Democrats who supported an energy tax were jeopardizing their corporate interests. Because campaign finance laws were murky—made even less transparent today, thanks to the atrocious *Citizens United v. Federal Election Commission* Supreme Court decision in 2010—there's no way of telling how much money they funneled into the campaign against me.

I am also convinced that Koch Industries' concern over their corporate bottom line, as well as their own philosophical views, made funding my opponent a sound investment, with an anticipated positive return. This was also known as "let's fund the other guy," and spend whatever is necessary to smear and even ruin his opponent.

Things have only gotten worse. Now a handful of supremely rich families can steer millions toward any campaign or candidate of their choosing, whether that means supporting a senator in their home state or a representative from a district hundreds of miles away. They can do so entirely cloaked in secrecy, thanks to nefarious political operatives steering bundled millions of dollars toward politicians via PACs and super PACs, the mother of all corruption. It's all completely legal, but in my opinion, it's highly unethical.

Political party resources have been outstripped by super PACs since the *Citizens United* ruling opened the floodgate of dark money campaign expenditures. This deregulation effort now resembles the arms race between the United States and the Soviet Union, with each side trying to remove all barriers and rules preventing them from raising unlimited contributions. The political parties promulgated this development to fight fire with fire, but the result just further increases the importance of high-net-worth donors and further marginalizes most of the voters in our political system.

As a result, donations flow directly to candidates rather than to either party, which results in extreme candidates finding success by simply embracing a single issue that wealthy donors care about, like eliminating the estate tax. As long as a candidate supports a pet issue of wealthy constituents, unscrupulous donors will turn a blind eye to the zany, radical, or outright insane policy views that candidate may hold in any number of other issues. It is the height of irresponsibility to invest in candidates to protect or extend things like tax benefits without regard for the rest of the dangerous nonsense that comes along with supporting that candidate.

All of this has had a paralyzing effect on our legislative bodies at state and federal levels. There are only twenty-four hours in a day, and once you subtract time for sleeping, eating, traveling to and from the district, and hours upon hours for fundraising, there is little time left to shape policy, engage in true debate, build relationships with your colleagues, and put in any genuine effort to move the country forward.

This also doesn't take into account the fact that most dollars are given to preserve the status quo. Donors ask that you don't do something legislatively, for example, like create new regulations to address changed energy production such as fracking. Big donors generally do not support big ideas; they usually fight them. They also want to preserve the systemic inequality that exists in our country. One positive development on this front is how social media has empowered many small donors to contribute, offsetting some of the need for candidates to rely exclusively on the rich and powerful.

At the same time, this compounds the disconnect that average voters feel toward their elected officials. I would suggest that many voters on both sides have a legitimate belief that our political system is irrelevant to the lives of everyone except those at the financial top. Candidates offer this or that on income inequality or tax or social policy, but most of the public policy we need for a better America, like infrastructure investment and education reform, is completely stuck.

Voters are unhappy because they are not being served by a government paralyzed by money: political donations bind candidates to the views of a handful of Americans, stoking the flames of partisanship and keeping Congress from doing anything truly transformational. The system feeds itself via ruthless professional fundraisers who care little about the damage they are doing to the nation. They are much more interested in earning their consultancy fees from candidates who are convinced they can only win because they've engaged the best hired guns to essentially buy their way into office.

This dependence on fundraising has had an additional debilitating effect. We are turning away highly qualified candidates for office who simply want nothing to do with a system that requires them to constantly ask strangers for money. It is a privilege to ask someone for their vote. It is embarrassing to ask someone for their money. While candidates can be recruited to do the former, they are now turned off by the latter.

Add to that the personal attacks most candidates endure at the hand of their opponents and there's little motivation left to seek higher office. Citizens see political dysfunction causing policy gridlock, and fewer and fewer potential public servants view Washington, DC, as an opportunity to fulfill Daniel Webster's mandate: to do something worthy to be remembered.

We are not only alienating future senators and representatives—we are also turning off future federal bureaucrats, foreign service officers, and political appointees. Because fundraising is the single most determinative factor for congressional committee assignments and top leadership positions in the House or Senate, new members of Congress are told to raise money not only for their reelection but also for the party and their colleagues. That gives those wanting to rise within a committee little incentive to become issue experts and a lot of incentive to cozy up with that committee's corporate interests.

This is a recipe for failure as a democracy.

An all-too-comfortable relationship between members of Congress and the interest groups they regulate also contributes to making an incumbent member almost unbeatable. Back in 1976, when I took on incumbent congressman Garner Shriver, it was already considered a fool's errand to challenge a politician who was seeking reelection and did not have a scandal dragging him or her down. While there are wave elections that sweep an unexpectedly considerable number of sitting members out of office, most of the time the incumbent enjoys a clear advantage over the challenger and handily wins reelection.

One other thing we can do to make our politics better is to end the extreme politicization in gerrymandering of member districts. One of the reasons our election campaigns are uncompetitive is that congressional districts are drawn by most state legislatures in a partisan manner with the sole purpose of keeping each seat safely in the hands of whichever party happens to control the redistricting process following a census.

These gerrymandered districts (named after a salamander-shaped Massachusetts district then governor Elbridge Gerry created in 1812) produce almost no competition on Election Day because the outcome is pretty much predetermined. That leaves the real contest to the favored party's primary, where very few eligible voters determine the eventual representative of that seat. This has also led to more extreme candidates winning primaries, since the 10 percent of eligible voters who do show up for a primary tend to be on the far right or left.

Gerrymandering is one of the truly bipartisan aspects of our electoral system because given the opportunity, both parties gleefully reshape congressional districts. Only a few states have adopted a nonpartisan or bipartisan redistricting process because whichever party cedes its advantage to a neutral body also gives up its sure grip on the seat.

Part of the discussion about gerrymandering should also analyze whether our nation is served best by holding onto a two-party system. We are a multiparty nation with differing political points of view within each party that form a coalition under one of two labels: "Republican" or "Democrat." In recent years, we have allowed this within-the-party coalition to yield to the most extreme political persuasions within the party, which effectively diminishes the voices of reason that each party's moderates bring to the table.

Two-party labels no longer allow for a broad definition of *liberal* or *conservative*. Politicians are loath to work with each other because there's no political gain from crossing the aisle. Though some politicians actually do work with "them," it is not the norm. In fact, the opposite is true: your party's primary voters will punish you for being too close to members from the other party, but few politicians get punished for being too close to a super PAC moving unregulated dark money.

Our current system produces too many one-issue voters who make a single question (usually a social issue, such as abortion) their litmus test for support and are willing to accept a host of fringe positions on any other topic. Gerrymandering and our primaries process support the continuation of the two-party system to the detriment of our ability to elect the best and the brightest. This system also punishes the moderate candidate who has a much harder time winning a primary than a general election.

Beyond tribal politics, the influence of money, recruiting top-notch candidates, and gerrymandering, the viciousness of our political rhetoric has reached new heights. I cannot recall a president of the United States bullying political opponents daily, either via Twitter, in speeches, or by sending out his press secretary or a nasty statement with no possibility of questions from the press.

As president, Donald Trump had little or no filter on anything he said or did. His use of Twitter did not allow for any depth of discussion and only triggered friction and confusion because of the way he used it. He remained in constant campaign mode, and his announcements, whether confined to 280 characters or a two-hour speech, were aimed at a single audience: his own voters. Every other president in the history of our nation has approached the job with a willingness to unite, and a recognition that he is responsible to all Americans, not just the ones who voted for him.

What message does this send to young Americans who need to trust their government, engage in the political process, be responsible citizens, and work for change? It turns them off and makes them run for the hills rather than run for office.

We should not forget, however, that Donald Trump is not the source of our tribal politics and hyper-partisan rhetoric, but rather its logical product. He is also a product of our national obsession with TV and celebrity. Those same politicians who want to meet a Hollywood actor were dazzled by Trump because they had seen him on TV for so long.

By abandoning civility, empathy, and a willingness to collaborate, we have enshrined a different type of leader than what our nation used to demand. The goal for all who care about democracy needs to be that we return to leadership based on integrity, good character, sound morals, and a vision to move the country forward rather than suppress those who think or look or sound different.

We most certainly can regulate campaign finance better. In this age of social media, elections will be fundamentally different in the future, and the traditional model that candidates can simply be outspent by buying TV airtime may eventually become a thing of the past. In a rational system of government, there is absolutely no reason why members of Congress should spend more time fundraising than legislating.

At a minimum, it should be prohibited for members of Congress to dial for dollars while Congress is meeting or in session. That would at least eliminate the immorality of a member simultaneously raising money from a corporate supporter and working or voting on an issue important to that corporate entity. Fundraising should simply be banned while Congress is in session to eliminate even the appearance of a quid pro quo. It would also free members to do what they were sent to Washington to do—legislate.

Running for office should be based on wanting to change the country for the good and contributing big ideas. By making the path toward a candidacy and electoral success much less focused on fundraising and much more focused on policy, we will encourage big thinkers to pick up the mantle. Let's support these idealists by allowing them to create solutions rather than exploratory committees.

Let's also embrace the notion of professional politicians who have made public service their calling. In the age of Trump, where our own president disparaged Washington, DC, as a swamp filled with despicable creatures either running the government or working for it, we somehow have become persuaded that political experience is a detriment.

I prefer experienced pilots to fly my plane and experienced surgeons at the operating table. Why would I want *in*experienced legislators to formulate our laws or lead our country. This notion that by having worked in government, a candidate for office is somehow tainted is completely nonsensical. Let's stop falling for candidates who run for Congress or the White House by denouncing the institutions to which they want to be elected. We need individuals of character and integrity, who possess a moral compass as well as a healthy respect for our representative democracy.

Former Arizona senator Jeff Flake retired from Congress because his moral compass prevented him from blindly siding with the president from his own party. I respect him for that and completely agree with him that Congress must pursue strong, independent, and bipartisan oversight of the actions undertaken by the White House and all the cabinet departments. Donald Trump seemed disinterested in learning that the White House must deal with Congress, the courts, and the media, all of which are empowered by the Constitution to provide checks and balances to keep our democracy from turning into something sinister.

John F. Kennedy (JFK) wrote an outstanding book called *Profiles in Courage*, which highlights the integrity of eight US senators. In each of the stories, their actions went against their perceived self-interests, as they probably would have benefited politically by staying on the sidelines rather than taking a stand and following their moral compass. History showed that voters rewarded them for doing the right thing.

Since much of my current work focuses on bringing Republicans and Democrats together, if I were to write a sequel to JFK's book, my theme would be bipartisanship. Let's recognize those elected officials who cross the political aisle and are willing to approach colleagues with a sense of empathy and a commitment to collaboration.

In the era of Trump, American journalists have risen to the challenge of covering his bizarre and dangerous ways. Unfortunately, in the process of doing their job, they have also given him a bullhorn to promote his bigotry.

But our journalists need to rediscover a degree of professionalism that abhors any implication of bias. It's easy to go on social media and see the political views of almost any journalist. This erodes their credibility and gives space for actual peddlers of fake news to spin lies and propagandize on behalf of their masters. Professional journalists should seek information and the truth, no matter where the story takes them, and must always be conscious of being accused of bias. The First Amendment protects our freedom of speech and a free press and encourages the fourth estate to look over our leaders' shoulders, which remains as vital to our democracy as our system of checks and balances.

We need to push society to move toward a more unified and civil place. The first step is restoring civic education into America's classrooms. Though largely a state responsibility, we need to eliminate the ignorance of so many Americans, especially the next generation, who need to be taught the skills necessary to make informed decisions when it comes to their vote. They know little of the basic tools of public service: listening to opinions, making your own argument, building trust, and engaging in the art of compromise.

There it is again: compromise.

Remember comedian Jay Leno's shtick called "Jay Walking," where he asked folks on the street simple questions, like how many branches of government there are? The answers usually revealed that too many citizens are woefully and ridiculously uninformed.

We need a real push for young Americans to strengthen their communities by performing public service. While I am not advocating conscription or a draft, I believe we all would benefit as a society if young adults were incentivized by thoughtful and realistic options for public service. All Americans between the ages of eighteen and twenty-five should have an opportunity to come together under a service umbrella, including military and civilian programs. This would give our next generation of citizens a way to interact with people of different economic backgrounds, races, cultures, and levels of education.

Much like the greatest generation who fought in World War II and returned home to see the country safely through the Cold War, America would benefit enormously from a citizenry working together on the common purpose of moving the country forward. Sadly, this is a missing ingredient in American democracy, especially considering our public school system, where economic class and race are still enormous factors in determining the quality of our children's education.

We know that all power flows from an educated, informed, and engaged citizenry. Grassroots efforts could achieve proper and objective congressional redistricting, based on actual census data rather than partisan politics. A large citizen movement might be able to enact even bigger changes to the system, which could spur politicians to behave better. Citizens, as a whole, should demand government action on everyday issues, such as a national effort to improve America's infrastructure or our entire education system. Most importantly, if politicians know that an educated, informed, and engaged citizenry is watching their every public move, they will be committed to constitutional principles, especially First Amendment rights, freedoms of expression, and separation of powers to preserve a check on the executive branch.

I am convinced and optimistic that what has made America great for hundreds of years is still alive and well: our sense of community, our willingness to help and support each other in times of crisis, and the strength we derive from our diversity. We have abundant resources in our people: bright minds that can pursue and receive top-notch educations, can-do attitudes toward problem solving, and an overarching entrepreneurial spirit that has made us the strongest economy on the planet. Our schools, religious institutions, and community groups can all do a better job extolling the values of respect, good character, and compromise. Our complex social and political challenges cannot be fixed with magic bullets, but I remain optimistic because I remember American history.

We have always overcome times of great divisiveness, whether it was the Civil War, McCarthyism, the Vietnam War, or Watergate. Throughout those challenging times, we have demonstrated that we are a resilient country with a destiny unequal in human history.

Adlai Stevenson said, "America is much more than a geographical fact. It is a political and moral fact, the first community in which men set out in principle to institutionalize freedom, responsible government, and human equality."

Bill Clinton shared a notion that "there is nothing wrong with America that cannot be cured by what is right with America."

Both of these great speakers reminded us of our nation's exceptionalism. Now, in this time of division and hyperpartisanship, we need to focus on the great strength of our democracy, which means delivering tangible results for the American people by thinking big—rather than the great weakness of democracy, which is just saying "no." Some of the brightest moments in our country occur when citizens come together from all walks of life to serve, putting aside their differences for the common good. That's the America we all love, and that's the genuinely American DNA that has made us who we are and that continues to make us great.

I often think of Daniel Burnham, an American architect and urban designer, who opined on the difference between having small ideas and pushing hard for big ones, when he said, "Make no little plans; they have no magic to stir men's blood and probably themselves will not be realized. Make big plans; aim high in hope and work."

In politics, shying away from big ideas might keep you in office a bit longer, but it defies the purpose of being there. If we think small, how will we ever manage to rebuild America's infrastructure, explore space, or cure diseases? If we think small, how can we be a worldwide leader in the search for freedom and liberty? If we think small, how will we ever erase our growing national debt?

Economists estimate that we will be in the red to the tune of $30 trillion by the end of the decade. Only twenty years ago, we had four years of balanced budgets. This demonstrates that restoring fiscal responsibility can be done while still engaging in big plans for the future.

The key is leadership, character, and courage.

That means compromise.

Our leaders need courage to make tough choices, like creating a sensible but fairer tax system, restraining the growth of federal spending on entitlement programs, and just good old effective management practices. That means some candidates of character may risk losing an election, if necessary.

We recently saw character and courage in the votes of a select few Republican House and Senate members, most of whom risked their political careers on making unpopular votes on the impeachment and conviction of President Trump. In my judgment, these people put country over party, put deep personal values over obsequious support for a president who had committed unpardonable offenses against the country. They made sacrifices for the larger historic good. Not every elected official, including yours truly, can honestly say that we always voted courageously on every hot divisive political issue. But these folks wrestled carefully, independently, and thoughtfully and did not compromise their principles. In most cases, compromise is needed to make the system work, but in others, fear of losing a political race is an enormous sign of weakness. Personal dignity and respect are more important than a committee chairmanship.

Perhaps the example of my life you have read about here has defined what a moderate is and how moderation is a necessary ingredient for our country to move forward. Based on my experiences, in politics and life, it can lead people to deal with issues and conflicts—and each other—in a healthy and productive way. It's simply better than any rigid ideological political philosophy. That's my opinion, and I'm sticking to it. I don't care how much you think compromise won't work. I'm not budging on my view. It's compromise or bust!

All joking aside, one can hold conservative or liberal political views, but if you are a jackass with a closed mind or have little to no empathy for what your adversary or competitor is feeling, or what struggles one has faced, you are not only a jerk but you will never be a positive force to solve any of our nation's problems.

That is what being in elected office is all about. Don't be a jerk!

If you have the ability to listen, if you can cultivate a general sense of empathy and are respectful in tone and substance, you can still advance any of your liberal or conservative views with a sensible and moderate tone, and you may even find that people will listen to you much more and consider your position in a reasonable way. You may even change some minds, or, quite surprisingly, when you listen, too, you may even change your own mind.

Our nation's great leaders have certainly mastered the art of active listening. Will our current crop of politicians ever learn from the wisdom of our past leaders?

Whether you agreed with him or not on specific issues, former senator Everett Dirksen once said quite a wise thing, which most politicians today could do well to emulate: "I am a man of principle. And my first principle is flexibility."

You see, principles and flexibility are not inconsistent with one another. They are necessary tools for creating a genuinely bipartisan and effective government because, as we know all too well, the alternative is gridlock. Dirksen and LBJ were examples of politicians who used both techniques to work across the aisle to achieve great things for our country, especially when it came to the civil rights laws of the 1960s.

I had the privilege of a long and successful career in public service, shaped by outstanding public servants from both sides of the aisle. We always found much more in common than what divided us politically. We always found ways to work together because we never forgot that we are stronger together than standing alone.

Is America vulnerable? Yes, of course it is. Our democracy is only as strong as our commitment to perfecting it, and right now our country faces huge challenges on multiple fronts. In spite of that, I am optimistic that the opportunities are even greater than the challenges. We are an extraordinarily resilient nation, founded on common sense principles, and the bedrock of our exceptionalism is the ability of the American people to persist, sometimes by taking two steps forward in response to when we falter and regress. Our Kansas state motto, "ad astra per aspera," or "to the stars through difficulties," is especially relevant now. We must maintain our determination to overcome adversity and find a better way, as this is what separates America from so many other nations. Each of us must turn our hopes into responsible actions, and together "we shall overcome."

Hopefully your experience will mirror mine in some respects and you will enjoy a productive, happy, and enriching life. Oh yeah, and have some fun along the way. Tell a joke, be humble, be yourself. Remember the words of Yakov Smirnov, reflecting on this remarkable place where we are privileged to live.

"What a country!"

NOTE

From chapter 14 of *Laughing at Myself: My Education in Congress, on the Farm, and at the Movies,* by Dan Glickman. Published by University Press of Kansas, ©2021, www.kansaspress.ku.edu. Minor updating edits have been made to the original work. Used by permission of publisher.

DAN GLICKMAN *is a Senior Fellow at the Bipartisan Policy Center and is a former Secretary of the US Department of Agriculture and a former Democratic member of the US House of Representatives from Kansas.*

WHY BIPARTISANSHIP IS SUCH HARD WORK

MARJORIE RANDON HERSHEY

INTRODUCTION: WHY BIPARTISANSHIP MATTERS FOR DEMOCRACY AND GOVERNANCE

One of the many dramas that played out in Washington, DC, in 2023 evoked especially bad memories. A decade earlier, in the summer of 2013, the division between Republicans and Democrats in Congress was so bitter that the two parties could not agree on a bill to fund government operations. Government spending hit the permitted limit on accumulating debt and had to shut down. The Washington Monument was closed to visitors. Parents and children were turned away from national parks. Public approval of Congress dropped even lower than usual, to around 10 percent. International markets downgraded the federal government's credit rating for the first time in history.

Eventually, the parties reached a compromise and government programs were funded again. Yet Congress had not learned its lesson. In 2023, congressional Republicans refused for months to vote to raise the debt limit, though failing to do so would force the federal government to default on its debts and again risk its credit rating, unless Democrats agreed to make deep cuts in social programs.

The lack of bipartisanship has real consequences—not just the closure of important public services but also the damage done to confidence in governance. It threatens the belief that the US government can respond to crises as well as to more mundane national needs. Why, then, is bipartisanship so hard to achieve? This chapter will examine how bipartisanship is defined, how and why it has ebbed and flowed over time, and what can be done to promote bipartisan cooperation.

WHAT'S BIPARTISANSHIP?

Because they live in a nation composed of multitudes of different ethnicities, ages, occupations, and experiences, Americans will not agree on every issue. Democracy does not require that. Rather, democracy requires using procedures that let us express and try to resolve our inevitable disagreements without resorting to violence. Among those procedures are political parties. Parties are a democracy's primary means of reducing the number of alternatives for solving a particular problem to a manageable number and mobilizing support for those alternatives.

Bipartisanship then refers to the effort by different parties to reach common ground, either in forming a new policy or at least in creating greater mutual understanding. That, in turn, requires compromise: each side will need to move at least a little from its original preference. Although many politicians prefer to think of bipartisanship as limited to concessions from their opponents, as in the idea that "We're ready to cooperate right now. All you need to do is go along with what we want" (Babington 2010), bipartisanship is the opposite of "my way or the highway." It can refer to the appointments of opposition party identifiers to jobs in the executive branch or the courts. It can involve people persuading one another to accept two sets of policies—one favored by one party, the other by the opposing party—as a package deal.

As Lee Hamilton, a longtime member of Congress, writes (Hamilton 2023): "To get anything done in Congress or a state legislature, you've got to get a majority of the votes—and often, that means you have to get votes from the other side.... I'd argue that it's one of the virtues of our system, because it means that, on a regular basis, politicians have to consider what people who don't agree with them think." In practical terms, if a policy is to survive, then it must appeal to future Congress members of both parties, as well as voters with a diversity of views, or it will later face the threat of repeal.

Bipartisanship is especially crucial to US politics because the American version of democracy is unique. Most democracies, such as the United Kingdom's, are majoritarian: the party (or coalition) that elects a majority of representatives to Parliament or Congress then takes control of the national government. Because that party or coalition has a majority of legislative seats, it has the power to move its agenda into law, and at the next election, the voters decide whether they liked the results. There is usually no need for bipartisan cooperation. As one journalist put it, "If you believe in majority rule, forget about making converts: Assemble a majority and start ruling with it" (Shafer 2021).

The US political system works differently. Members of the legislature are elected as individuals, not as members of party lists. They are nominated by voters in primary elections, not by a party organization, so they do not have to follow a party line on issues. Members of the US House are elected on a different time schedule than are senators and the president. The three branches of the national government each have the power to check and balance one another's actions. These institutional features were adopted in the US Constitution precisely to limit majority rule, to prevent majorities from tyrannizing over the rest of the population. Winning a majority, then, even in both houses of Congress does not guarantee a party the power to pass its preferred policies. The majority party will probably need the votes of at least some members of the opposition party to pass bills. In short, even majorities often need bipartisan cooperation in American politics. Cooperation can reassure the public that a proposed policy benefits more than just the majority party's supporters.

WHY THE AMERICAN FRAMERS HOPED FOR BIPARTISANSHIP BUT OFTEN REVERTED TO PARTISANSHIP

If bipartisanship is so necessary in US politics, then why does it seem so rare? Since the beginning, bipartisan cooperation has been hard to achieve. Even inducing the thirteen North American colonies in the 1770s to come together as the United States was painstaking. Creating a new nation took long, heated debates, refusals to compromise, claims of betrayal, fiery protests, and all the other challenges that today often attend the birth of major programs. Pre-revolutionary migrants had not come to a *United States*; they had come to fish or build ships in Massachusetts or to grow tobacco or cotton in Virginia. The colonies had different systems of governance, their economies were based on different products, and their populations differed in ethnic origin, religion, and other important characteristics. The various colonies reacted differently to the taxes and oppressive regulations imposed by the British Parliament. Many colonists, especially those who had prospered under British rule, strongly opposed the idea of separating from Britain.

Even once the idea of independence had been accepted by many colonial leaders, George Washington as commander in chief of the Continental army found it excruciatingly difficult to convince the various colonies, as well as the factions in the weak Continental Congress, to send the money and troops needed to fight the British army. Different factions questioned why troops from Maryland, or those steeped in the egalitarian traditions of New England, should have to obey a general from Virginia. When Washington tried to bring British sympathizers into the colonial fold, he permitted them to "cleanse" themselves of disloyalty simply by pledging allegiance to the "United States," a legal entity that did not exist yet, rather than to their home colony or state. This outraged many members of Congress, who were still loyal primarily to their own state. Many expected the several colonies to remain separate nations even after independence was won—neighborly at times, but not united (Flexner 1984, 100, 85).

Once a United States was established, this divide continued between proponents of a strengthened national government, who came to call themselves Federalists, and those who preferred to keep power in the hands of the state governments. Federalists, led by Alexander Hamilton, wanted to jump-start a new American economy by creating a national bank and empowering the national government to absorb the states' war debts. Anti-federalists, largely from southern states with agrarian economies, feared that a more powerful national government would take power from the states. These two partisan forces, though not yet organized as political parties, remained locked in strong opposition. They avoided stalemate at times by some creative horse-trading, as when Hamilton's economic proposals, strongly favored by northern Federalists, passed Congress together with a bill favored by southerners and anti-federalists, establishing a permanent national capital in the South (see Aldrich and Grant 1993). But partisan divisions were as big a barrier to bipartisanship in the early Republic as they are today.

Partisanship benefits a democracy. It clarifies voters' choices on complicated issues by providing alternative visions of what can be done. Any issue has several possible answers, each of which benefit some people and impose costs on others. Although citizens may agree on goals at the most abstract level—that they want the best possible system of education, for example—they inevitably differ on how to reach those goals, depending on their economic, social, demographic, and other characteristics (Madison 1787). Some may feel that the best possible education can be achieved only through giving parents vouchers to pay tuition at private schools. Others favor charter schools or stronger public education or greater parental controls or limited teachers' unions or stronger teachers' unions. Partisanship gives citizens a tool to focus their debates on a few alternatives rather than a cacophony of differing views. Trying to eliminate partisanship altogether, even if it were possible, deprives the polity of a valuable tool for resolving issues.

Yet partisanship can provoke bitter conflict. As Washington warned, partisanship can be like fire: used properly, it serves many purposes, but when unquenched, it can consume everything in its path. Bipartisanship—bringing together the values and proponents of both parties—can help lessen the dangers of partisanship without losing its value. The benefits can be seen in one of the earliest challenges faced by the new Republic. The anti-federalists' successors—the Republicans under the leadership of Thomas Jefferson— had their first major victory in the hard-fought national election of 1800. After a tie in the Electoral College, the presidential contest was decided by the House of Representatives. In a controversial move, the House narrowly picked Jefferson. For the first time in the US, then, the ruling Federalists would have to give up power: not just the presidency but also the leadership of Congress. Around the world at that time, there was no precedent for a ruling party to peacefully turn political control over to their opponents. The Federalists could have simply refused to cede power. But they didn't. They stepped aside in favor of their victorious opponents.

It was a striking act of bipartisan cooperation, in which a powerful, shared value—a belief that the survival of the Constitution they had created was at stake, and with it the integrity of the nation they had risked their lives to establish—caused partisan interests to take a back seat. Thus, a major act of bipartisanship emerged in the American Republic. Federalists did not cede the presidency because they felt their rivals would do a perfectly good job. Both sides believed intensely in their cause and objected strongly to their opponents' plans. There was personal animosity combined with ideological animus; David McCullough writes of Federalist leader Alexander Hamilton that the hostility between Hamilton and Jefferson "had reached the point where they could hardly bear to be in the same room. Each was certain the other was a dangerous man intent on dominating the government" (McCullough 2002, 436). But democracy trumped partisanship.

WHEN HAS BIPARTISANSHIP APPEARED
SINCE THE EARLY YEARS?

This major step in the history of democracy has been followed by many long years of partisan rancor. The partisan disputes of the 1800s came to a head in the devastating Civil War of the 1860s, in which hundreds of thousands of Americans died in a failing effort to settle the debate over the rights of Black Americans and the power of the federal government versus the states.

In particular, the era since the mid-1990s has been characterized by strong partisanship in Congress, elections, and national political debate. Party-line votes have increased to record levels (see Hershey 2021, 304–308). The signature legislation of presidential administrations beginning with Bill Clinton's in the 1990s has often been rejected by Congress members of the other party (see McCormick 1997). The presidencies of Barack Obama and Donald Trump produced stunning levels of party polarization. An index compiled yearly by Georgetown University reports that there was less bipartisanship in Congress during 2021 than in previous years (see McCourt 2022).

WHAT FORCES TEND TO INCREASE PARTISAN DIVISION?

Why is partisanship so pervasive? Consider a classic experiment known as "Robbers Cave." A group of middle-school-aged boys were divided into two comparable groups. Before they knew of the other group's existence, each group quickly developed norms and hierarchies and took on a group name. When the two groups met, they began trading insults. As they competed in games, hostilities increased, even though the stakes were small and the groups were composed of similar people. As conflict grew, each group became more cohesive internally (Sherif 1956). In short, psychologists have long found evidence of a tendency for people to divide into in-groups and out-groups and to develop negative feelings toward the out-group, even when there is little basis for conflict between them.

Yet some conditions are more likely to promote conflict or cooperation than others. What has caused heightened partisan divisions in current American politics?

Gerrymandering

Members of the US House and state legislatures are elected from legislative districts, in contrast to the US Senate, whose members are chosen at large, by all the voters in a state. Every ten years, after the US Census results are announced, the US Supreme Court requires that these US House and state legislative districts be redrawn so that all districts within a given state are equal in population.

In most states, state legislatures draw the district lines. Voters in a few states have used initiatives and referenda to require that legislative district lines be drawn by independent, bipartisan commissions, but most states have been unable by law or unwilling to do this (McDonald 2004; but see Henderson et al., 2018). All states except one (Nebraska) elect their state legislators on partisan ballots, and all but a handful of state legislators are Democrats or Republicans (Hershey 2021, ch. 2).

Not surprisingly, these partisan state legislators want to redraw district lines to enhance their own party's chances in upcoming elections. This gerrymandering—dividing a state into election districts to benefit one party and dilute the voting strength of the other party—has been standard practice since the early days of the Republic (Engstrom 2013). Current state legislators have become very skilled at it; legislative majority parties can now use a variety of sophisticated computer programs to maximize their chances of drawing the map most favorable to their party. Standard methods of gerrymandering are to "pack" the other party's voters into a small number of districts where it will be forced to win upcoming elections by wasteful majorities, or to "crack" the other party's supporters among several legislative districts, so that it can win only a few such districts (Morrison and Bryan 2019).

The result is to skew later election results in favor of the party that dominates the state legislature. The skew is often substantial; in Indiana, for instance, the statewide partisan "normal vote" (as measured by the percentage of the vote received on average by candidates for the lesser-known statewide offices: state treasurer and secretary of state) is between 56 and 58 percent Republican. Yet in the last two state legislative elections, because of gerrymandering by a Republican-dominated state legislature, Republicans have won a veto-proof 70–80 percent of legislative seats. This process occurs in many other states, including those dominated by Democrats as well as Republicans. Why is this allowed to happen? The Supreme Court has stated clearly that it won't intervene, because it views partisan gerrymandering as a political issue to be decided by elected officials; the Court has overturned gerrymanders only if they threaten representation for protected minorities such as Black Americans (Liptak 2019).

The ability to gerrymander heightens the partisan atmosphere in a state legislature; what one party gains, the other party loses, so both parties' futures are on the line. Gerrymandering also reduces the competitiveness of state legislative and US House seats. Whether a legislature redraws district lines to favor the dominant party or to protect incumbents of both parties, it is likely to create safe districts for the favored candidates. Elections thus become less competitive, and the disadvantaged party in a district will find it harder and harder to recruit capable candidates and raise enough money to run a credible campaign.

Therefore, although American politics can be highly competitive at the national level in presidential races and the competition for control of both houses of Congress, other US elections have become much less competitive. Journalist Bill Bishop showed that in 1976, when Jimmy Carter beat Gerald Ford by just two percentage points in the popular vote, most Americans experienced a competitive presidential race; almost three-quarters of the public lived in counties where one presidential candidate won with less than 60 percent of the vote. Only 27 percent of the public lived in a county that was won by a landslide (more than 60 percent). By 2004, although the presidential race was comparably close, nearly half of all counties recorded landslides for one presidential candidate (Bishop 2008). US House races, which used to be competitive in the 1800s, are no longer; a House incumbent who runs for reelection typically has a 95 percent chance of succeeding. In US House races since 2012, for example, only between 5 and 10 percent of elections were rated as realistically winnable by either party (for 2022 statistics, see Cook Political report). Senate races, though a little more competitive, are still largely one-sided.

This decline in competitiveness takes its toll on bipartisanship as well. In a race where one party is almost assured of winning—a so-called safe district—the dominant party's candidate has no need to appeal to the other party's voters; he or she can win without their support. Once the dominant party's candidate wins that party's primary election, victory in the general election is all but guaranteed. The only real threat to that candidate's success, then, is a strong opponent in the primary. Turnout in party primaries is typically low, often only half the turnout in general elections. Primary voters tend to be the party's most intense supporters, often more ideologically extreme (right-wing among Republicans, left-wing among Democrats; see Hershey and Birkhead 2019) and more resistant to compromise (Davis 2019) than other party voters. Because these activists comprise such a large part of the primary turnout, candidates in a one-party district need to focus their attention on those more intense party voters—the party's so-called base. These base voters usually prefer a legislator who votes a strong partisan line in Congress; a representative who works collaboratively with opposition legislators is seen as a traitor by many primary voters. This motivates elected officials to become more partisan in their rhetoric and congressional voting records (Babington 2010). As a result, primaries in safe House districts have produced new legislators (especially among Republicans) who tend to be more extreme than the legislators they replaced (DeSilver 2022).

In short, the hard-fought competition between the two parties for the White House and control of the US House and Senate has recently been built on the backs of large numbers of safe Republican and Democratic districts. Gerrymandering has contributed to these safe seats, which results in more ideologically extreme representatives who are reluctant to compromise with the opposition party (Anderson et al. 2020). Some states have adopted reforms such as nonpartisan and top two primaries to encourage moderation, but to this point, these reforms have not consistently accomplished that goal (see Hershey 2021, 202; McGhee and Shor 2017).

Gerrymandering isn't the only cause of this decline in competitive districts; competition has also declined in elections for the US Senate and other offices where redistricting does not occur. Researchers have noted a rise in *voluntary political segregation*. In a mobile society, people often prefer to live in areas where people like themselves already live. Conservatives and Republicans are more likely to want to live in small towns and rural areas where there is a high density of churches and other traditional institutions. These areas tend to vote Republican. In contrast, liberals and Democrats disproportionately prefer to live in cities with considerable racial and ethnic diversity, which tend to elect Democrats (see DeSilver 2014). Communities become more homogeneous in their social and cultural preferences. As a result, urban areas become more Democratic and rural areas and small towns become more Republican and consequently less competitive, even without gerrymandering.

PARTY AND IDEOLOGICAL POLARIZATION

Closely aligned with these trends has been the striking increase in party and ideological polarization of American political life. This polarization has two closely related components: increased ideological distance between the two parties and greater homogeneity of views within each party. Polarization was especially marked in the late 1800s and reemerged in the late 1900s.

The recent polarization has its roots in a change in the makeup of the two parties' supporting coalitions that began a century ago. The Democratic Party had been dominated by the White South for most of its history—the heirs of the states' rights, anti-federalist tradition. But when the Great Depression hit the US in the early 1930s, the newly elected Democratic president, Franklin Roosevelt, was pressured by desperate economic times and reformist party colleagues to greatly expand *federal* social services, especially to lower-income people hit hard by the economic collapse. Among those drawn to the party by these expanded federal social services were Black Americans. As more and more Blacks started voting Democratic, the Democratic Party nationally became an uneasy coalition of strange bedfellows: Blacks, lower-income Whites, socially conservative southerners (whose traditional support for Democrats was maintained by the economic devastation of the South during the Depression), minority religious groups, and urban wage workers. With this large coalition, the Democrats became the majority party during the Depression, but their majority was fractured by group conflict.

Many northern liberals welcomed the increasing flow of Blacks to the Democratic Party as a way to push the national party into greater commitment to civil rights legislation. They eventually succeeded: during the Democratic Kennedy and Johnson presidencies in the 1960s, a Democratic-majority Congress succeeded in passing the landmark Civil Rights Act in 1964 and the equally important Voting Rights Act in 1965, helping to secure the right to vote for Black Americans in states (mainly southern) where they had long been turned away from the polls.

More conservative southern Whites, long a mainstay of Democratic voting strength, reacted with distaste. They distanced themselves from the national Democratic leadership. The party's White southern wing slowly shrank from the 1940s through the 1960s. At the same time, many Republicans, tired of having spent three decades as the minority party since the 1930s, searched for ways to attract more voters. Impressed with the organizational strength of evangelical Christian groups, Republican leaders increasingly appealed to conservative White former Democrats in the South. This slow but important party realignment was largely complete by the mid-1990s, when Republicans won control of the US House for the first time in forty years on a wave of southern White support (see Hershey 2021, chap. 7). The transformation was remarkable; although in the mid-1900s there were many conservative (southern) Democrats and liberal (northeastern) Republicans, by the 1990s conservative Democrats had become an endangered species and liberal Republicans saw themselves as unwelcome in their own party.

This realignment made each party's supporters more homogeneous and widened the gulf in views between Democrats and Republicans. The movement of conservative White southerners from Democratic to loyal Republican made the Republican Party more consistently conservative, and the loss of those conservative White southerners made the Democratic Party more liberal to moderate. Partisanship again became a reliable predictor of voting behavior, and straight-party-ticket voting reasserted itself increasingly after the mid-1990s (Theriault 2008).

Congress members' voting behavior also became more consistently partisan. A recent study found that on average, Republican and Democratic Congress members are farther apart in views on issues now than they have been in half a century (DeSilver 2022). As this distance on issues grew, it became riskier for legislators to vote for bills sponsored by the other party. Congressional scholar Sarah Binder writes, "When ideological and electoral incentives propel the parties to the [ideological] wings, abandoning the political center, lawmakers struggle to find broadly palatable solutions to the range of problems they face" (Binder 2013, 14). And a few extreme partisans in each party have received a great deal of media coverage for broadcasting conspiracy theories and uncivil language about the other party, calling members of the opposition "groomers" and "traitors"—and were rewarded with a lot of campaign contributions from hyperpartisan voters (see Herndon 2021).

Change in the Issue Agenda

At the heart of this growing party polarization was a shift in the types of issues that have dominated the political agenda. In the late 1800s and early 1900s, elections were typically fought on economic issues. Other issues were very much at play during this time, of course, especially race and women's rights, but were not discussed as frequently. But as Republicans increasingly saw an opportunity to attract White southern conservative support in the mid-1900s, Republican leaders realized that these voters were more likely to be attracted by culturally conservative appeals than by economic issues. Republicans found those culturally conservative appeals in the issues of abortion, religion in American public life, traditional values, and veiled appeals to racism. Supreme Court decisions legalizing abortion, government regulation of religious schools and radio programming, and growing acceptance of the rights of LGBTQ+ people alarmed socially conservative White southerners and slowly, steadily, pushed them into the Republican camp. This movement sped up during the 1980s presidency of Ronald Reagan, who referred explicitly to the need to protect traditional values. These new Republicans' socially conservative views made these cultural issues more and more important to the party's leadership.

Economic issues lend themselves to bipartisanship more easily than do cultural issues. If Democrats would like to increase spending on social services by $60 billion and Republicans want no increase at all, it might be possible to reach a bipartisan agreement on an increase of, say, $20 to $40 billion, or to balance a $50 million increase with a comparable increase in the defense budget. When legislators focus on abortion or the treatment of transgender people, the standard methods of meeting halfway or balancing both sides' needs don't work well.

Even in recent elections, although economic issues remain at the top of most Americans' priority list, abortion and other values issues have grown in importance. In 2022 exit polls, for instance, 31 percent of respondents identified inflation as their primary concern, but abortion was cited by a full 27 percent as their major issue in voting (CNN 2022). Because these cultural issues have mattered so much in expanding Republican candidates' voter appeal, condemnation of abortion, LGBTQ+ rights, and the treatment of transgen-der individuals continue to hold a leading position on the Republican Party's agenda. The party's challenge, then, is to balance the strong commitment of its activists to these cultural issues while not turning off Republican voters less motivated by these "culture wars."

Close Partisan Parity at the National Level

This shift in the parties' issue agendas has made it easier for Republican candi-dates to win elections, especially in the South. As a result, Republicans, who were the minority party in the US House for forty years until 1994, have been able to win control of the House and the Senate more than half the time since then (see Lee 2013, 777). When the current minority party can dream of becom-ing the majority, not just in the distant future but maybe even in the next elec-tion, why should it be willing to work with the opposition to pass bills? Doesn't it make better strategic sense to oppose everything the other party proposes, force the majority party into votes that are difficult to defend to constituents, and therefore increase the minority party's chance of gaining control in the next election? The result motivates the parties to focus on advertising their talking points rather than creating policy. With so many intense primary voters pressing for ideological purity in their representatives, candidates are tempted to take more extreme positions, which can become a roadblock when Congress members try to shift to crafting viable public policies.

"Negative partisanship"

Another aspect of polarization is that people's party identification is now closely related to their race, ideology, and religiosity. This increasing align-ment of important identities has led to greater hostility between Republicans and Democrats. This "negative partisanship" began to increase in the 1980s and has reached new heights in the past decade. Both parties' supporters have become substantially more negative toward the other party. The percentage of Democrats and Democratic-leaning independents holding an unfavorable view of the Republican Party increased from 57 percent to 81 percent during the past two decades, and the proportion of Republicans and Republican-leaning independents with an unfavorable opinion of Democrats rose from 68 percent in 1994 to 81 percent in 2017. A study in 2014 reported that about a third of each party's identifiers say that the other side's policies "are so misguided that they threaten the nation's well-being"—and the percentage rises substantially among respondents who are politically active (Pew 2014). Many partisans now feel stronger hostility toward the other party than they feel affection for their own party (Pew 2017; see also Iyengar and Krupenkin 2018).

Such hostile feelings make bipartisanship even more difficult to achieve. In fact, when asked whether they prefer public officials who compromise with people who disagree or whether officials should stick to their positions, 52 percent of Republican respondents prefer the latter, whereas 69 percent of self-identified Democrats choose compromise (Pew 2017).

One-sided Media

Media outlets have also been greatly affected by party polarization. Media polarization is nothing new in the United States. For at least the first century of the US, the only media available to American readers were partisan media. Technology leading to the creation of national networks led to the economic need to appeal to a broad, undifferentiated audience. But the biased sources had never gone away, and with the end of implementation of the Fairness Doctrine and the success of Rush Limbaugh on radio and Fox News on TV, as well as the introduction of online news sources that could survive with relatively small, curated audiences, partisan media allow readers and viewers to wrap themselves entirely in media designed for people who share their partisan views (Prior 2008). When many voters expose themselves only to media that express a single point of view, bipartisanship becomes harder to imagine.

YET BIPARTISANSHIP SURVIVES

These forces limiting bipartisanship may seem overwhelming—and, in fact, they often are. *But although bipartisanship has suffered major blows, it is not disappearing.*

Although partisan voting has increased in the US House and the Senate, bipartisanship can also be found in important policy areas. Major federal programs such as Medicare and its prescription drug benefit plan had bipartisan support on final passage. So did the increase in the federal minimum wage in 2007, expansion of the Violence Against Women Act in 2013 and its reauthorization in 2022, and criminal justice reform in 2018. In fact, a careful study (Curry and Lee 2019) finds that *most* legislation that passed both houses and became law between 1973 and 2016, including landmark legislation, had substantial bipartisan support. *Successful* legislative coalitions are almost as bipartisan now as they were in the 1970s.

In short, although bills may pass one house of Congress along party lines, the majority party can't usually go it alone in getting bills through Congress as a whole. Even in the face of party polarization, and even when both houses of Congress are controlled by the same party, bills with bipartisan support are more likely to get enough votes to become law (see Harbridge et al. 2023). So, "When majority parties succeed on their agenda priorities, they usually do so with support from a majority of the minority party in at least one chamber and with the endorsement of one or more of the minority party's top leaders" (Curry and Lee 2019, 47).

A good example of bipartisan achievement is the long-term survival of the SNAP (Supplemental Nutrition Assistance Program), more popularly known as "food stamps." In the late 1930s and early 1940s, the food stamp program was set up to deal with widespread hunger during the Great Depression and to meet the needs of farmers at a time when markets were disrupted by the threat of world war. The program lapsed, but it returned as a pilot program in the early 1960s. Congress then passed the bipartisan Food Stamp Act of 1964, which provided people on government relief access to nutritional foods. The program was revised several times in the 1970s. Another major bipartisan reform was passed in 2008 over President G. W. Bush's veto, to further reduce fraud and protect users' privacy.

What led to bipartisan support in this case? Food stamps were designed to benefit constituencies of both major parties. By expanding the market for farmers' surplus production and sales at grocery stores, as well as crop insurance and farm price supports, the program served groups that tended to vote Republican. It also provided food for low-income families, who are likely to vote Democratic. Food stamp users lived in more Republican rural and small-town areas as well as more Democratic big cities and in states represented by Republicans as well as Democrats. Former Republican Senate leader Robert Dole helped lead support for the program in cooperation with Democratic Senator George McGovern and others. Because SNAP was crafted to benefit the constituencies of both parties in Congress, it was able to weather a highly partisan atmosphere.

Efforts at bipartisanship do fail, of course. Think of the Affordable Care Act ("Obamacare"), passed in 2010, making affordable health insurance available to a larger proportion of Americans, particularly lower-income and younger people. Every one of the Republicans in both the US House of Representatives and the US Senate voted no, and almost every Democrat voted yes. In the subsequent presidential term of Donald Trump, every House Democrat voted against the Republican tax cut bill of 2017. Under the next president, Joe

Biden, the $1.9 trillion pandemic legislation of 2021 was passed without a single Republican vote in either chamber. Bipartisanship isn't easy to achieve.

In many other cases, however, even a united majority party can't ram its legislation through both houses of Congress without the agreement of at least a substantial number of members of the minority party. That is consistent with the many features of the US political system intended to fracture political power, to keep transient popular majorities from becoming dictatorial. A majority in public sentiment at any given time for a particular policy—say, more effective controls on the purchasing and use of guns—can be stymied by a series of institutional hurdles. Although members of the US House are elected every two years and therefore assumed to be responsive to public opinion, their election occurs at the same time as only one-third of the members of the Senate and only in every other House election with the vote for president. A wave of popular sentiment in one election year, then, will not be felt to the same extent in the Senate as it is in the House, and it may not coincide with a presidential race at all. The division of Congress into two houses produces institutional rivalries and differences that work against majority rule. The constitutional provision that each branch of the federal government can veto the actions of the other two also interferes with the direct translation of majority public opinion into law. All these institutional features make it difficult for a majority party in one house of Congress—and sometimes, in Congress as a whole—to push its agenda into law.

Other non-constitutional forces can combine to produce either a bipartisan outcome or no legislation at all. The continuing threat of the Senate filibuster, in which any Senate bill must get at least sixty votes to pass rather than a simple majority, means that no bills will pass the Senate without at least some support from the minority party, because the majority has rarely held more than fifty-nine Senate seats. Because the number of moderates in the Senate has declined, the majority party is unlikely to be able to reach sixty votes just by picking off a few moderate minority senators; getting to sixty usually requires working with minority party leaders to bring enough votes on board. These institutional rules make it harder for the majority party to push bills through without help from their minority colleagues. Even the more cohesive majority parties of recent Congresses have not been able to move their agenda into law without substantial bipartisan support.

As a result, during the past four decades, bills that became law were supported, on average, by more than 70 percent of members of the House minority party; the average is only slightly lower in the Senate (Curry and Lee 2019, 51). This has been true of major pieces of legislation, not just low-visibility bills.

For example, during the first two years of the Biden presidency, which has faced exceptionally high rates of party conflict, a bipartisan group of senators negotiated the first gun control legislation to pass Congress in thirty years, and bipartisan votes were responsible for the $1.2 trillion infrastructure law passed in 2021 and laws dealing with hate crimes, postal delivery, violence against women, and other important issues. Majority parties during this time have only occasionally been able to enact parts of their congressional agenda into law when a majority of the other party votes no.

Researchers have found even more evidence of bipartisanship in other parts of the lawmaking process. Most systematic studies of congressional behavior focus on roll-call voting: the dramatic and often public occasions when members of Congress cast their official ballots on the legislation being debated. It is in these roll-call vote studies that we see clearest evidence of party polarization and increasing partisanship (see Theriault 2008). Because roll-call votes meet the media's definition of news—they are clear-cut, conflict-filled, and visible—they receive more media coverage than most other congressional activities, and because they are easily measurable, they understandably attract the lion's share of attention from congressional scholars.

Roll-call votes are only part of what Congress does, however. Voice votes—those in which individual members' votes are not recorded, but the chair judges whether the yeas or nays have greater support—tend to be more bipartisan than roll-call votes (Harbridge 2015, ch. 1). There's added evidence of bipartisan cooperation in decisions to cosponsor bills. It is not unusual for a bill to have cosponsors from the minority party, though the number of these signers may be small. Congress members often brag to their constituents that they have cosponsored bills with members of the other party (Harbridge 2015, 33). The process of gaining cosponsors is not a public one, however. So "bipartisanship, in short, is not dead. It is just hidden from view" (Harbridge 2015, 3). Yet the compromises made to achieve these cosponsorships, and the committee and subcommittee delibertions, are baked into the bills that are then subject to roll calls.

At times, Congress shows bipartisanship in exercising its oversight responsibilities: investigating the activities of the executive branch and other salient issues. Oversight gets more attention when it is confrontational; the hearings of the January 6 committee investigating the 2021 attempted coup at the US Capitol received much more media coverage and public attention than did, for instance, the work of the House Select Committee on the Modernization of Congress. Yet the latter oversight committee, made up of six Republicans and six Democrats, issued ninety-seven unanimous recommendations in 2020 on how to change the House and increase the chances for bipartisanship. Recommendations ranged from bringing back some form of earmarks (benefits specifically for one district, which can often be used as sweeteners to bring about compromise) to setting aside space in the Capitol for Congress members of both parties to relax. The committee's cochair noted that bipartisanship could help raise Congress's standing with the public: "The fact that Congress, according to recent polling, is held in lower regard than head lice, colonoscopies and the band Nickelback is some indication that the public doesn't hold Congress in high regard" (Davis 2020, quoting Rep. Tom Graves, R-GA).

Members of Congress often claim that their bills are bipartisan, even when, objectively, the bills have not involved bipartisan sponsors or compromises (Westwood 2022). Claiming the symbolism of bipartisanship doesn't change the reality. But it does suggest that Congress members realize that being known to cooperate with the other party can be effective in campaigns. Presidents, too, often make bipartisan appeals in their rhetoric and at least some of their behavior. By doing so, presidents may increase their support among independent voters, who are not a large portion of the electorate but can make a real difference in close races (Villalobos et al., 2011). Finally, legislators (especially those in the minority party) who engage in bipartisan cooperation are more effective at moving their bills through Congress (see Volden and Wiseman 2016).

So we have a fascinating puzzle. On the one hand, signs of party polarization are shot through US politics. Partisan appeals appear frequently in Congress members' campaign ads, speeches, and roll-call voting behavior. Congressional party leaders are more and more likely to bring partisan bills to the floor, and members show greater unity in their party-line votes than before. Journalists and members of the public see bipartisan cooperation as almost nonexistent; consider the recent National Public Radio story titled, "A Tale Of Bipartisanship In Congress—No, Seriously" (Davis 2020).

On the other hand, there is systematic evidence that this is not the whole story. When legislation *passes* Congress, as opposed to simply being introduced and debated, it frequently has support from substantial numbers of minority-party legislators. The powerful pull of party and ideological polarization leads candidates and legislators to make a great deal of partisan noise and to associate the other party's activities with every type of sin and dishonor. As a result, "Legislative votes that distinguish the parties abound, but these votes are very rarely the enactment of laws. In many cases, they are messaging efforts that have no effect on public policy. On the occasions when majority parties do succeed in lawmaking, they rarely do so over the opposition of the minority party. Most lawmaking accomplishments are bipartisan, allowing both parties to claim credit" (Curry and Lee 2019, 60).

One reason for the widespread assumption that bipartisanship is dead is that it is typically under-reported. A recent study (quoted in De Vise 2023) found that the most hyperpartisan members of Congress got four times the coverage in major media platforms as did the least hyperpartisan members. That is likely to continue, given that drama, conflict, and anger are more likely to draw audiences to news platforms than substantive coverage of what Congress is doing at a given time (Hershey 2021, 241–242).

WHAT CIRCUMSTANCES ENCOURAGE BIPARTISAN COOPERATION?

What are the types of issues that tend to stimulate bipartisan cooperation?

On average, bipartisanship occurs more often in foreign policy than in domestic policy. International threats have often been the crucible of bipartisanship (Bryan and Tama 2022), especially when the nation is at war. After the terrorist attacks of September 11, 2001, both congressional parties signed on to the establishment of a National Commission on Terrorist Attacks Upon the United States, more commonly known as the 9/11 Commission, headed by a Republican and a Democrat. When the nation faces a mortal threat, bipartisanship is not as difficult to achieve, though it may wane as the crisis evolves.

A notable example of bipartisan cooperation in foreign policy was the extensive work by Senators Richard Lugar (R-IN) and Sam Nunn (D-GA) to pass the Cooperative Threat Reduction legislation in the 1980s and 1990s. At a time when the Soviet Union was disintegrating, the cooperation between Nunn and Lugar prevented the many Soviet-held nuclear weapons from falling into the hands of hostile regimes and terrorist organizations. Another more recent example of bipartisanship is demonstrated by members of both parties have condemned China's problematic human rights record and its alleged programs to foment discord among Americans through the internet and other means.

Bipartisan voting is easier to achieve on less controversial pieces of legislation. In polarized times, it is harder for the minority party's Congress members to support the majority's bills on issues that receive a lot of media coverage and public attention. By giving the majority party a win, the minority fears enhancing its opponent's standing and future election success. But "when something has low salience, its passage isn't seen as conceding ground to the other side" (Bazelon and Yglesias 2021). When dealing with low-profile issues, a few members on each side may have the space to educate themselves on the issue and find ways to benefit both parties while those who thrive on partisan division are attuned elsewhere. Others (Mellow and Trubowitz 2005) show that bipartisanship is more likely when the two major parties are diverse geographically, though this geographic diversity has often been lacking in the American parties.

At times, strategic members of Congress from both parties have been able to come together when the party leaders themselves were unable or unwilling to reach a compromise. These negotiators, typically termed "the Gang of [insert number]" by reporters, have prompted significant bipartisan legislation. After the 2004 elections, for instance, President George W. Bush's nominations of conservatives to federal appellate court judgeships led to a partisan stalemate. In the Republican-controlled Senate, Democrats successfully blocked the nominations by threatening a filibuster. Frustrated Senate Republicans in turn threatened to invoke what was called the "nuclear option"—changing Senate rules so that filibusters could no longer be used to stop judicial nominations. It was called the "nuclear option" because it was expected to blow up the relationships between the parties. The stalemate was broken by the "Gang of 14"—seven Democratic and seven Republican senators, meeting apart from their colleagues and the Senate leadership. They negotiated a written agreement that if the Democratic minority would quit filibustering Bush's judicial nominees, the Republican majority would drop its threat to invoke the nuclear option. (That agreement lasted until 2013, when the Senate Democratic leadership did move forward with the nuclear option, which was expanded by a Republican-dominated Senate leadership in 2017.)

These efforts have had varying degrees of success. A "Gang of Six" worked toward a bipartisan Senate agreement on health care reform in 2009. Though negotiations lasted for months, no compromise developed. But two later "gangs" were more successful. A large "Gang of 20"—a fifth of all Senate members—formed in 2019 to explore several areas of possible collaboration, including infrastructure, immigration, and raising the minimum wage. Another "gang" of eight Democratic and Republican leaders of the House and Senate, as well as the chairs and ranking members of the House and Senate Intelligence Committees, formed in 2023 to investigate classified documents found on the properties of former President Trump, former Vice President Mike Pence, and President Biden. These small groups of motivated participants give both parties' lawmakers the chance to attempt a workable compromise without the glare of publicity that can heighten partisanship.

Gang formation is one of the unorthodox ways in which Congress has come to handle legislation during the past three decades (see Sinclair 2016).

Congressional party leaders have taken increasingly important roles in negotiating on bills. Leaders often bypass standing committees in bringing bills
they favor to a vote—a major change from the traditional practice in which
these committees took the lead in honing legislation before it came to a vote.
But at least to this point, the increased power of congressional party leaders
has not stamped out bipartisanship. In fact, the current ability of legislative
party leaders to bypass committee deliberation can increase the flexibility
and secrecy that facilitate bipartisan negotiation (Curry and Lee 2020, ch. 6).

In short, research shows that there has been room for both heightened party
voting *and* several important collaborations between the parties in Congress in
recent decades, including on landmark bills. Members of Congress still need
to satisfy the strong partisan demands that stem from the more intense, often
more extreme voters in their party's primary. Otherwise, their careers in Washington, DC, will soon come to an end. But even though these primary voters
are often allergic to compromise between the parties, they have not yet been
able to prevent all bipartisan collaboration.

Bipartisanship remains hard to achieve; a variety of electoral and institutional incentives are stacked against it. It is easier to clear those hurdles under
some circumstances than others: among members of Congress whose districts
remain competitive, when international threats are present, and on domestic
issues that manage to evade the harsh light of intense media scrutiny. Yet it
remains the case that if a bill is to stand a good chance of becoming law, it will
probably need at least some buy-in from the minority party.

WHAT CAN BE DONE TO ENCOURAGE BIPARTISANSHIP?

What can be done to redress the balance between partisan and bipartisan efforts? One possible answer comes from the Robbers Cave experimenters, who
reported that boys developed strong loyalties toward their group and hostility
toward another group though there was no apparent basis for conflict between
them. The researchers found that simply bringing the two groups together for
fun activities didn't reduce the hostility between them. But when the groups
were put to work on achieving valued goals that took cooperation to achieve—
for instance, dealing with a problem they all faced—eventually the two groups
stopped fighting and began working together.

One way to apply this answer to Congress would be to encourage a common
understanding, among members, of the central facts of an issue. Although legislators are likely to see any issue through a partisan lens, encouraging members
to share the sources of their information, question witnesses out of camera

range, and work to establish a common body of knowledge can put extremist claims in context. So-called conflict entrepreneurs (Ripley 2021) can more easily whip up dissension when legislators are working from mutually exclusive sets of facts. A richer research and informational environment for all members could be provided if substantially more resources were invested in the Congressional Research Service (https://crsreports.congress.gov/Home/About), which now conducts bipartisan research when requested by members or committee staffs. Greatly increased funding and staffing as well as regular briefings on current issues could strengthen this vital service, along with a focus on the relationship between proposed policies and the protection of democratic norms.

Another possible answer is to further encourage and support the informal, bipartisan caucuses of Congress members particularly concerned with a given issue, known as "legislative membership organizations," such as the Rural Caucus, the Military Veterans Caucus, and the Bipartisan Women's Caucus (Butler and Sommerfeld 2017). These caucuses promote the development of "weak ties" among members (see Granovetter 1973)—the acquaintanceships and loose social connections that promote the flow of information across individuals. These casual connections expose individuals to sources of information outside of the "echo chambers" in which they and their closest contacts are embedded. As a result, they can broaden individual Congress members' perspectives and expand their factual knowledge. To the extent that legislative membership organizations promote the development of weak ties, they can not only generate shared bodies of knowledge but also serve as incubators for bipartisan bills. Some researchers find (see Ringe and Victor 2013) that Congress members are more likely to create bills with bipartisan co-sponsorship when they share membership in a caucus on that issue.

Another important answer is to build social trust. In the book *Bowling Alone* (Putnam 2000), political scientist Robert Putnam found that the social bonds that connect individuals have frayed in recent decades. People are less likely to know their neighbors, get together with friends, belong to organizations that meet face-to-face, and as the title suggests, belong to bowling leagues, even though more people bowl now than ever before. These changes erode interpersonal trust, known as "social capital," which is as important to a nation as is economic or physical capital. A certain level of interpersonal trust is necessary for people to risk cooperating; they need to feel reasonably sure that the other negotiators are acting in good faith.

In Congress, programs that help members get to know one another across party lines can enhance interpersonal trust. It is easier to demonize people we don't know. By breaking down the cultural isolation that divides Republicans from Democrats, urban from rural legislators, southerners from northeastern- ers, and those who value government from those who despise it, Congress members can better understand why others hold different beliefs from their own. In earlier decades, members of Congress were more likely to live in Wash- ington, DC, and to attend events outside of the Capitol together. Now, when members are urged to spend hours every day on the phone raising money for reelection and when maintaining a home in the district and visiting frequently have become important markers of concern about constituents, members are simply less likely to interact socially with one another. This lack of communica- tion can heighten distrust.

Encouraging bipartisan cooperation, as well as civil partisanship, can help soften the damaging effects of party and ideological polarization in American political life. As Representative Hamilton (2023) points out, "In the end, a battle over public policy isn't about momentary wins or losses, but about creating sustainable policy that's accepted by a broad cross- section of the population. . . . In legislative terms, this means finding a path to bipartisan cooperation." That, in turn, is necessary to sustain the democratic institutions that so many generations have worked for so long to protect.

WORKS CITED

Aldrich, John H., and Ruth W. Grant. 1993. "The Antifederalists, the First Con- gress, and the First Parties." *Journal of Politics* 55, no. 2 (May): 295–326.

Anderson, Sarah E., Daniel M. Butler, and Laurel Harbridge-Yong. 2020. *Rejecting Compromise: Legislators' Fear of Primary Voters.* Cambridge: Cambridge Univer- sity Press.

Babington, Charles. 2010. "Despite All the Nice Talk, Partisanship Reigns." Asso- ciated Press, Feb. 9, 2010. https://www.nbcnews.com/id/wbna35312826.

Bazelon, Simon, and Matthew Yglesias. 2021. "The Rise and Importance of Secret Congress." *Slow Boring,* June 21. https://www.slowboring.com/p/the-rise -and-importance-of-secret.

Binder, Sarah. 2014. "Divided We Govern?" Brookings Center for Effective Public Management, May. https://www.brookings.edu/wp-content/uploads/2016/06 /BrookingsCEPM_Polarized_figReplacedTextRevTableRev.pdf.

Bishop, Bill. 2008. *The Big Sort.* New York: Houghton Mifflin.

Bryan, James D., and Jordan Tama. 2022. "The Prevalence of Bipartisanship in U.S. Foreign Policy." *International Politics* 59: 874–897.

Butler, Stuart M., and Matthew Sommerfeld. 2017. "Could Caucuses Help Rebuild Bipartisanship on Capitol Hill?" Brookings Institution, February 9. https://www.brookings.edu/research/could-caucuses-help-rebuild -bipartisanship-on-capitol-hill/.

CNN. 2022. "2022 Exit Polls." Accessed Dec. 4, 2023. https://www.cnn.com /election/2022/exit-polls/national-results/house/o.

Cook Political Report. 2022. Accessed Dec. 4, 2023. https://www.cookpolitical .com/ratings/house-race-ratings?mod=article_inline.

Curry, James M., and Frances E. Lee. 2019. "Non-Party Government: Bipartisan Lawmaking and Party Power in Congress." Perspectives on Politics 17, no. 1: 47–65.

Curry, James M., and Frances E. Lee. 2020. The Limits of Party. Chicago: University of Chicago Press.

Davis, Nicholas T. 2019. "Identity Sorting and Political Compromise." American Politics Research 47, no. 2 (Sept.): 391–414.

Davis, Susan. 2020. "A Tale of Bipartisanship in Congress—No, Seriously." National Public Radio, December 26. https://www.npr.org/2020/12/26 /949286593/a-tale-of-bipartisanship-in-congress-no-seriously.

DeSilver, Drew. 2014. "How the Most Ideologically Polarized Americans Live Different Lives." Pew Research Center, June 13. https://www.pewresearch.org /fact-tank/2014/06/13/big-houses-art-museums-and-in-laws-how-the-most -ideologically-polarized-americans-live-different-lives/.

DeSilver, Drew. 2022. "The Polarization in Today's Congress Has Roots That Go Back Decades." Pew Research Center, March 10. https://www.pewresearch .org/fact-tank/2022/03/10/the-polarization-in-todays-congress-has-roots -that-go-back-decades/.

De Vise, Daniel. 2023. "'Hyper-partisan' Politicians Get Four Times the News Coverage of Bipartisan Colleagues." The Hill, March 13. https://thehill.com /homenews/media/3894486-hyper-partisan-politicians-get-four-times-the -news-coverage-of-bipartisan-colleagues/.

Engstrom, Erik J. 2013. Partisan Gerrymandering and the Construction of American Democracy. Ann Arbor: University of Michigan Press.

Flexner, James Thomas. 1984. Washington: The Indispensable Man. New York: New American Library.

Granovetter, Mark S. 1973. "The Strength of Weak Ties." American Journal of Sociology 78, no. 6 (May): 1360–1380.

Hamilton, Lee. 2023. "Our System Can't Work without Compromise." Indiana University Center on Representative Government, March 23. https://corg .iu.edu/programs/hamilton-views/comments-on-congress/Our%20System %20Cant%20Work%20Without%20Compromise.html.

Harbridge, Laurel. 2015. *Is Bipartisanship Dead?* New York: Cambridge University Press.

Harbridge, Laurel, Neil Malhotra, and Brian F. Harrison. 2014. "Public Preferences for Bipartisanship in the Policymaking Process." *Legislative Studies Quarterly* 39, no. 3 (Aug.): 327–355.

Harbridge-Yong, Laurel, Craig Volden, and Alan E. Wiseman. 2023. "The Bipartisan Path to Effective Lawmaking." *Journal of Politics* 85, no. 3 (July). https://doi.org/10.1086/723805.

Henderson, John A., Brian T. Hamel, and Aaron M. Goldzimer. 2018. "Gerrymandering Incumbency." *Journal of Politics* 80 (#3 July): 1011–1016.

Herndon, Astead W. 2021. "In Iowa, Gaetz and Greene Pick Up Where Trump Left Off." *New York Times*, August 21. https://www.nytimes.com/2021/08/21/us/politics/marjorie-taylor-greene-matt-gaetz-iowa.html.

Hershey, Marjorie Randon. 2021. *Party Politics in America*, 18th ed. New York: Routledge.

Hershey, Marjorie Randon, and Nathaniel E. Birkhead. 2019. "Assessing the Ideological Extremism of American Party Activists." *Party Politics* 25, no. 4: 495–506.

Iyengar, Shanto, and Masha Krupenkin. 2018. "The Strengthening of Partisan Affect." *Advances in Political Psychology* 39, S1 (Feb.): 201–218.

Lee, Frances E. 2013. "Presidents and Party Teams." *Presidential Studies Quarterly* 43, no. 4 (Oct.): 775–791.

Liptak, Adam. 2019. "Supreme Court Bars Challenges to Partisan Gerrymandering." *New York Times* June 27, 2019, p. A1.

Madison, James. Federalist Number 10, November 22, 1787. https://founders.archives.gov/documents/Madison/01-10-02-0178.

McCourt School of Public Policy. 2022. "The Lugar Center and McCourt School unveil Bipartisan Index rankings for the 117th Congress." Georgetown University, May 3. https://mccourt.georgetown.edu/news/bipartisan-index-rankings-117th-congress/.

McCullough, David. 2002. *John Adams*. New York: Simon & Schuster.

McDonald, Michael P. 2004. "A Comparative Analysis of Redistricting Institutions in the United States, 2001–02." *State Politics & Policy Quarterly* 4, no. (Winter): 371–395.

McGhee, Eric, and Boris Shor. 2017. "Has the Top Two Primary Elected More Moderates?" *Perspectives on Politics* 15, no. 4 (Sept.): 1053–1066.

Mellow, Nicole, and Peter Trubowitz. 2005. "Red Versus Blue." *Political Geography* 24: 659–677.

Morrison, Peter A., and Thomas M. Bryan. 2019. "Unmasking 'Packing' and 'Cracking' for Racial or Partisan Purposes." In *Redistricting*, by Morrison and Bryan, pp. 75–85. New York: Springer.

Pew Research Center. 2017. "The Partisan Divide on Political Values Grows Even Wider." October 5. https://www.pewresearch.org/politics/2017/10/05/8-partisan-animosity-personal-politics-views-of-trump/.

Pew Research Center. 2014. "Growing Partisan Antipathy." June 12. https://www.pewresearch.org/politics/2014/06/12/section-2-growing-partisan-antipathy/.

Putnam, Robert D. 2000. *Bowling Alone.* New York: Simon & Schuster.

Ringe, Nils, and Jennifer Nicoll Victor with Christopher J. Carman. 2013. *Bridging the Information Gap.* Ann Arbor: University of Michigan Press.

Ripley, Amanda. 2021. *High Conflict.* New York: Simon & Schuster.

Shafer, Jack. 2021. "'Bipartisanship' Is Dead in Washington. That's Fine." *Politico,* May 28. https://www.politico.com/news/magazine/2021/05/28/bipartisan-congress-dead-washington-491372.

Sherif, Muzafer. 1956. "Experiments in Group Conflict." *Scientific American* 195, pp. 54–58. https://www.jstor.org/stable/24941808.

Sinclair, Barbara. 2016. *Unorthodox Lawmaking.* Washington, DC: CQ Press.

Theriault, Sean M. 2008. *Party Polarization in Congress.* Cambridge: Cambridge University Press.

Villalobos, Jose, Justin S. Vaughn, and Julia R. Azari. 2011. "Bipartisanship in an Increasingly Partisan Era." Paper presented at the 2011 Annual Meeting of the Western Political Science Association. https://papers.ssrn.com/sol3/papers.cfm?abstract_id=1766730.

Volden, Craig, and Alan E. Wiseman. 2016. "Are Bipartisan Lawmakers More Effective?" Center for the Study of Democratic Institutions, Vanderbilt University. https://my.vanderbilt.edu/alanwiseman/files/2016/12/volden_wiseman_CSDI_WP_4_2016.pdf.

Westwood, Sean J. 2022. "The Partisanship of Bipartisanship: How Representatives Use Bipartisan Assertions to Cultivate Support." *Political Behavior* 44 (Sept 2022): 1411–1435. https://doi.org/10.1007/s11109-020-09659-6.

MARJORIE RANDON HERSHEY *is Professor Emeritus of Political Science at Indiana University Bloomington.*

PART II

BIPARTISANSHIP AT WORK

FIVE

WHAT BIPARTISANSHIP REALLY LOOKS LIKE

ANDRÉ CARSON

PARTISANSHIP TRADITIONALLY REFERS TO FOLLOWING general principles and policies of a particular party or group. For me, a life-long Democrat, that means policies that advance fairness and equal opportunities for everyone. It also means supporting and strengthening social safety net programs, like Social Security and Medicare. The Grand Old Party, or GOP, has long touted its belief in limited government and free markets to economic advancement. Left and right. But no one side is always right or always wrong. As elected representatives, members of Congress must work together to find consensus. And this is often found in the middle, not out on the far ends of the spectrum.

The ability to work with people across the political aisle is often referred to as being bipartisan. But bipartisanship alone is not always a good thing, particularly if it's a bad policy being pushed under the "bipartisan" banner. However, good policies that have grown out of dialogue and consensus often bring the recognition of agreement and the good will to pass with a majority of votes.

In the House of Representatives, it's important to remember that the magic number to pass a bill is 218 votes. Very rarely do the same 218 people vote the same way on vote after vote. Each vote is unique and different. We hear a lot about "straight, party-line votes." But less attention goes to those other votes. Votes that reflect local, regional, or personal priorities that defy party lines. Speaker Tip O'Neill was right, "All politics is local." Or it can be.

This differs from a new and disturbing trend of hyperpartisan extremism that has emerged over the last few years, and which reached its worst yet in 2023: rather than simply disagreeing with someone else's opinion, it became common to see viciously personal hyperpartisan attacks that demonize, vilify, and possibly threaten those with whom they disagree. I don't need to name names for you to come up with examples that make you cringe, or think, "That's not how our elected officials are supposed to act."

But the extremists haven't taken over completely yet. I believe if more people of good will and common sense stay engaged in our civic discussions, we can restore some of the civil discourse that most Americans want—for the common good. These breakthroughs of bipartisanship don't often get press attention because there's no shouting. There are encouraging examples if you know where to look.

When I was asked to write about bipartisanship for this collection, I knew I had plenty to talk about. Bipartisanship isn't just a buzzword for me—as a Hoosier and the representative of Indiana's Seventh Congressional District in the US House of Representatives since 2008; I live it every day.

Over time, Congress has developed a reputation for being slow, inefficient, and sometimes chaotic. Congressional job approval was at its highest following September 11, 2001 (Gallup.com 2001), but a poll in May 2023 showed disapproval of Congress sitting at 77 percent (Gallup.com 2023). That's not good for the People's House. But it's important to note that sometimes what is perceived as "slowness" is really the hard, painstaking work of compromising. This includes debating in committees (real debate means listening with open ears and minds, learning about different perspectives, and not spewing a prepared diatribe when your mind is already made up). It includes marking up bills to change them—perhaps from one extreme or another, to consensus language that can end up passing by voice votes because improvements have been made. This process is described as sausage-making for a reason. It can be time consuming and messy. But if done well, with good intent and sound policy ingredients, the result is beneficial.

At some point in recent years, it has become more common on both sides to deliver blows that used to be off limits. Instead of talking to one another in hearings or on the House floor, attacks are made for the cameras. Disagreements playing out in a twenty-four-hour news cycle, amplified by hyperpartisan pundits who are seeking more clicks and more revenue and not acting in the best interest of the whole country. It's no wonder most everyday Americans find the activities at the US Capitol to be something they turn away from instead of staying engaged.

In reality, behind the scenes, Congress is slightly more . . . normal. Representatives share elevator conversations, walk together for votes, and we gather on the House floor to conduct business, but between votes, folks have been known to share photos of family members—or even talk about the latest episode of

Succession. After hours, we may chat in group messages about legislation or about what new food options are in the cafeteria. Personally, I still brag about the Indiana-based Steak 'n Shake that opened in the Rayburn Cafeteria.

Congress, as a whole, is probably tamer than what people are sometimes led to believe. Perhaps I'm biased, but I also believe there is something special about Hoosiers and our ability to extend hospitality to anyone.

That's Hoosier hospitality. And it translates to real bills, real policies, and real change for everyday Americans.

The nature of politics in the twenty-first century can be quite loud—whether it's splashy, click-bait headlines or commentators yelling at each other on TV. But again, the accomplishments of day-to-day work in Congress don't have to be the loudest or showiest in the room. Sometimes they're a bit quieter. There are three examples that come to mind when I reflect on successful, bipartisan efforts that have, or will have, enormous impacts on Americans' lives.

REBUILDING AMERICA WITH THE
BIPARTISAN INFRASTRUCTURE LAW

I can't talk about bipartisanship without talking about the Bipartisan Infrastructure Law—a historic, once-in-a-generation investment in our nation's crumbling infrastructure. As a senior Member of the Transportation and Infrastructure Committee, I have long worked to expand funding and equitable access to our nation's infrastructure. There's no such thing as a Democratic road or a Republican bridge, only roads and bridges. No matter what side of the aisle you fall on, infrastructure is important to everyone.

But it's not just roads and bridges. In the twenty-first century, access to high-speed internet isn't a luxury—it's a human right. In 2011, the United Nations released a report arguing that denying internet to citizens goes against international law, at a time when roughly two-thirds of Syria's internet access was dark. Especially in rural, remote parts of Indiana, internet is scarce, making it difficult to access health information, find and apply for jobs, apply for social services and benefits, and even participate in our democracy.

Access to clean drinking water, sadly, is another piece of the infrastructure puzzle that needs significant improvement. In Indianapolis, the Keystone Corridor Ground Water Contamination site will be one of twenty-two Environmental Protection Agency "Superfund" sites to transform this contaminated property, spur job creation, and ensure long-term access to safe drinking water.

Another aspect of the Bipartisan Infrastructure Law that will bring us into the future is electric vehicle (EV) infrastructure. According to the US Bureau of Labor Statistics, EV sales in the United States could reach 40 percent of total passenger car sales by 2030 (Colato and Ice 2023). EVs produce zero tailpipe emissions, meaning that they don't contribute to air pollution the same way gas-powered vehicles do, and they can travel four times as far as a traditional car given the same amount of energy. Although EVs require fewer trips to the gas station or the mechanic for oil changes, they do require a place to charge. While some folks only need a standard 110V outlet in their home garage, public charging stations are essential. I'm working to ensure Black neighborhoods don't get left behind in this important infrastructure by calling on the Department of Transportation to make equitable EV infrastructure in minority neighborhoods a priority.

It's all thanks to the Bipartisan Infrastructure Law. Working across the aisle is leading us toward a cleaner, greener, and brighter future.

DIAGNOSTICS TESTING WITH CONGRESSMAN PENCE

In May of 2023, on the same day former vice president Mike Pence announced he was running for president in 2024, I introduced a bill with another member of the Pence family—Congressman Greg Pence.

As the dean of the Indiana delegation, I work closely with my fellow Hoosiers in Congress, including Congressman Pence, who has represented Indiana's Sixth District since 2019. At face value, we might be a bit of an odd couple. Our politics differ, but our values and dedication to Hoosiers line up more than you might think.

Believe it or not, Congressman Pence and I have always had a great working relationship. This year we introduced a bill together, the bipartisan Diagnostics Testing Preparedness Plan Act to address the urgent need that arose during the pandemic: the availability and strength of diagnostic testing, one of the best tools we have to treat public health crises early and effectively. The COVID-19 pandemic revealed gaps in our current system, making it clear that to address any public health crisis—from a once-in-a-generation pandemic to a bad flu season—we can't rely on foreign countries for supplies, and our private/public partnerships and coordination need to be drastically improved.

At the time of this writing, our Diagnostics Testing bill has passed out of committee. The bill is co-led by another Hoosier Republican, Congressman Dr. Larry Bucshon, as well as a Democrat from Washington State, Congresswoman Dr. Kim Schrier.

Roche Diagnostic, a world leader in diagnostic testing, is headquartered in my district in Indianapolis. I'm proud of this bill and what it will mean for keeping Americans safe and healthy. But I'm even more proud that it corrects a perception many have about modern-day politics. Bipartisan bills in 2023 are still possible, and the results will translate into more jobs, more opportunities, and a stronger public health system.

FLYING INTO A STRONGER FUTURE

For years, I partnered with the late dean of the House, Don Young, to lead a bill that passed the House with broad, bipartisan support.

Don Young, a staunch conservative, represented the entire expanse of Alaska and its majestic wilderness. He was a pilot himself, and he shared my concerns about the need to improve America's aviation sector. We both agreed on the need for more diversity among our pilots, mechanics, and new engineers. We also agreed that we must expand educational and STEM opportunities to bring more young people into the aviation workforce, to improve safety and to better connect and serve Americans everywhere.

Don Young sadly passed away while flying back to his district, before our bill passed the House, but his reputation for working with people across the aisle, like me, had a big impact on the success of our bipartisan and bicameral bill, the National Center for the Advancement of Aviation Act. I have a new Republican partner on the bill, fellow midwesterner Pete Stauber, for the 118th Congress. I'm happy to report that we passed the bill a second time, in the newest FAA Reauthorization bill, and I believe this time it will pass the Senate and reach the president's desk.

The aviation industry drives our economy in Indiana and across the country. While it may not be the most attention-grabbing issue with debates featured on cable television, the future of this industry depends on our work. This is another example where an agreement actually gets ignored, while absurd disagreements make headlines.

HONORING CIVIL RIGHTS ICONS

In 2018, America was arguably at the height of division. Two years into the Trump presidency, it felt like neither side could agree on anything. I personally was feeling frustrated, especially by the administration's anti-Muslim executive orders and anti-Muslim policies, and I routinely spoke out against these cruel policies.

In the midst of what seemed like chaos, the Indiana delegation was quietly working together on an issue of great importance to our state and the entire country. We recognized the fiftieth anniversary of the heartbreaking assassinations in 1968 of both Dr. Martin Luther King Jr. and Senator Robert F. Kennedy—just a few months apart. *TIME* magazine published an anniversary edition that described 1968 as a year that could have torn the country apart, especially with the outburst of pent-up pain that resulted in so many urban riots across the country. But the city of Indianapolis did not erupt in violence, and I believe that was the result of the plea for peace and nonviolence made by Senator Kennedy—without a script and with the heartfelt experience of losing a loved one to violence.

The Kennedy-King National Commemorative Site Act enshrines the Landmark for Peace Memorial in Indianapolis where Senator Robert F. Kennedy delivered his historic, moving speech on the day Dr. King was killed. Traveling with Senator Kennedy that day was John Lewis, who later worked with me when I introduced a bill to preserve this site as a part of the National Park System and include it in the African American Civil Rights Network. With myself, Senator Todd Young, Senator Joe Donnelly, and Representative Susan Brooks, the entire Indiana delegation worked together, and the bill was passed by a Republican-led House, by an evenly split Senate, and then signed into law by President Trump. This was a true bipartisan effort.

Robert Kennedy spoke that fateful day in 1968 with a timeless message: "What we need in the United States is not division; what we need in the United States is not hatred; what we need in the United States is not violence and lawlessness, but is love, and wisdom, and compassion toward one another, and a feeling of justice toward those who still suffer within our country, whether they be white or whether they be black."

The idea of "Hoosier hospitality" may induce some eye-rolling, but in the halls of Congress, it's true. The Landmark for Peace Memorial is an opportunity for everyone in our state and our country to reflect, learn, and feel a call to action for the ongoing battle for civil rights.

I'll always remember Robert Kennedy's words, and now, Indianapolis visitors and residents will too.

Love and wisdom. Compassion. Selflessness. Service. These are all words I aspire to live out every day in Congress. For me, this role is not about personal recognition or accolades. It's not about being the loudest in the room, or the one who finds division instead of common ground. That does not mean I don't stand up to bigotry, racism, xenophobia, or injustice. But it does mean I find the times and places where common ground can be reached—otherwise we would not be able to make any progress at all.

The search for consensus and balance can be challenging, but it's simple: we can have decency in government again. We can have courtesy, and we can have compromise. Despite what internet comment sections and the echo chambers of cable news want you to believe about our country, despite the ideological arguments that can tear families apart over Thanksgiving dinner, it's still possible to work across the aisle to get things done. It takes open ears, open minds, and open hearts. As a Hoosier, I know there's more to agree over than to disagree, if we listen and learn about our neighbors' experiences.

WORKS CITED

Colato, Javier, and Lindsey Ice. 2023. "Charging into the Future: The Transition to Electric Vehicles," *Beyond the Numbers* 12, no. 4 (February 2023). www.bls.gov /opub/btn/volume-12/charging-into-the-future-the-transition-to-electric -vehicles.htm.

Gallup.com. 2001. "Do You Approve or Disapprove of the Way Congress Is Handling Its Job?" October 11–14, 2001. www.news.gallup.com/poll/1600/congress -public.aspx.

———. 2023. "Do You Approve or Disapprove of the Way Congress Is Handling Its Job?" May 1–24, 2023. www.news.gallup.com/poll/1600/congress-public .aspx.

ANDRÉ CARSON *is a Democratic member of the United States House of Representatives from Indiana.*

SIX

—w—

BIPARTISANSHIP AND LEADERSHIP

OLYMPIA SNOWE

IN 1997, I WAS HONORED to address the graduating class of the John F. Kennedy School of Government at Harvard. I told them I intended to speak about the great test facing our nation's political leaders: making government work. At that time—twenty-six years ago—I asserted it was a task made more daunting by the mounting chorus of partisanship that had engulfed our nation's politics.

Little could I have known that chorus would swell into a cacophony.

At the start of my address, I presented my thesis that the fundamental themes of leadership and the public good—forever and eternally intertwined—were too often the missing ingredients from contemporary political debate. I proposed this predicament forces those of us dedicated to public service to ask the question: Can we govern?

My answer was, and remains today, that we can—as long we do not lose sight of the two enduring elements, indeed, two testaments to our remarkable resolve as a people and a nation: a notion of the public good combined with the leadership to attain that public good.

I don't arrive at this question as some kind of above-the-fray Monday morning quarterback. I spent thirty-four years in elected office, serving in four different legislative bodies during the past three decades.

My journey to public service began on the road to the state House in Augusta, Maine. I was a young widow, running for the legislative seat that had been held by my late husband. And I was honored when the people of my hometown of Auburn elected me to represent them in the Maine House of Representatives.

I felt then, as I do now, that public service was a high calling. It was and is my deepest conviction that no pursuit is as valuable or worthier than the simple idea of helping others, of enabling individuals to improve their lives, of softening the hardest days and brightening the darkest. Put simply, I felt that as a public servant, my job was to solve problems.

I reference my early days of public life because I've reflected many times on this period, which stands in bold contrast to the political ethos that exists today.

In Augusta, I found that politics and public life were positive and constructive endeavors. Once the elections were over, my colleagues in the Maine legislature and I put campaigns and party labels behind us to enact laws that genuinely improved the lives of the citizens of our state.

I often reference what I call the Augusta Model. It provides a compelling allegory on politics, circa 1975. While it may sound quaint or dated, it provides a blueprint for governing that should neither be lost to history nor assumed to be impossible now to replicate. As I have frequently told audiences I have spoken to throughout the country since my retirement from the Senate in 2013, we should not—and need not—accept the current status quo as the new normal.

My years in the Maine legislature were an extremely positive and formative experience. Making laws was a hands-on process. I focused on the issues and learned how we could work together as legislators to help our constituents in practical ways. There was cross-party voting, and although we had fights, we were usually able to work through our political differences and find solutions.

We had one of our major and instructive cross-party successes early in my career. Several days before adjournment of the legislative session, I was appointed by the Speaker of the Maine House of Representatives to a bipartisan, bicameral group of legislators given something out of a *Mission Impossible* script. Our assignment was to develop a constitutional amendment to disband an antiquated government entity called the Executive Council. This body was an unelected, anachronistic holdover from 1820 that solely confirmed gubernatorial appointments in the state. Many previous sessions had tried and failed to dissolve it.

We in the group were, frankly, skeptical about our mission, given past, failed efforts to disband this administrative dinosaur. And not to mention we were in the final, hectic days of the legislative session—hardly an opportune time to try to abolish anything, let alone a 150-year-old political institution.

Our first meeting took place at a restaurant, over dinner, after a day in the legislature, and was run by the Senate and House chairs of the group. We huddled over our plates to start sketching out a plan and then returned for the legislative session, which was running late into the night. Sometimes, it helps to have a more informal setting away from the swirl of legislative chambers and offices, and something as simple as breaking bread together to create a more convivial mood.

I have always remembered the resoluteness with which we approached our task. We researched the question. We considered the concerns of our colleagues. We negotiated. We reached a consensus recommendation. And, despite being tasked with this project in the midst of the final flurry of the session, we passed our legislation creating a confirmation process through both houses of the Maine legislature and it was ultimately approved by referendum.

This successful effort had an important influence on me. I saw that anything is possible, even under difficult circumstances and time constraints, as long as you put forth a good-faith effort to solve a problem and have enough legislators who share a spirit of cooperation.

In 1978, I was elected to Congress as a legislator, a Republican, and a woman—not necessarily in that order—with a commitment to help my country, my state, and my party. Above all else, however, I continued to believe a legislator is a problem-solver and allowed my tenure to be guided by that basic tenet.

As such, being a Republican did not preclude my willingness to work with legislators who were at different points on the political spectrum. Often a bill would be written off by some legislators because of who was presenting it. But that was never a factor in my thinking on an issue when I was looking for an essential legislative partnership. It was the issue that was paramount.

Indeed, my first defining experience in Washington, DC—after service in the Maine State House of Representatives and Maine Senate—demonstrated that problems can be solved, even under the most unlikely of conditions.

When I first came to Washington in January 1979 as the US representative from Maine's Second Congressional District, it became clear to me rather quickly that Congress was practically oblivious to a critical set of issues: those of particular importance to our nation's women. This observation was not fueled by a supercharged sense of radical feminism or aggrieved group politics. It was simply the truth.

I was, after all, one of only seventeen women members in the US House and Senate in 1979. To put this in perspective, that was less than 3 percent of the entire US Congress—in a nation in which women made up 54 percent of the electorate. From the outset, it was clear to me, and to each of us as women, that we were far too few to be divided among ourselves along partisan lines. We recognized that we held not only a tremendous responsibility, but an obligation to "go to bat" for the women of America. We knew full well that our success or our failure rested solely on our shoulders and our ability to collaborate on issues that were essential for America's women—and that if we didn't fight for those issues together, no one would.

Thankfully, I had been preceded by a remarkable group of women. Two years previous, Elizabeth Holtzman, a pro-choice Democrat, and Margaret Heckler, a pro-life Republican, had put aside their differences over abortion and formed the Congressional Caucus for Women's Issues (Women's Caucus), which worked in a bipartisan spirit to advance issues of importance to the women in the House of Representatives. Their mission was to work on issues that united them, rather than divided them, issues that required changing laws to reflect women's changing role in society, and their dual responsibilities of work and family.

I joined the Women's Caucus when I entered Congress in 1979, along with Geraldine Ferrarro and Nancy Kassebaum. And in 1983, I became cochair with Pat Schroeder of Colorado, where I served until I moved to the Senate in 1995.

Incredibly, there was a time in America when society accepted deadbeat dads, and child support was considered strictly a woman's problem; when pensions were canceled without a spouse's approval; when family and medical leave wasn't the law of the land. But working together, across the political aisle, we changed all that.

In one particular year, in a historic milestone we enacted thirty separate bills on women's issues encompassing education, health, defense, taxes, family leave, abortion rights, and childhood immunization. And when our laws failed to reflect women's dual roles at home and in the workplace, the Women's Caucus championed the Economic Equity Act, including many provisions that were ultimately enacted targeting employment opportunities, women in business, economic justice, even expanding the dependent care tax credit to assist millions of working families struggling with childcare or elderly-dependent care.

This was also an era when women unbelievably were systematically excluded from potentially life-saving clinical medical trials. There was the now-infamous physician's health study at the National Institutes of Health, our premier research facility in America, if not the world, which examined the ability of aspirin to prevent heart attacks that included twenty-two thousand men, and not one woman, even though heart attacks are the leading cause of death in women. Yet, working across party lines, we produced watershed policy changes that, to this day, are resulting in life-saving medical discoveries for America's women.

Outraged by these studies and others like them, as cochairs of the Women's Caucus, Congresswoman Pat Schroeder and I asked the then General Accounting Office (GAO) in 1989 to document inequities in medical research at the National Institutes of Health. The findings of this GAO study spurred the

Women's Caucus to introduce in the US House of Representatives its first Women's Health Equity Act, landmark legislation on women's health that was also championed in the US Senate by Senator Barbara Mikulski.

Under our leadership, we secured more funding and attracted more attention to breast cancer, osteoporosis, and cervical cancer research. It is now required that women be included in vital drug and medical trials where once they were excluded. And my own legislation created an Office of Women's Health Research at the National Institutes of Health where, once also, there was none.

This was the Augusta Model all over again. It was a case study of legislators reaching across party lines to research, consider, negotiate and then pass legislation addressing a critical policy issue. Those of us who led the charge for these women's issues certainly did not agree on everything. But we shared a common vision on the needs of women, and we did not allow our differing views on abortion or our partisan affiliations to stand in our way.

Throughout my career, I have seen how difficult objectives could be accomplished when legislators from both sides actually sat down together. I remember when President Reagan assumed office in 1981, as America suffered under double-digit inflation, double-digit unemployment, and an astronomical prime lending rate of 20 percent, he recognized the value of building a coalition of Democrats, who became known as the "Boll Weevils," and of moderate Republicans, called the "Gypsy Moths," to pass a budget that was a cornerstone of his bold recovery plan. Although, I have always wondered about the significance of naming members of Congress after destructive insects!

Even after I was elected in 1994 to the US Senate, vestiges of this kind of cooperative disposition remained on Capitol Hill.

In my early years in the Senate, there was a formal effort to bring together potentially like-minded legislators from both parties. The Senate Centrist Coalition, which I joined, was formed by Senators John Chafee (R-RI) and John Breaux (D-LA) during the 1994 health reform debate to bridge the political divide. The coalition lapsed for a time after the government shutdowns of 1995 and 1996. After President Clinton's impeachment trial in the Senate, and after Senator Chafee passed away in 1999, Senator Breaux and I thought it was imperative that we revive the coalition to help foster the spirit of bipartisanship and together we cochaired the coalition.

The group was a force for bridging the political divide to drive a tangible agenda for change. I well recall how in 1996, despite the volatile atmosphere in the aftermath of the historic government shutdown, a large, bipartisan group of us met weekly for months to craft an alternative plan to balance the federal budget. And while it didn't ultimately pass, people were shocked by how close we came, and it served as a prelude to passing a balanced budget in 1997 that produced four consecutive years of budget surpluses for the first time since 1930.

Somewhat remarkably, in retrospect the 1990s were something of a case study in how the legislative process could be fruitful despite bitter political confrontations. After the 1995 and 1996 government shutdowns, President Clinton, Speaker Newt Gingrich, and Senate Majority Leader Trent Lott came together to forge bipartisan coalitions on important legislation in the Clinton years. They played a key role in the 1995 attempt to overhaul the welfare system and managed to make changes in the Senate to the House's more stringent proposals, paving a middle road between conservative Republicans and liberal Democrats. Ultimately, twenty Republicans joined Democrats to excise the "family cap" from the House bill, a provision that would stop welfare payments to children whose parents were themselves on welfare.

It was also clear we would have to address the imperative of access to safe and affordable childcare before passing any meaningful welfare reform legislation. And for many of us, we refused to accept defeat as an option.

At a critical juncture for the bill, a group of us requested a meeting with then Majority Leader Bob Dole to explain what we needed for increased funding for childcare. Incidentally, when there was a major policy issue he would customarily instruct us to meet in his conference room at 8:30 in the morning and tell us in his familiar refrain to "work it out." So, he agreed to our request and he sat down with us. He listened. And then he dispatched one of our group to the Democratic cloakroom to find Senator Dodd, who was leading the bill for his side of the aisle.

Unfortunately, we still weren't able to arrive at an agreement. So the majority leader took to the floor to lament the inability to come to an accord. And when he mentioned the dollar figure he'd offered, Senator Dodd grabbed a mic and said he'd never been given that number. It was truly one of those moments when everyone was listening and you could hear a pin drop. We held our breath until Majority Leader Dole and Senator Dodd emerged from their huddle, and we had a deal. And that proved to be a turning point for the bill which went on to pass with an overwhelming bipartisan vote in 1996.

A *Congressional Quarterly* piece on the welfare bill identified seven moderate Republicans who were instrumental in putting together a piece of legislation that the Senate as a whole could agree on. As I said, "We knew we could be the counterweight on the floor" between Democrats and our more conservative fellow Republicans. The seven of us didn't agree on everything. Describing the outcome, Senator Pete Domenici (R-NM) said, "Everyone's going to have something in this bill they don't like."

This is a key tenet in bipartisan consensus building. To get a lot of what you want, you may have to accept a little of what you don't want. Welfare reform was another example of how the Senate can address issues at the forefront of our national agenda, either by informally identifying willing partners both within the party and across partisan lines, or in other instances with groups specifically formed to facilitate bipartisan cooperation.

There were efforts that were more individual as well. Early in my Senate tenure, I worked with Senator Paul Simon (D-IL) on student loans. What later came to be called Stafford Loans had been instrumental in my ability to attend and graduate from the University of Maine. So I was alarmed when, in 1995, the original Senate budget resolution included more than $13 billion in cuts in student loan funding. Fellow Budget Committee member Senator Spence Abraham (R-MI) and I, and others, offered an amendment providing offsets in order to restore $6.3 billion to the program, yet it lost on the Senate floor by a vote of 39–60.

But I refused to take "no" for an answer. Consequently, two days later, Democrat and fellow Budget Committee member Paul Simon and I sought to restore an even larger amount, $9.4 billion. After just two days, we passed our amendment by an overwhelming vote of 67–32. We were successful because of an open amendment process and an atmosphere of legislative possibility.

The following year also proved how vestiges of this kind of cooperative disposition remained on Capitol Hill. It was a cross-aisle alliance between Democratic Senator Jay Rockefeller of West Virginia and me that produced the so-called E-Rate program in 1996. This was a landmark law ensuring every library and classroom in America would be wired to the revolutionary resources of the internet, which one publication has ranked as fourth in a list of innovations and initiatives that have helped shape education technology over the past generation.

Originally, as a member of the Senate Commerce Committee, which had jurisdiction over the issue, I had drafted my own provision, and Jay, also a member of the committee, had authored a measure to make the burgeoning field of telemedicine more affordable and accessible to health care professionals. One early morning, prior to the continuation of the markup of the Telecommunications Act we each sought to amend, Jay called me to suggest we combine our two amendments. And I said, "Jay, that's a great idea, let's do it!" So we offered our Snowe-Rockefeller amendment.

This story is significant because we had been instructed by the Republican chairman of the committee that the leadership was anxious to get the bill completed, and therefore was discouraging Republicans from offering any amendments. The reauthorization of the Telecom Act was proving contentious, and leadership was concerned that a prolonged markup would undercut momentum and support for the bill. But in my view, deferring our amendment for the floor lessened the possibility of its success. And if no amendments had been allowed, the E-Rate program would never have come to fruition.

I had indicated to Jay that my intentions were to move forward, but Jay was still nervous because he knew there was considerable pressure to forgo amendments. In fact, he kept coming up to me during the markup and asking, "You're still going to do this, right?" I assured him not to worry, I was planning on it!

One key point that the E-Rate program exemplifies is the rich and fertile ground of the open amendment process in committees and on the floor. It demonstrates how the germ of an idea can flourish into a powerful act of law, and that we cannot even imagine what we are missing when amendments are not considered—an occurrence that is increasingly frequent today, as the entire committee process in Congress has been diminished. This erosion does a grave disservice, not only to the legislative process but, most critically, to the nation.

Later, I teamed up with Senator Ted Kennedy (D-MA) on a number of issues, such as the patient bill of rights. Senator Ron Wyden (D-OR) and I collaborated closely on prescription drug coverage and a host of issues when we both served in the House. And Senator Dianne Feinstein (D-CA) and I collaborated on landmark legislation requiring greater fuel economy for America's entire automobile fleet, to promote a healthier environment and reduce our dependence on foreign oil. Senator Jack Reed (D-RI) and I partnered on home heating assistance, and, pairing with Barbara Boxer (D-CA), we passed an airline passenger bill of rights.

Why did we collaborate? Because we were in agreement on a particular piece of legislation. If a legislator is prepared to build a consensus to solve a problem, there is no limit to what he or she can achieve.

During the tax debates we had in Congress in 2001, I moved heaven and earth along with my bipartisan partner on the Senate Finance Committee, Senator Blanche Lincoln (D-AR), to make the Child Tax Credit refundable. Amid all the tax cuts, I wanted to make certain that Americans at the lower end of the income scale would benefit. The Earned Income Tax Credit is unique in being refundable—meaning that, even if a person's income is too small to incur any tax liability, the government still pays the full credit or the difference if the credit reduces the liability to zero, so that low-income earners will receive the full amount in all circumstances. Republicans opposed my approach, but I believed it was a matter of fairness that we extend the Child Tax Credit to an additional thirty-seven million families, and refundability was the only means of doing so.

Senators Baucus and Breaux took me aside to ask if I would vote against the 2001 tax package if the refundable Child Tax Credit was not included. They were both members of the House-Senate conference committee and my vote could prove pivotal to the bill's final passage, so they would have to transmit my answer back to the committee. I responded that I would have to vote "no." It turned out that President Bush also supported the provision, and as the conference met late into the night before the vote on the following day, the president called them to urge them to retain my measure. As a result, the refundable credit, with increases built in over ten years, was included in the $1.35 trillion tax cut package. It became only the second refundable tax credit ever.

Ultimately, we extended a consequential tax credit to an additional thirty-seven million American families and fifty-five million children nationwide. As I have expressed to President Bush, I will be eternally grateful for that call.

And in a shining example of what's possible with civility and bipartisan teamwork, Ted Kennedy, the "Liberal Lion of the Senate," and I coauthored the landmark Genetic Information Nondiscrimination Act (GINA)—to stop insurance companies and employers from denying or dropping coverage or making employment decisions based on genetic tests, so individuals wouldn't forgo those potentially life-saving tests. At that juncture, Democrats were in the majority—and traditionally, the chair of a committee takes the lead name on legislation. But Ted approached me and said essentially that, because my work on GINA had made it possible, it should be "Snowe-Kennedy" not "Kennedy-Snowe"—a magnanimous legislative gesture. It took persistence and years to get it done, but I'm proud to say GINA passed in 2008 and has been referred to as "the first major civil rights act of the twenty-first century."

The point is, there are templates for working together effectively in the US Congress on behalf of the American people. That isn't to say that arriving at compromise was easy by any means. It never is. But lawmakers can undertake the difficult work, if they choose to do so.

On occasion, it is the very institution of the Senate itself that is preserved when we stake out common ground. In 2005, for example, I joined the so-called Gang of 14, comprising seven Republicans and seven Democrats, which was formed to avert an institutional crisis as a result of repeated, systematic filibuster of President Bush's judicial nominees that had been a corrosive force on the Senate. In response, the Republican majority was seeking to break the logjam by exercising the so-called nuclear option, that would have jettisoned long-standing Senate rules requiring sixty votes to end a filibuster.

That sixty-vote threshold had always been a bulwark protecting the rights of the minority, but would have become just a simple majority vote. Yet, just as we were about to cross this political Rubicon, the Gang of 14 forged a pact based on mutual trust, that we would only support a filibuster of judicial nominees under what we labeled "extraordinary circumstances," and we would oppose the "nuclear option." This agreement embodied the very manifestation of the power of consensus building.

It is regrettable that the sixty-vote threshold was later jettisoned for non-Supreme Court judicial nominees in 2013, which opened the door for eliminating the filibuster for Supreme Court nominees in 2017. Because what makes the Senate unique, and what situates the institution better than any other to secure the continued greatness of our nation, is that balance between accommodation of the minority and primacy of the majority. Moreover, it has been proven time and again that today's majority in the Senate can become tomorrow's minority and vice versa, and each is tempted to employ the other's old tactics.

Ultimately, it is only when we minimize the political barriers that we can maximize the effectiveness of our governing institutions. I always think of the sage words of the late Republican Senator Alan Simpson of Wyoming, who once said that if you can't compromise without compromising your principles, you better never be a legislator, you better never go into business, and for God's sake you better never get married!

What is fundamentally required is a willingness to listen and to work with those with whom we disagree, and to respect differing views; to acknowledge you don't have a monopoly on good ideas; to accept that you won't typically get 100 percent of what you seek, and therefore attempt to work through the differences.

It is also critical to understand that, in fact, we generally have more in common than meets the eye, and there is value in incorporating and respecting different perspectives in addressing shared concerns. We all have our own backgrounds and subsequent viewpoints.

I often point to the example of the women in the US Senate when I served in that chamber. In 1999, the nine of us who were in the Senate wrote a book called *Nine and Counting* to paint a portrait of how women from incredibly diverse backgrounds could overcome barriers to achieve extraordinary goals. And certainly, just as I had experienced in the House in the Congressional Caucus for Women's Issues, we did have disagreements over policy, even within our respective parties. But in my experience, if I approached a female Senate colleague to join me as a partner on an issue, I would invariably find a willing participant and an active listener, someone prepared to help construct a viable solution.

It is a spirit that's encapsulated in the ritual the women of the US Senate had of gathering on a monthly basis for dinner. The tradition was initiated by Democratic Senator Barbara Mikulski along with former Republican Senator Kay Bailey Hutchison, and the beauty of these dinners is that we always kept them light, informal, and off the record. What we said there, stayed there— sort of like Vegas, we used to joke, but not exactly! There was no set agenda or planned strategy sessions. Instead, we shared thoughts on everything from our families to issues we were working on to what might be happening in our respective states.

So, in 2012, after I had announced I was leaving the Senate because I didn't believe the excessive partisanship would change in the short term, I was especially looking forward to the retirement dinner that Barbara and the senators had arranged for me and for Kay, who was also retiring at the end of that year. But unfortunately, as it turned out, that dinner had to be limited to just a reception. Why? Because we had to leave early to attend the Republican dinner for departing Republican senators. The Democratic dinner had been held the night before for their retiring senators. And that was regrettable, because customarily, in the past, those dinners for departing senators had been held jointly. And I couldn't help but think that, even the act of leaving the Senate had become partisan. Yet by contrast, our women's dinners were always a free-flowing discussion in an environment of mutual respect—which is fertile ground for future cooperation on legislation.

Which brings me to a final point: relationships matter.

In 2013, I jointed the Bipartisan Policy Center (BPC) as a senior fellow and a member of the board of directors. My first major undertaking was to cochair BPC's Commission on Political Reform. We examined and made a series of recommendations in the areas of electoral reform, congressional reform, and bolstering the civic life and contributions of Americans.

One of the major themes that emerged was that members of Congress simply do not have the opportunity to get to know one another as fellow human beings to the extent they did in the past. In prior decades, lawmakers didn't return home as often. Travel took longer and was more arduous. Members frequently stayed in Washington on weekends. Often, they even moved their families to the nation's capital—something that largely has become an anathema. Husbands and wives of lawmakers would get to know one another socially. Families would see each other and interact at their children's sporting events.

These kinds of encounters across party lines have become much more rare. On top of that, members of Congress fly in on Monday evenings, have about two and a half days filled with nonstop committee hearings, constituent meetings, votes, and fundraising activities. Then, they return home Thursday afternoon or evening. There is virtually no time or opportunity to truly get to know their colleagues from the other side of the aisle and what makes them tick.

We will not return to the days when lawmakers remained in Washington, because it is vital to spend time with constituents. Nor was there ever, frankly, some golden age of bipartisanship when everyone got along. And it would not be fair to say that building relationships of trust among members across the parties is sufficient alone to address today's caustic and hyperpartisan environment. Yet, it is indisputable that these bonds are an essential predicate to a functional legislative process.

That is why organizations like the BPC are a vital bulwark against the forces of division that have a stake in maintaining the status quo, and the misaligned political incentives that dissuade lawmakers from working with each other. There are many more in Congress who actually want to get things done than would appear to the untrained eye or are portrayed in the media. But they require our support, from outside the institution.

BPC brings together former elected and administration officials, along with respected policy experts, to develop actionable solutions to help improve the lives of all Americans. They also work to create an environment more conducive to getting things done for those in Congress willing to work together to solve problems. One such program is BPC's American Congressional Exchange (ACE).

Under the ACE program, members of Congress from opposite parties travel to each other's congressional districts. Through visits to places as diverse as factories, small businesses, military installations, health care facilities, tribal councils, universities, even religious institutions, these cross-party pairings experience firsthand the pressures their colleagues face, the challenges and opportunities for their constituents, and the driving forces in regions of this country that are far different from their own. Lawmakers get to understand each other outside the crucible of Washington: why their colleagues speak as they speak, vote as they vote, and fight for the causes they embrace. As one ACE participant has said, "If you really want to know where someone is coming from, you should see where they actually come from."

Clearly, not every lawmaker will be interested in such an experience. Yet, all that is required is a critical mass of members who are invested in making the system work better. Indeed, I find it exceedingly encouraging that, of the more than fifty participants in ACE so far, easily two-thirds are not what anyone would consider "moderate" or in the political center.

So I remain optimistic. What is required now is for leaders at both ends of Pennsylvania Avenue and on both sides of the aisle to make their political points, have their votes, but then ultimately coming together for the common good to meet our country's challenges. Simply put, it is time for our leaders to lead, and for all of us to make our voices heard at the ballot box. For it is true that, in a representative democracy, we ultimately get the government we demand—and if we demand and value bipartisanship, we will get it.

As I expressed to that Harvard graduating class, we live in a nation—the Great Experiment—that was born because it came together, rose up, and threw off, at the time, the largest standing army in the world. A nation where neither the Western frontier nor the frontier of space could contain our people. Where the scourge of polio and yellow fever could not survive the onslaught of medical and scientific expertise. Where the world turned for leadership during the torments of the last century.

Every time—every single time—our people and our national leadership responded assertively, decisively, convincingly. This is the legacy we have inherited, and for which we are now all responsible.

OLYMPIA SNOWE *is a Board Member of the Bipartisan Policy Center and a former Republican member of the US Senate and the US House of Representatives from Maine.*

BIPARTISANSHIP AND MEDICARE PAYMENT REFORM

ALLYSON Y. SCHWARTZ AND
CHARLENE MACDONALD

INTRODUCTION

Health policy debates in the United States start with the knowledge that there is little that Republicans and Democrats agree on in principle. When they agree there is a problem to be addressed, their approach to solutions is very different. Broadly speaking, Republicans stand for less government intervention, lower government spending and more individual responsibility. Democrats are willing to spend government funds for health care by expanding access to coverage and lowering costs for consumers while demanding more from the health sector by establishing greater accountability from providers. Democrats tend to initiate new federal health policies while Republicans are more inclined to allow the private sector or states to take the initiative. These very different approaches rarely align.

Adding to that basic ideological misalignment, health care is a political lightening rod in modern politics. Our health care system grows and changes due to market forces, scientific and technological advancements and changes in public policy. Making changes to Medicare, the government health program that covers adults sixty-five years or older and those with disabilities, is particularly high stakes politically for many reasons. First and foremost, Medicare is considered a promise made to millions of Americans who spent a lifetime of work to earn this coverage. Medicare also serves as a benchmark for health benefits and costs for nearly every other American with either employer health insurance or other public coverage. In addition, ongoing financial pressures on Medicare due to rising costs and an increasing number of seniors threaten its sustainability.

Finally, seniors are very sensitive to any change to Medicare, as are all the providers who are paid by the program. Both are strong constituencies who are taken very seriously by both Republican and Democratic policymakers. New legislation brought by either party has political consequences. The biggest recent example, the passage of the Affordable Care Act, also known as "Obamacare," not only led to heavily funded attacks on Democrats and subsequent electoral losses for Democratic members of Congress but to deep animosity between the parties. Both led to real hesitancy to engage in any significant health care legislation by either party.

Adding to the pressure on policymakers are the demographics of significant population growth of the people eligible for Medicare. The number of seniors is projected to more than double in number to eighty million people by 2046. The added cost of caring for this population is already evident. Medicare's increasing cost to government is projected to total over half a trillion dollars annually.[1] The call to contain costs in public programs like Medicare is ever-present but considered too difficult to tackle.

One of the few areas that has been promoted by some in both parties to reduce cost spending are new care delivery initiatives targeted at improving health while slowing the growth in costs. This approach was first introduced by President Bill Clinton in the late 1990s, advanced by President George W. Bush in the early 2000s, followed by support from the administrations of President Obama and President Trump. Both Congressional action and regulation by these quite different administrations worked to advance new care delivery models in Medicare.

These initiatives are quietly underway, but face resistance from many professional and trade organizations that represent organized medicine. Their advocacy typically seeks to maintain the status quo and counter the need to address the financial sustainability of Medicare. They continue to call for increases in provider payments, particularly for physicians, hospitals, and nursing homes. Members of Congress on both sides of the aisle are fully aware of the fact that health care is 20 percent of the US economy and their policies have an impact not only on beneficiaries but also on millions of people who work in health care institutions and industries in their districts. Actions they take can have a profound impact on the people and businesses they represent; therefore, they are cautious in approaching changes to health policy.

This ideological, political, and policy environment means building bipartisan support is rarely easy. New policies are hard-fought within Congress and must be negotiated with numerous powerful stakeholder groups that are eager to get involved and often at odds with one another. Hospitals, physicians, other health care providers, insurers, employers, unions, pharmaceutical companies, nursing homes, home care providers, caregivers, suppliers, innovators, employers, and patient advocacy organizations all seek to shape legislation to meet their needs.

This chapter offers one example of the willingness of Republicans and Democrats to act to address a significant health issue, one of their own making, that needed to be undone. The policy, known as the Medicare Sustainable Growth Rate (SGR), was enacted in 1997 to contain the cost of physician services in Medicare. The law called for mandatory cuts to Medicare physician payments if spending exceeded an inflationary growth rate. Year after year, from the late 1990s until 2015, Congress acted to suspend implementation of the SGR to avoid cuts to physician payments. As the years passed, there was growing recognition inside and outside of Washington that this blunt instrument of cuts to all physicians was not going to work. It was born out of the need to reduce spending in Medicare during a budget crisis and it was fundamentally flawed. Unlike virtually every other health care issue of the day, Democrats and Republicans came to agree on the need to repeal the SGR.

Yet, action on permanent repeal was stymied by the cost. As implementation was suspended each year, the anticipated savings were considered debt in the budget, requiring any permanent repeal to "pay for" the accumulated "debt" to the budget. In 2011, the Congressional Budget Office (CBO) projected cost of such legislation to exceed $300 billion, making the task of repeal seem simply too expensive to tackle. So, lawmakers continued to suspend it every year, hoping to find a remedy sometime in the future. Few policymakers wanted to think about how to make up for the expected savings in the federal budget that were projected to come from containing the rate of growth in spending on physician services. Even fewer, on or off the Hill, had contemplated a viable replacement.

This chapter tells the story of finally dealing with this untenable situation by repealing the SGR, finding the replacement payment system for physicians, and agreeing on how to pay for it. Congress passed the repeal in what became the Medicare Access and CHIP Reauthorization Act (MACRA), in March 2015. This chapter illustrates that new policy—even transformative policy—can and does happen, and it can happen with the support of both Republicans and Democrats with keenly different views of government's role in health care.

THE VISION FOR A NEW PAYMENT MODEL

This chapter also tells the story of the effort to advance the move to value-based care. This vision for health care requires a move away from paying doctors and hospitals for individual medical services known as "fee-for-service." US health care often excels in acute care and clinical discoveries, but it is lacking in many ways. Those failures can be blamed in part by fee-for-service payment because it creates the wrong incentives for payers and providers. It incentivizes physicians and health systems to provide high-volume, costly procedures in expensive settings over lower-cost interactions with health professionals in lower-cost settings. It ignores social needs and provides little financial gain to provide coordinated, ongoing care for those with complex chronic conditions, even as it is known that these patients are many in number and their care is costly.

In addition, there is little measurement of quality or accountability for improving the health status of patients or populations. These gaps contribute to inequity in outcomes for minorities, uneven access to care depending on geography and income, and inadequate availability to mental health and behavioral services or social services.

The current fee-for-service payment and the delivery system has resulted in a care that is fragmented, expensive, and often wasteful. Researchers, practitioners, and many policymakers know the system of payment must change if the goal is to both help people live healthier lives and to generate savings in spending on health care for individuals and the nation.

A value-based payment system, in contrast to fee-for-service, encourages prevention, early intervention, and continuity of care. It incentivizes a focus on patient-centered primary care and care coordination among providers. It provides the opportunity to address social risk and add benefits. It encourages a team-based care delivery model and demands quality measurement that focuses on improving the health of patients and populations. In addition, it allows for innovations in care delivery that address care in the community and greater consumer convenience and engagement. This way of paying for and delivering care can move the US health care system to provide better care at lower cost.

In the story of SGR reform, policymakers and health care stakeholders seized the moment of financial crisis in provider payments to create a new payment model for physicians built on value-based payment. With advice and counsel from experts and advocates, leaders from both parties ended a failed policy that threatened annual cuts to physicians. They replaced it with a new, voluntary payment model intended to transform care delivery to improve care and outcomes at lower costs.

MACRA passed in 2015, by a wide bipartisan vote in both the House and the Senate. This chapter describes how this happened in an environment of deep ideological divide. The work on improving health care delivery built on prior policy changes and the evidence of their effectiveness. The Patient Protection and Affordable Care Act (ACA), passed in 2010, was significant in advancing major changes in health care coverage and delivery. It provided expanded access to meaningful, affordable coverage and primary care; advanced managed care; established quality accountability that rewards high performance; and established an innovation center within the Centers for Medicare and Medicaid Services (known as the Center for Medicare and Medicaid Innovation), which allowed for new initiatives intended to improve patient outcomes while reducing costs. Other prior legislation, such as the laws enacted to support adoption of electronic data sharing, advance new technologies, establish patient-centered medical homes, accountable care organizations, Special Needs Plans (SNPs) in Medicare Advantage, and Programs of All-Inclusive Care for the Elderly (PACE) for those who are dually eligible for Medicare and Medicaid, were all important to moving physicians away from fee-for-service care to more value-based care.

MACRA built on these efforts and moved the adoption of value-based payments further. It also ended uncertainty for physicians, allowed professional associations to focus on the future for medical professionals and their patients, and showed that bipartisan agreement on a complex health issue could be achieved. Below is the story of how it got done.

THE SUSTAINABLE GROWTH RATE
AND HOW IT FAILED

In the late 1990s, among President Bill Clinton's signature achievements was a bipartisan deal to eliminate the country's budget deficit through a package of reforms to federal spending, including changes to Medicare. As early as the 1990s, it was already clear that Medicare was financially unsustainable due to the aging population. Medicare would grow even more strained as those born between 1946 to 1964, often called the baby boomers, began to age into Medicare. To address these cost concerns, Congress enacted changes to payments for hospitals, nursing homes and other Medicare providers, including physicians.[2] This was done through the budget reconciliation process, a legislative maneuver requiring a simple majority for passage. That historic agreement, the Balanced Budget Act of 1997 (BBA), established a new method for physician payments.

These changes were designed to lower Medicare costs by capping annual increases in physician reimbursements based on the rate of growth in the overall economy. The SGR was intended to constrain overall increases for physicians' services. Payments would be cut for the following year if overall national spending on physicians' services exceeded inflation in the prior year. The idea was that anticipation of cuts would compel physicians to find a way to reduce costs. Budget analysts projected the SGR would contribute billions in savings to taxpayers in future years.

However, policymakers failed to anticipate how difficult it would be for physicians to reduce spending on their own, without guidance or direction. Nor did they account for the realities of human behavior, particularly that of individual physicians faced with the threat of cuts to reimbursements.

For the first few years, growth in spending on physician services initially hovered around the rate of inflation, thus avoiding automatic cuts to physician payment rates. By 2002, health care utilization and costs began to rise more rapidly, outpacing the Consumer Price Index, a leading indicator of inflation. For the first time, an automatic 4.8 percent cut was applied to physician payments. The pushback from physician groups was clear and strong: physicians alone were not at fault. They said physicians should not be held financially at risk for rising costs. The cuts were considered untenable by physicians and their associations. Joe Antos of the American Enterprise Institute said, "Physicians were more resistant to taking financial risk than anticipated. With annual cuts anticipated ever year by physicians, it made it ever worse. SGR was unsustainable."

The SGR's system-wide threat was not changing the individual physician's behavior and did not reign in overall spending. In fact, it was doing just the opposite. Instead of working together to bring down costs, the threat of insufficient payments for services drove physicians and hospitals to protect their revenue streams by increasing the volume of care provided. This in turn drove up the rate of growth in federal spending on physician services.

Subsequent cuts triggered by the SGR were ultimately averted each year through congressional action to delay the cuts. This in turn postponed the realization of projected savings for the federal budget that were to come from lower spending. This annual suspension of the cuts came to be known as the "doc fix." Without implementation of these cuts and the savings to the federal budget that were to result, the difference between actual spending on Medicare physician services and the projected spending in the budget continued to grow. It was expected that if SGR were to be repealed, those projected savings would have to be compensated for by reduced spending for physicians or other providers in Medicare. This made any effort to permanently repeal the SGR very costly. Physicians worried about the possibility of steep reductions in their reimbursements and charged their lobbyists in Washington, DC, with making repeal of SGR their top legislative priority.

As annual battles over the doc fix continued though President George W. Bush's administration in the early 2000s, the strength of the physician lobby grew. The SGR served as a rallying cry for the American Medical Association and other physician professional groups. Policymakers on the Hill were growing frustrated by the demands for increased spending without a commitment from organized medicine to hold physicians accountable for the quality and cost of the care they were delivering to Medicare beneficiaries. Some were simply weary of the annual fight year after year to suspend the SGR that seemed to have no resolution. Dr. Douglas Holtz-Eakin with the American Action Forum said, "SGR was a failure. Passed as part of a budget reconciliation bill to achieve physician payment reductions—it was clear, it was never going to be implemented and everyone knew it."

With the election of President Obama and a Democratic "super majority" in Congress in 2008, Democrats seized the opportunity to pass historic health reform legislation that would not only expand coverage to twenty million more Americans, but also build upon the Bush administration's value-based care policies. Despite a massive lobbying push by organized medicine, the ACA passed Congress by a razor thin margin in 2010. No Republican member of the House or Senate voted for this legislation. The ACA continued to be hard-fought politically, even after it was implemented. Votes sponsored by Republicans to repeal the ACA were held almost weekly for years.

One of the issues that the ACA did not address was the repeal of the SGR, primarily due to the significant cost associated with repeal. However, the new Center for Medicare and Medicaid Innovation, established by the ACA, did start to test new payment models in Medicare. These new models rewarded providers for delivering higher quality, higher value care with the requirement that they also achieve cost savings for the government. There were also demonstration programs to test new incentives for primary care physicians and new regulations established for stronger quality accountability within Medicare Advantage, the managed care option in Medicare.

Even with new incentives and options afforded to providers under the law, adoption of new value-based care payment models was hindered by the misaligned incentives inherent in the underlying fee-for-service system. Few physicians were prepared to sign up for the new payment models. The adoption of financial risk for care by physicians was slow. The looming threat of SGR cuts remained.

There was widespread recognition of the need for SGR repeal on both sides of the aisle. However, the extreme partisan division over health care policy in the wake of that bruising battle over the ACA drove lawmakers on both sides of the aisle to largely disengage on any bipartisan efforts on major health issues. Despite a ballooning price tag for repeal from the Congressional Budget Office and increasing calls from providers for lawmakers to act, Congress continued to delay with annual short-term suspensions of the SGR.

CRISIS CREATES OPPORTUNITY

The country faced a potential crisis over the need to increase the debt ceiling in 2011. Republicans and Democrats sought a way to came together to avoid default and attempted to force bipartisanship through the creation of the Joint Committee on Deficit Reduction, colloquially known as the "Super Committee." The Super Committee was charged with reaching agreement on a plan to reduce the federal deficit by $1.2 trillion, in exchange for an agreement to lift the debt ceiling. Failing to reach agreement would result in automatic cuts to both mandatory and discretionary spending, a threat intended to meet both Republican and Democratic priorities.

At the same time, but independent of the work of the Super Committee, a member of Congress from Pennsylvania, Democratic Congresswoman Allyson Y. Schwartz, who was a member of the Ways and Means Committee, but not of the Super Committee, had started work to find a way to deal with the SGR. Schwartz was active in the development and passage of the ACA and was known in the House for crafting new ideas in health care and getting a number of those passed. She included elements of value-based payments in these bills and was interested in resolving the SGR dilemma. Schwartz had already tasked her staff to develop a proposal for repeal and replacement, bringing in the idea to advance a new payment system. They developed both a proposal and a strategy that involved extensive meetings with stakeholders from medical societies to seniors' advocates to think tanks.

They met individually with influential organizations like the American Medical Association, American College of Physicians, American Academy of Family Physicians, and the American Osteopathic Association and with multiple other health care interest groups. The purpose was to solicit their advice on the proposal to replace the fee-for-service system with alternative payment models. This was a way both to get their input and hopefully to bring them onboard to support the bill.

Believing that a big bipartisan deal represented the best opportunity to repeal the SGR, Congresswoman Schwartz and stakeholders in the provider community urged members of the Super Committee to incorporate SGR repeal into the deal on the debt. This was the first time an SGR repeal proposal included a framework to replace the physician payment system with a path to transition to alternative payment model.

Schwartz reached out to members of the Super Committee individually, including cochair Senator Patty Murray (D-WA), Senator Jon Kyl (R-NV) Senator Max Baucus (D-MT), and Representative Dave Camp (R-MI), among others, urging them to prioritize Medicare physician payments in their negotiations. On November 16, 2011, she sent a letter to the Super Committee to repeal the SGR and laid out a framework for replacement.[3] This letter drew positive attention to the proposal that would not only repeal the SGR, but also replace it with value-based payment systems. Members of the Super Committee were interested but the work of the Super Committee was already in trouble.

In the end, the Super Committee failed to reach a broader agreement on the debt ceiling. Once again, SGR repeal and Medicare physician payment policy fell by the wayside. In January of 2012, Congress passed yet another suspension at the eleventh hour to stave off a looming 27 percent cut in physician payments.

MOVEMENT TO REPLACE THE SGR

This failure of the Super Committee and yet another "doc fix" gave Schwartz the opportunity to flesh out her proposed framework into comprehensive legislation. It also gave her more time to build support among health care industry stakeholders and to court potential Republican cosponsors. Over the next several months, she continued to seek out her Democratic and Republican colleagues in Congress to gain their support for this new payment model that would incentivize value-based care, reward patient-centered primary care, and gradually reduce increases in payment for physicians who remained in fee-for-service. She resisted pressure to do repeal alone. Many medical societies—particularly those representing specialists—agreed with the call for SGR repeal but were wary of new payment systems that would disrupt the status quo. Inside Congress, Democrats were interested while Republicans held back. As discussions progressed, the idea that repeal alone would fall short and a replacement would be needed was planted. Former Representative Senator Bill Cassidy (R-LA) said, "I remember I thought her ideas went too far. I was intrigued. I knew we wanted repeal but not sure we were ready for a new payment model. Looking back, it was a good idea. Value-based payments are the future."

Recognizing that Republican leadership in control of the House would only consider legislation endorsed by the powerful Republican Doctors Caucus ("Doc Caucus"), Schwartz targeted the members of the Doc Caucus as potential sponsors of her legislation. Several sat on relevant committees and most of them represented the most conservative wing of the Republic party at that time. Nonetheless, the thought was that they were physicians before they were members of Congress and they had committed to repeal the SGR. There had to be an opening. Schwartz's willingness to cross party lines to hear out their ideas and share her own vision held a certain intrigue for even the most partisan among them. It helped that the congresswoman had worked with several members of the Doc Caucus on other health issues and developed a level of trust with them.

The Doc Caucus very much wanted SGR repeal, but they had not addressed a possible new payment system and were hesitant to define one. Representative Michael Burgess (R-TX), chair of the Energy and Commerce Committee, had introduced bills every session to permanently repeal the SGR since he was first elected to Congress. His bills included both repeal and future increases for doctors, with particular concern for solo practitioners and small practices. To pay for the repeal and payment increases in his 2012 bill, Burgess relied on provisions in the bill to repeal key elements of the ACA. These included repeal of the mandate on individuals to purchase health insurance and end government subsidies to make coverage more affordable. It was attractive to Republicans but a nonstarter for Democrats. Burgess's goal was to gain Republican votes and meet the expectations of some of the leading professional medical associations. He did not take Democratic support into consideration. Burgess said, "Repeal was important to me. It was one of the reasons I came to Congress, and I led the way every session. I came up with changes to the formula for physician fee schedule to end SGR and reimburse doctors fairly after years of no increases. I wanted to see it happen. We had the majority, and I was not thinking about making the effort bipartisan. Only later did I recognize that we needed to get it passed in the Senate with its Democratic majority."

Months of early morning breakfasts in the Members' Dining Room of the US Capitol between Schwartz and each of her potential Republican allies in the Doc Caucus attracted curious looks from other members. She sought to build momentum for what she believed could be a bipartisan proposal to overhaul the country's physician payment system. One by one, potential cosponsors would cautiously engage and then decline. They cited concerns that the bill was overly ambitious. Some may have been concerned about crossing the aisle on any Democratic health proposal. Then Schwartz's office reached out to Representative Joe Heck (R-NV), an osteopathic physician elected in a competitive district outside Las Vegas in the Republican wave of 2010.

Both members were born in Queens, NY, educated in Pennsylvania, and later came to represent moderate districts on opposite sides of the country.

Congressman Heck was also a member of the American Osteopathic Association (AOA). Before responding to Schwartz's outreach, Representative Heck approached the AOA to discuss the SGR repeal proposal. AOA was an early supporter of the Schwartz proposal, saying it aligned with their ideas for physician payment reform and as an association, they supported it. Heck appreciated their position and followed up with Schwartz's office to hear more. He liked what he heard and agreed to sign on as the lead Republican cosponsor. Schwartz and Heck believed that the country urgently needed to move toward value-based care and that physician payment reform would be key to unlocking that transformation. A bipartisan partnership was established. Heck said,

> After talking to AOA, I reached out to Schwartz's office. I liked the legislation she proposed. I wanted to take on something meaningful on healthcare. This proposal was consistent with my own belief that primary care was key to improving health. I checked with Speaker Boehner. He said if I could get the Doc Caucus approval, he would be okay with it. So, I went to work. They were resistant to me as a new member coming to them with this proposal and it took lots of conversation. Getting acceptance from outside medical groups—which Congresswoman Schwartz did—helped a lot.

Despite pressure from the Democratic Congressional Campaign Committee not to collaborate with Heck, who the party viewed as vulnerable to a Democratic challenge in the upcoming midterm elections, Schwartz welcomed Heck's partnership. On March 21, 2012, the duo introduced the Medicare Physician Payment Innovation Act. This was the first legislation that would not only repeal the widely disparaged SGR formula but would also incentivize providers to transition to innovative payment models.

Although repeal of the SGR was then estimated to cost $300 billion, Schwartz continued to build support for her legislation during the 112th Congress, elevating the issue in the press and at every opportunity in Congressional deliberations, including in her role as a member of the Ways and Means Committee. She lobbied other Democrats for their support and reached out to leaders of key committees on both sides of the aisle. The outreach often elicited an interested but lukewarm reaction. While they all wanted the SGR repealed, none were focused on developing a replacement policy. Even if they liked the policy ideas, few were ready to embrace the proposed bill.

Schwartz, determined to turn mild interest into commitment, continued to reach out to the medical associations and other interested parties. There were more meetings to seek their input and support. It worked. Dozens of professional societies and trade associations endorsed the Schwartz legislation, engaging their members and lobbying members of Congress. More than forty organizations agreed to sign a letter of support. All the while Congressman Heck worked the Doc Caucus, knowing their support was critical to House Speaker John Boehner's final approval to move the bill forward. While most were hesitant to sign on to the nascent reform proposal, they were engaged early and often and were ultimately essential to the success of the effort. Shawn Martin, then head of goverment affairs, AOA, said,

> It was hard to imagine bipartisan health legislation post-ACA, but AOA
> represented doctors, many of them in primary care. We knew we had
> to keep advocating for the important role they could play in improving
> healthcare. We were early supporters of the move to value-based care
> and supported Congresswoman Schwartz's bill. Having an osteopath in
> Congress was good for us and I encouraged him to get involved. As one of
> our own, Congressman Heck was great in helping to get our members to
> support the bill. They were all in on repeal of SGR and many got on board
> with the replacement payment changes as well. Both mattered to us. We
> were willing to reach out to other medical associations. It took a while,
> but in the end, they were all telling members of Congress why it was so
> important.

By the start of 2011, it was clear that repeal and replacement of the SGR was gaining momentum on and off the Hill. While Schwartz juggled her Congressional responsibilities with her run for governor of Pennsylvania, Congressional leaders charged the committees of jurisdiction in both the House and Senate with readying a new Medicare physician payment system in preparation for a potential vote on SGR repeal. The Senate Finance, House Ways and Means, and House Energy and Commerce committees got to work on the first major bipartisan health reform effort following the passage of the ACA. Committee staff had the specialized expertise, as well as the unique access to resources and experts inside and outside of government, that were needed to craft payment policy that could stand the test of time. As a member of the House Ways and Means Committee, Schwartz's proposal was readily available to the committees at the start of their work and provided a foundation to build on.

After well over a year of deliberations, in 2014, the committees agreed to a policy proposal based on the Schwartz legislation's concept and goals which provided a period of stability for providers and set out a transition to alternative payment models. Just before the 112th Congress was about to adjourn in December 2014, all three committees of jurisdiction passed the historic legislation out of committee with strong bipartisan support. The bill did not reach the House floor for a vote, but agreement by the key committees on the replacement language was done. The committee work would be important in the next session. Still, with Schwartz leaving Congress in the new year and a 27 percent cut to physician payments scheduled to take effect in March of 2015, the future for Medicare physician payment remained uncertain.

HOW IT CAME TOGETHER

In January of 2015, lobbyists were skeptical and began to anticipate another short-term fix to the looming cuts to physician payments. Hopes for a permanent repeal of the SGR had dimmed when the committees' legislation failed to reach the floor of either chamber in late 2014 after years of hard work, coalition building and negotiation. Congressional leaders in the House, however, remained undeterred. Bipartisan agreement on health policy was increasingly rare but Speaker John Boehner and Minority Leader Nancy Pelosi were each privately determined not to let the opportunity pass. With the policy work on replacement done and ready, the question that remained was how to begin the politically fraught process of negotiating policies to offset the roughly $300 billion cost of the legislation. Speaker Boehner said, "I was clear. We were going to repeal the SGR permanently. It was a priority for me and for the Republican Conference. We were tired of dealing with the doc fix every year with no solution. It had to get done. I told the Doc Caucus to find a way. Their support was key to getting the Republicans on board."

Pelosi's second-in-command, Minority Whip Steny Hoyer (D-MD), had a reputation for being willing to cross party lines and encouraged his staff to do the same, both formally and informally. His newest staff member, Charlene MacDonald, who formerly served as health adviser to Schwartz, had built a relationship with Charlotte Ivancic, senior health adviser to House Speaker John Boehner (R-OH). They had bonded over their experience working on the federal budget and comparing notes on their bosses' respective priorities. MacDonald decided to reach out to Ivancic to see if they could work on the repeal together. The two huddled over coffee in the Carry-out, a popular gathering spot for leadership staff in the basement of the Capitol. They found one area of common ground: physician payment reform.

Ivancic was interested but knew that the House Republicans conference would demand reforms to entitlements to pay for the package. She acknowledged that such reforms had long been considered a nonstarter for many Democrats. MacDonald took a chance, telling her Republican colleague that Democratic

Minority Leader Nancy Pelosi's office had expressed some openness to limited
Medicare reforms, provided they were enacted alongside policies to strengthen
protections and benefits for beneficiaries. Cautiously optimistic, she suggested
to Ivancic that it was worth a serious conversation with Minority Leader Pelosi's
longtime trusted health adviser, Wendell Primus. Ivancic was open to the discussion and Primus readily agreed. The Democrats wanted SGR permanently
repealed as well. He knew the committees had already agreed on the new payment system, so the substance of the bill was done. The two issues to be worked
out were, first, how to pay for the cost of the bill and second, how to get both
Democrats and Republicans to agree.

The major hurdle to passage was agreeing on how to pay for the cost of repeal. The Congressional Budget Office estimated the cost of repeal was now
$300 billion. The CBO required budgetary offsets in that amount to cover
these costs but offsets in that amount would be hard to find. Ivancic proposed
that they try to limit the cost of the bill only to new spending, suggesting that
once the law was repealed, the anticipated savings would be deleted from the
budget. The change was dramatic, bringing the amount down to an estimated
$130 billion. Speaker Boehner agreed, as did CBO. Ivancic said, "Bringing down
the cost was the game changer for us. We didn't have to deal with the substance
since that was already done by the committees, so tackling the cost in a way that
would be acceptable to both sides was our challenge. When Speaker Boehner
agreed to only covering the cost of the new spending rather than the theoreti-
cal savings that never occurred, it was suddenly doable." The three negotiators,
Ivancic, Primus, and MacDonald, went to work.

With high hopes but low expectations, Ivancic, Primus, and MacDonald
began meeting regularly in a small, windowless room in the Speaker's office,
sketching out a bipartisan plan to cut billions of dollars in federal spending to
cover the costs of repeal. They brought in support from outside experts, including the Congressional Budget Office, the Medicare Office of the Actuary,
MedPac (the government agency that advises Congress on Medicare issues),
and the Bipartisan Policy Center. They also brought in a few key committee
staffers sworn to secrecy about the delicate negotiations. Together, they sought
to balance political sensitivities, policy considerations, and the need to identify
sufficient savings. They wanted to bring Congressional leaders the bill that was
"paid for" to satisfy the budget hawks on both sides of the aisle. It was a lot to
put together in a short time. Ashley Ridlon, the former lead of Bipartisan Policy
Center Action, said, "There were lots of ideas of other policies that could be
added once the legislation looked like it would move. Many were given serious
attention but then had to be set aside, including some BPC's recommendations.

We talked about the ideas and the costs. It was a well thought out process even with the tight timeline. BPC Action was pleased to be a part of this process and proud of the final bill."

Negotiations over the cost offsets stumbled as the group came to the realization that some of their ideas to pay for the bill would increase rather than reduce federal spending. With the clock ticking, they abandoned plans to pair physician payment reform with an ambitious overhaul of the Medicare benefits structure. Instead, they focused in on targeted reforms that would produce savings to Medicare by reducing scheduled increases in hospital payments over the subsequent years, among other reductions in non-physician provider payments. These were changes to Medicare that Minority Leader Pelosi could accept. They also agreed to add revenue to support Medicare by increasing cost sharing for the wealthiest beneficiaries. Republicans agreed. the result would improve financial sustainability for the Medicare Trust Fund, a priority for both parties and an added win.

Republicans also agreed to a two-year extension of the Children's Health Insurance Program (CHIP). This was an addition that pleased Democrats and Republican Senator Hatch, then chair of the Senate Finance Committee, who was a fan of the program. Additional funding for Federally Qualified Health Centers (FQHCs) was included, with a last minute ask from House Republicans that the Hyde Amendment be applied. This amendment which prohibited use of federal funds for abortions already applied to FQHCs, it was not a new restriction, and it was agreed to. While other additions were also included, no changes were made to the ACA and no limitations were made to Medicare.

The small circle of negotiators and bill writers began to slowly expand to others. They received cautious support of key leaders on both sides. The members and staff on relevant committees who had been involved in drafting language on the repeal and replacement were key to final acceptance. They were ready with the substance of the replacement and very much wanted it passed by the full House. They agreed to accept the leadership team's proposal. Wendell Primus said,

> The goal was clear, and the time was short. There were so many people involved. I knew it was best to stay with a small group to work out the how to pay for the bill. We took the chance to work on it quietly. Finding the offsets and adding other provisions that Republicans and Democrats wanted and would be agreed to was not easy. As people saw that the bill might move, there were new ideas and new asks. Presenting the hard-fought language and getting everyone on board made us nervous.

Committee staff was so invested, we were not sure how they would react. But it all came together; everyone was on board.

Outside groups of providers like the AOA and American College of Physicians wanted to see this bill move and maintained their advocacy throughout the months of debate. The American Medical Association finally agreed, as well. Repealing the SGR permanently was "the priority." It took years to get to this point and they didn't want to lose this chance to finally fix it. They weren't sure about the new payment model, but it was voluntary, so it was acceptable.

The bill also provided modest increases in payment in fee-for-service which was helpful in gaining their support. With the support of the AMA and so many other physician groups, the Doc Caucus agreed. They were ready to support the bill that would repeal SGR after almost a decade of pushing to see this happen. It would be a win for them. They gave Boehner the sign-off on the policy he needed to bring other Republicans along. The Speaker was ready to move forward. Joe Heck said, "The Doc Caucus could not say no to full repeal of SGR and the cost was not paid for by doctors. The doctors finally got a commitment to some modest increases. It was a pretty good deal. It was not the bill they would have written but it got the job done. We promised the Speaker we would find a way and we did. It sure felt like a win, and they agreed."

Democrats were ready to move ahead as well. They were comfortable with the concepts in the new payment model. They had supported the previous efforts to encourage primary care, bundled payments and ACOs. They liked the direction and were hopeful about where this could lead in better care for their constituents. Medicare was intact and the Medicare Trust Fund received additional revenue from the increase in Medicare taxes on wealthier earners. They were also pleased with the inclusion of the reauthorization of CHIP and funding for FQHCs, both high priorities for the Democratic Caucus. The bill was a big win for them as well.

The final legislation was sound. It was good policy, and it was largely paid for. As envisioned by Congresswoman Schwartz, it achieved the original goal of permanent repeal of the SGR and replaced it with a new value-based payment system.

On March 26, 2015, Boehner and Pelosi brought to the House floor the bill that would once again transform the US health care system, but this time with bipartisan support. The "aye" votes began to roll in slowly at first, as members waited to see how their colleagues would vote. Then as aye votes came in one after another, it became clear that passage was inevitable. It was overwhelming bipartisan. The House passed the Medicare and CHIP Reauthorization Act by a vote of 392–37. Schwartz looked on from the House floor, surrounded by former colleagues who had picked up the mantle and delivered a rare bipartisan victory on health care. Having let the House take the lead, the Senate moved swiftly without making any changes to the House bill. The Senate vote was strongly bipartisan as well, with a vote of 92–8 on April 14, 2015. The bill was signed into law by President Obama just two days later, on April 16, 2015. Chris Jennings, founder and president of Jennings Policy Strategies, said, "SGR repeal needed to happen after lingering for years. That it included good policy on physician payment and had overwhelming bipartisan support was even better."

A few weeks later, members and staff from both sides of the aisle were invited to gather with President Obama on the White House lawn to celebrate the end of a flawed policy and the beginning of a new era for health care payment and delivery.

CONCLUSION

What started as a call to Congress to lift uncertainty for doctors and end fifteen years of short-term fixes to a broken system became legislation to transform physician payment and enhance care for Medicare beneficiaries.

The legislation not only removed a constant political problem for Republicans and Democrats but set Medicare on a path away from fee-for-service and toward value-based care. It offered providers incentives to reform health delivery and emphasized primary, patient-centered, integrated care with quality accountability for improved care.

The legislation was not just a fiscal "fix" but rather a new health policy. The process came together because there was urgency, a starting point of agreement, and willingness to find a solution. It ended a deeply flawed policy and brought new opportunities for physicians and the health system more broadly to innovate with new ways of meeting patients' needs and improve health of all Americans.

MACRA was instrumental in moving that transformation forward. As MACRA comes due for reauthorization in 2025, it offers an opportunity for members of Congress from both parties to learn from the experience of MACRA to advance the move away from fee-for-service toward value-based payments.

The lessons of how SGR came together suggest that bipartisanship is there when the leadership of both parties share a goal and accept that they will work together to achieve it. Key committees took a bill with a clear vision from a Democratic congresswoman and a willing Republican partner and paved the way forward. Final negotiations by a few determined senior staff took a chance to trust each other. They found a way to pay for the cost of the bill and add provisions to satisfy one side without losing the other.

Outside interest groups took bold steps in offering early, consistent, and strong support. Experts offered counsel to make the result sound policy and fiscally responsible. All were essential to the outcome that was ultimately supported by almost everyone in both the House and the Senate, Democrats and Republicans alike.

The hope is that this is not just a story from the past but a message of hope for the future.

NOTES

We are thankful to the people who offered their recollections through interviews and whom we quoted in this chapter. They were invaluable in helping to inform this chapter. They included Joe Heck, John Boehner, Bill Cassidy, Mike Burgess, Wendell Primus, Charlotte Ivancic, Shawn Martin, Joe Antos, Doug Holtz-Eakin, Chris Jennings, and Ashley Ridlon. We also want to thank all those who participated in drafting the language, those who offered ideas and criticisms, those who advocated for the bill and the members of Congress and the Senate who voted for the final bill making it a bipartisan victory.

1. 2011 Annual Report of the Boards of Trustees of the Federal Hospital Insurance and Federal Supplementary Medical Insurance Trust Funds. https://www .cms.gov/Research-Statistics-Data-and-Systems/Statistics-Trends-and-Reports /ReportsTrustFunds/downloads/tr2011.pdf.

2. CRS Report for Congress, Medicare Provisions in the Balanced Budget Act of 1997 (BBA 97, P.L. 105-33). https://www.everycrsreport.com/files/19970818_97 -802_0347a1fe70af1b6bbce038af2c217186942cd7cc.pdf.

3. KFF Health News, Facing Pressure from All Sides, Deficit Panel Keeps Hands Off Health Law, November 16, 2011. https://kffhealthnews.org/morning -breakout/super-committee-news-18/.

ALLYSON Y. SCHWARTZ *is a former member of the US House of Representatives from Pennsylvania (2005–2015), former health care executive, current senior health adviser to the Bipartisan Policy Center among other health and civic organizations.*

CHARLENE MACDONALD *is a trade association executive who has served as a senior health adviser to Representative Schwartz and other senior Congressional leaders.*

EIGHT

—〰—

LEGIONS OF COSPONSORS
FOR THE MILITARY

JASON ALTMIRE

In the middle of every difficulty lies opportunity.

—ALBERT EINSTEIN

IT IS POSSIBLE TO FIND compromise and consensus even in the most bitterly partisan debates. Such was the case in 2011, when the nation watched as Republicans and Democrats in Washington, DC, engaged in a dangerous game of chicken with nearly catastrophic consequences. Despite a legislative debacle that created tension and bitterness among its members, Congress was able to come together in support of a cause on which we can all agree—support of our nation's military veterans. This is the story of how that issue proved that bipartisanship is not dead, and how, even in the midst of one of the most contentious debates in recent memory, members of Congress can still work together to overcome the politics-as-usual inertia of the institution.

When I first announced my candidacy for Congress in 2006, I made the need for members of Congress to work together more effectively a key part of my platform. I pledged that, if elected, I would seek bipartisan solutions and work to find compromise on difficult legislative issues. I was fortunate to win my first race and to be reelected in 2008 and 2010, despite the fact that I was a Democrat running in a congressional district with a decidedly Republican lean.

The majority of members of Congress represent districts that are overwhelmingly partisan in their makeup—either solidly red or solidly blue. This makes it more difficult for those representatives to seek compromise with members of the opposing party because their own party leadership demands loyalty and discourages positions that stray from party priorities and orthodoxy. Unlike those members of Congress, I represented a district that was politically mixed, giving me the benefit of hearing both sides of most issues whenever I traveled around the district.

On many of the key issues of the day, such as health care, American involvement in the overseas military conflicts in the Middle East, immigration, foreign trade, and education, there was a strong difference of opinion among my constituents depending on which political party was promoting the policies. However, there was at least one issue on which the majority of both sides would always agree—support of our nation's military veterans.

Because the western Pennsylvania district I represented had one of the largest populations of military veterans of any district in the country, I made veterans' issues a priority throughout my time in office. Given the importance of those issues and the support my proposals often received from the national veterans' service organizations, I was able to establish a strong record of legislative success on matters pertinent to veterans. Over the course of my three terms in office, I was able to shepherd nine different initiatives relating to veterans' policy through the legislative process, each of which became law.

On many of these veterans' issues, I worked closely with the American Legion, which had a strong presence in my district, including a former national commander of the Legion. I developed a solid working relationship with both the local and the national American Legion organizations, even though I had not served in the military myself.

I learned through experience that one of the best ways to establish credibility and to successfully position a bill for passage through the bitterly divided Congress was to find a lead Republican cosponsor for each bill I introduced. I had done so on several of my legislative initiatives that had become law, regardless of which party was in control of Congress at the time. Through this approach, I had seen successful enactment of my bills in both Democratic- and Republican-led Congresses, signed into law by both President George W. Bush and President Barack Obama.

One of my proudest achievements during my time in office was the "Special Recognition" award I received at the national meeting of the American Legion in March 2010. It signified the importance of the work we were doing together as well as our mutual appreciation of the relationship we had built.

Given that strong working relationship, I was not surprised when the American Legion's top liaison to the House of Representatives approached me in March 2011 about an issue that had long been one of the Legion's key concerns—the modernization of the organization's congressional charter.

Because it had been nearly a century since Congress established the American Legion's charter, there was a need to update some of the terms and clear up various ambiguities that existed. I was happy to help and agreed to introduce the modernization legislation with the goal of passing it through Congress by the end of the year.

Unfortunately, this task would not be easy. Despite the relatively noncontroversial nature of the legislation, moving legislation that was sponsored by a Democratic member through the Republican-led House of Representatives would be out of the ordinary, given the partisan political climate in the country and in Congress. Making matters worse, the congressional debate over the federal government's budget and fiscal policies would soon dominate the discussions and make it nearly impossible for House members to focus on anything else.

In the fall of 2010, it became clear that Democrats in Congress were heading for political disaster. The dialogue of the first midterm election of President Barack Obama's tenure in the White House was driven mainly by the Tea Party, a new political phenomenon that stormed the country with relentless force.

Followers of the Tea Party movement were motivated by the unprecedented government spending that had been injected into the economy following the 2008 financial crisis and the early months of the Obama administration. Although most economists would agree that the spending helped avert a financial catastrophe, a sizable portion of the American people were furious about what they perceived to be out-of-control government spending. They responded by organizing what would become one of the most powerful political movements in American history.

A thirty-year-old Seattle school teacher and blogger named Keli Carender is credited with organizing the first Tea Party protest, gathering more than one hundred people in her hometown to voice opposition to President Obama's 2009 stimulus bill. Shortly thereafter, a brash cable news business reporter took to the floor of the Chicago Mercantile Exchange to offer a rambling diatribe that would become a catalyst for the movement. Calling for a "Chicago Tea Party," CNBC's Rick Santelli screamed into the camera that Obama's policies were rewarding bad behavior by unscrupulous actors in the financial services industry. The video quickly went viral, as did the Tea Party movement itself.

The 2010 midterm elections were all about government spending and overreach, and the tidal wave of discontent grew stronger week by week, reaching its peak just as the November elections arrived. In losing an incredible sixty-three seats, House Democrats suffered the worst electoral defeat of any party in Congress since Herbert Hoover was president. It was clear that Republicans, soon to be the majority in Congress, would ride that wave into 2011 and the opening of the 112th Congress. The new freshman Republican lawmakers knew they were responsible for the Republican majority, and they were determined to use that leverage to bring attention to their concerns about government spending.

That enormous leverage came to a head during the 2011 debate over an arcane budget requirement necessitating a vote of congressional approval for the nation to pay its bills. Commonly known as the "debt ceiling" vote, this budget practice dates back to 1917, when Congress created a budget mechanism designed to provide more flexibility to fund American military involvement in World War I. This vote allows Congress to raise the cap on federal spending in order to pay bills that have already been incurred. Usually a formality, the debt ceiling vote gave the Tea Party its first opportunity to extract firm commitments from President Obama and Democrats to reduce government spending. Hardliners among the new freshman Republicans did not miss this opportunity to weaponize the powerful tool they had been given.

In the fifty years leading up to the 2011 debate, the debt limit had been raised seventy-four times under presidents of both parties. Despite this fact, it quickly became apparent that the 2011 debt limit vote would be unlike the others. Recognizing the precarious situation, the Government Accountability Office in February 2011 issued a report laying out the options available to the government to manage debt and spending should there be delays in raising the debt ceiling, as well as the dire consequences of a failure to raise the limit in time to avert a government default. The Department of the Treasury went into further detail, explaining that "failing to raise the debt limit would ... cause the government to default on its obligations—an unprecedented event in American history." Most economists agreed that such a default would have catastrophic economic consequences, not only in the United States but around the world.

The debate over the debt ceiling in 2011 was a particularly contentious and partisan affair, with deep disagreements between Democrats and Republicans over how best to address the growing federal debt. Some of the most vehement disagreements that occurred during this debate included:

1. The role of government spending: Republicans insisted that any increase in the debt ceiling must be accompanied by significant cuts to government spending, particularly in areas such as entitlement programs and discretionary spending. Democrats, on the other hand, argued that spending cuts alone would not be enough to address the debt crisis and that a balanced approach that included tax and revenue increases was necessary.

2. The size of the debt ceiling increase: Republicans initially demanded that any increase in the debt ceiling be tied to a dollar-for-dollar reduction in federal spending. Democrats rejected this proposal, arguing that such a drastic reduction in spending would be harmful to the economy and would be politically unfeasible.

3. The timing of the debt ceiling increase: Republicans pushed for a short-term increase in the debt ceiling, arguing that it would force the government to address the debt crisis in a more timely and effective manner. Democrats argued that a short-term increase would only serve to prolong the uncertainty and instability surrounding the debt ceiling issue and cause more harm to an already weakened economy.

4. The use of the debt ceiling as a political weapon: Some Republicans argued that the debt ceiling should be used as a tool to force the Obama administration to make significant concessions on issues such as tax reform and entitlement spending. Democrats rejected this proposal, arguing that it was unwise to set the precedent of using the debt ceiling debate as a partisan political bargaining chip.

Overall, the debate regarding the debt ceiling in 2011 was characterized by deep ideological and political divisions, with both parties entrenched in their positions and unwilling to compromise. The resulting deadlock ultimately led to a downgrade of the US credit rating and contributed to a period of extreme economic uncertainty and volatility.

The clock continued to tick as the politicians in Washington dithered. The financial markets took notice, and throughout 2011, the major credit rating agencies warned that, as a result of the crisis, the US credit rating was in danger of being downgraded for the first time in American history. On April 4, 2011, Treasury Secretary Timothy Geithner informed Congress that when the debt limit was reached, the government had the authority to resort to "extraordinary measures," such as the sale of various financial assets, to move money around and briefly allow the government to continue to meet its obligations and temporarily extend the time available to avert default. Still, the acrimonious debate continued in Congress as both sides dug in their heels. With no compromise in sight, those extraordinary measures went into effect on May 16, 2011. Secretary Geithner informed Congress that unless Congress voted to raise the debt ceiling by August 2, 2011, the government would exhaust its ability to maneuver around the crisis and the nation would enter default.

As the deadline approached, the credit-rating agency Standard & Poor's followed through on its threat and downgraded the credit rating of the United States, citing the political instability that paralyzed the government and threatened to throw the nation into default. In both houses of Congress, tempers flared as partisans pointed fingers and cast blame for this unprecedented event. America, and the world, buckled up for the rough ride ahead, preparing for the worst.

It was against this backdrop that I decided to remind my colleagues in Congress that there were still some issues on which we could all agree. In the spring of 2011, I was approached by the American Legion about the need to modernize its charter, which was first authorized by Congress in 1919 and had not been updated to account for technology changes that had occurred over the past several decades. As a Democratic member of the House, and thus in the minority party, I worked with leaders from the Legion to assess the need and finalize the details, then agreed to introduce a bill to reauthorize the charter.

But first I had an idea.

Knowing the extreme animosity that existed in the House over the debt ceiling debate and other partisan disagreements, I decided to use this opportunity to demonstrate the bipartisan unity that was sorely lacking. In the overall scheme of things, this was a relatively insignificant issue compared to the debt limit debate that was dominating the national airwaves and the discussions on both ends of Pennsylvania Avenue. Nevertheless, modernizing the charter was long overdue and only Congress could do it. I set out to not only complete the task, but also to send a message of unity that I hoped would demonstrate for Congress and the nation that bipartisanship was possible even in the most polarizing times.

I worked for several weeks with the American Legion and legislative counsel in the House to ensure the bill was consistent with congressional rules while addressing the issues of concern to the Legion. The legislation, which would become H.R. 2369 of the 112th Congress, updated the American Legion's charter to take into account modern technological advances, such as the ability of Legion members to pay their dues online by credit card. Importantly, the bill also clarified the autonomous, independent status of American Legion posts and departments, a status that was ambiguous in the original charter written nearly a century before.

To best position the bill for the work ahead, I wanted to find a Republican co-sponsor who I knew would share my vision not only for the merits of the bill but also the message bipartisan passage would send to the House and the American people. After considering several options, I found the perfect partner.

First elected in 2008, Florida's then thirty-eight-year old Republican representative Tom Rooney was universally respected and had many friends on both sides of the aisle. A grandson of the legendary Pittsburgh Steelers founder, Art Rooney Sr., Tom earned a law degree from the University of Miami before enlisting in the US Army. Stationed at Fort Hood (now Fort Cavasos) in Texas and serving as a JAG officer in the years following the September 11, 2001, attacks, Tom spent more than four years on active duty. Afterward, he remained in the US Army Reserve. After two consecutive congressmen in Rooney's district had embarrassed themselves with humiliating personal scandals, Tom offered voters a clean-cut alternative straight out of central casting. He waged a successful campaign for Congress and quickly established a reputation in the House as a relationship builder and honest broker. We became friends and bonded over our common interests of sports and politics. After the bill language was finalized, I met with Tom to discuss the American Legion charter and he enthusiastically agreed to serve as the lead cosponsor of the bill, which we introduced on June 24, 2011.

After the bill's introduction, Tom and I began the routine process of collecting cosponsors. We sent out a joint "Dear Colleague" letter to those with whom we served in the House, asking for support and cosponsorship of H.R. 2369. The responses were both swift and enlightening. Responses came in almost immediately, with both Republican and Democratic House members asking to be listed as cosponsors. On July 7, 2011, as the debate on the debt ceiling was hitting its peak and mistrust among House members was near an all-time high, I submitted to the House clerk the first wave of new cosponsors for the bill, a bipartisan list of eighty-nine House members.

It was about this time I realized we had something special. My goal had been to get a critical mass of cosponsors necessary to pass the bill, and better yet, to make that list of cosponsors as bipartisan as possible. With this first wave of support, I knew we were well on our way. Little did I know we were on our way to not only enacting a change in the charter but also setting a record for the most cosponsors for any bill ever introduced in the history of the US House of Representatives.

With 435 voting members in the US House of Representatives, 218 votes are necessary to pass a bill when all members vote. For a bill to pass the House under the expedited "suspension of the rules" process, a two-thirds majority is necessary, which equates to 290 yea votes. Surpassing this number was my initial goal for cosponsors, which I speculated would show enough support to bring the bill to the floor for a vote.

At the time, members of Congress were required to be present in the House chamber to participate in roll call votes on bills and amendments. This meant that all members were together at the same place and the same time, offering the best opportunity to catch colleagues in person and discuss whatever business was at hand. For me, that business was increasing support for the American Legion bill.

After dropping the list of new cosponsors at the desk in the House on July 7, Tom and I spent the time during the multiple series of votes that were occurring that day to walk around the crowded House chamber to talk to our colleagues about the bill, asking them to join as cosponsors. Without rhyme or reason, I approached whichever members happened to be within my sight lines, focusing primarily on those with whom I had stronger personal relationships. Tom was doing the same. On that one day, ninety additional members agreed to join the effort, bringing our cosponsor total to 179 when I submitted the new names on July 8.

A similar pattern repeated itself each time the House was in session, and Tom and I also began to call and email our colleagues directly over the next several days and weeks. The number of cosponsors especially grew when the American Legion sent a letter to all House members in support of the bill.

Nathan Robinson, the staffer in my office in charge of the effort, was a military veteran himself. Nathan spent countless hours courting new cosponsors through contacts with his staff peers in other congressional offices. As the list grew, Nathan provided me with names of members who were *not* on the bill, which made it easier for me to seek out those colleagues to speak with them about the legislation.

During the month of August, Congress adjourns in order to give members several weeks at home in their districts. Because Congress had narrowly averted fiscal calamity on July 31 with an eleventh-hour deal extending the debt ceiling in exchange for deep spending cuts, the 2011 August recess gave members the opportunity to visit their constituents and try to explain the maddening dysfunction in Washington. The tension and bitterness in the House was palpable, so this recess also allowed time for tempers to subside.

After traveling around my congressional district visiting constituents and explaining the debt ceiling fiasco, I returned to Washington, DC, after Labor Day and continued work on the American Legion bill. By the end of September, the bill had more than 330 cosponsors, more than enough to pass the House. Under normal circumstances, this would at minimum be more than enough support for House leaders to bring up the bill for a vote, but these were anything but normal circumstances. It was about this time that I realized that, despite all my efforts to the contrary, partisan politics were now getting in the way of my bill.

The Speaker of the House of Representatives does not typically cosponsor bills, so it was not a concern to me when Speaker John Boehner (R-OH), with whom I had a cordial relationship, declined to sign on to the bill when I spoke to him about it. Nor did it strike me as unusual that the chairman of the House Committee on the Judiciary, Rep. Lamar Smith (R-TX), also stayed off the bill, which had been referred to his committee. What did concern me, however, was what my staffer Nathan Robinson and I were hearing about *why* the bill was not moving through committee.

While both Speaker Boehner and Chairman Smith indicated support for the bill, both were noticeably evasive the multiple times I asked them for updates on the status of the bill, hoping for clarity on when it would move through committee. Over time, it became clear the delay was due to the desire of Republican leadership to deny the Democratic bill sponsor—me—a political victory that would be beneficial to my reelection campaign the following year, when Republicans were planning to mount a challenge against me given the strong conservative lean of my western Pennsylvania district. Nathan was hearing as much at the staff level, and multiple House colleagues were passing along similar messages to me. Despite the popularity of the bill and the issue, Republican leadership was willing to stall consideration of the bill indefinitely.

We had to find a way around the bottleneck. Working with the American Legion throughout the process, Nathan and I compared notes and considered alternatives. As summer turned into fall, it became clear House leadership was not going to move the bill no matter how much support we assembled. To get around this obstacle, we turned to an unlikely source—the US Senate. If the bill could pass the Democratic-controlled Senate, it would be forwarded to the House for consideration. To force the issue, we worked with the American Legion to approach Senator Jon Tester (D-MT) and ask him to introduce the identical bill as the Senate companion to H.R. 2369. On October 3, he did just that. In an unlikely scenario for observers of the workings of Congress, the Senate moved the bill through at lightning speed, passing it unanimously by voice vote on October 6, three days after introduction.

With the ball now in their court, House leaders could no longer ignore the bill. The Senate companion legislation, which was word-for-word identical to the bill I had introduced months earlier, was received in the House and referred to the Judiciary Committee—the same committee where my bill had languished for months. It wasn't until December 6 that the House finally brought Sen. Tester's companion bill up for consideration, one day after my bill was finally passed out of the Judiciary Committee. By that time, H.R. 2369 had accumulated 432 cosponsors, the most for any congressional bill ever introduced.

On December 6, the day of the final vote in the House, I took to the podium on the House floor to speak about the significance of the moment.

In the well of the House, there are two podiums where members stand to speak during debate, one on the left, and one on the right. As members look toward the presiding officer, the podium from which Democrats usually speak is, perhaps appropriately, on the left. On this day, however, I wanted to send a message of unity, so I chose to speak from the podium on the right, the one from which Republicans usually spoke.

As author of the House bill, I acknowledged for my colleagues that the modernization of the American Legion's congressional charter was not the most important issue facing the country in these highly polarized times. To the contrary, it was relatively insignificant given the enormity of the political battles in which the House members were currently engaged. But the American Legion had asked for this change, and only Congress could amend and modernize the Legion's charter. It had to be done, and we were here to do it. But what was most important, I said, was that the House had come together to pass this bill in a rare bipartisan show of support. To honor our nation's veterans, we garnered a record number of cosponsors. I argued that this effort, however small it may be in comparison to the larger issues of the day, was a demonstration to the Congress, and to the American people, that there really are issues on which we can all agree and for which we can all work together. I told my colleagues that I hoped we could all learn from this experience and create a better and more collegial working environment moving forward.

As it had in the Senate, the bill passed unanimously. On December 13, 2011, President Obama signed it into law.

Time would go on and the political battles would continue. Few would argue that bipartisanship has increased in Congress since passage of the American Legion charter bill in 2011. In fact, by every conceivable measure, it has gotten much worse. But for all the angst and consternation about Congress's inability to work together in these current polarized times, it is my hope that the memory of the American Legion's charter modernization and the overwhelming support it received can serve as a reminder that it is still possible to achieve consensus and find areas where all members of Congress can agree. It is in that spirit that I hope current and future members of Congress will work together collaboratively and restore a measure of collegiality that has been sorely lacking in today's partisan political environment.

JASON ALTMIRE *is a former Democratic member of the US House of Representatives from Pennsylvania.*

NINE

—𝔐—

PUBLIC SAFETY IS NOT A
PARTISAN MATTER

CURT WELDON

IMAGINE WALKING DOWN CONSTITUTION AVENUE in Washington, DC, one night and seeing and hearing a screaming DC fire engine barreling toward some unknown fire or life-threatening situation. And on that truck, you spot folks who resemble elected members of the US Congress.

Or in the early afternoon, you are visiting the US Capitol to observe a legislative session and are startled by the sirens and air horns from hundreds of fire trucks parked along Constitution and Independence Avenues while dozens of members of Congress race over to a microphone on top of a flatbed truck trailer, above which flies an American flag connected to two raised aerial ladders with the dome of the Capitol Building as a backdrop!

Or, by chance, you observe a group of members of Congress and staffers gathered together in the Capitol parking lot using fire extinguishers to control and extinguish small fires deliberately set for training purposes.

Were these examples of members of Congress totally out of control? Absolutely not!

What you witnessed were members of Congress from both political parties from every state engaging and joining in operations and training activities working alongside and with DC firefighters. They were experiencing first-hand the role of firefighters and emergency services personnel that occur every day in every village, town, and city in America—and they were also making the case for a national interoperable emergency communication system for the nation.

These—and many similar—activities, were the work of the Congressional Fire Services Caucus and Institute, designed to awaken members of the US House and Senate to the role, activities, and needs of the more than one million firefighters and emergency services professionals, both paid and volunteer, working out of thirty thousand fire and emergency medical services (EMS) departments across America.

Conceived, founded, and organized in 1987, during my first term in Congress, the Congressional Fire Services Caucus is an example of members of Congress working together at their best. And thirty-six years later, that organization remains one of the largest, and most successful, bipartisan organizations in our nation's capital.

Representing your neighbors and friends in the US Congress is an honor few get to experience. Elevating your life's passion at the national level with leaders from all persuasions and political parties is a legacy envied by all who serve.

Elected in 1987 to serve in the US House as a Republican in a Congress overwhelmingly dominated by Democrats, presented an unusual challenge, but also an opportunity for me. Born and raised the youngest of nine children in Marcus Hook, Pennsylvania, a blue-collar industrial community along the banks of the Delaware River, I had no special stature nor inheritance worthy of recognition.

Becoming a teacher in disadvantaged communities in the border towns of Philadelphia gave me no special credentials that could empower success among the nation's leaders, especially with those of the opposite party. But I did have an attribute—a passion for community service—that had been ingrained in my soul by my father and eight older siblings. I was a volunteer firefighter who, at the age of twenty-eight, had the privilege and honor of becoming a fire chief.

And I knew that every other elected member of Congress had firefighters and EMS personnel, both paid and volunteer, working out of dozens of fire/EMS stations in their districts. Early in my congressional service, I met members from both political parties who had assisted and supported their fire/EMS departments during their careers.

Older than America itself, fire/EMS departments started in the 1700s in communities as volunteers organized and prepared to deal with any and all emergencies. Benjamin Franklin started one of the first departments in Philadelphia, while others were being organized in Boston and other villages and cities. Every village and town in America experienced a group of like-minded men and women who banded together to prepare and respond to disasters of every type imaginable. Most of these organizations were nonprofit and the members volunteered their services.

Raising funds through chicken dinners, tag days, fairs and other events, fire departments prepared for and responded to any, and all kinds of, disasters and emergency situations. Because of the community spirit involved—fire departments also organized patriotic celebrations, hosted parades, rescued cats in trees, pumped out flooded cellars, and offered their facilities to be used as voting centers. They rented out their buildings for wedding receptions, retirement parties and they hosted Boy Scout and Girl Scout meetings as well as other civic events. Fire departments became the heart and soul of our communities.

Firefighters and emergency medical service personnel respond to every type of disaster including fires, flood, hurricanes, tornadoes, explosions, accidents, terrorist incidents, and mass casualty events in every community. These domestic defenders have become known as the "backbone of our nation."

In the United States today, more than thirty thousand fire and EMS departments exist and are present in every state, every county, and every community, large and small. With many departments covering multiple jurisdictions, approximately fifty thousand fire and EMS stations exist in America. Eighty-five percent of these departments are volunteer or part volunteer/part paid. Volunteer fire departments are independent 501(c)(3) organizations who raise and manage their own budgets, purchase and maintain their equipment, train their members, maintain the fire stations, and serve all components of their communities.

As a lifelong firefighter, I have had the privilege of serving as a fire chief, a Pennsylvania State fire instructor, and a county-wide fire training director— all as a volunteer. I have devoted my life to the nation's fire service. In 1975 I served as deputy fire chief during one of the largest fire disasters ever to occur in the United States, the collision of two supertankers, which occurred at the dock of the BP Oil Refinery in my hometown of Marcus Hook. Incinerating twenty-nine crew members and burning out of control for forty-eight hours, the explosions and fire threatened our entire community, as well as the refinery.

I coauthored the technical publication "The Corinthos Disaster" and testified in federal court and before Congress as an expert witness, at the invitation of the member of Congress Bob Edgar and the House Energy and Commerce Committee on which he served. In 1978, Sun Oil Corporation's Marcus Hook oil refinery overfilled one of five man-made massive underground liquefied gas storage caverns, pumping Butane into the basements of local homes, destroying five homes, requiring me as fire chief and newly elected mayor to evacuate eighty families until the site could be secured.

My passion as a firefighter was shared by men and women in every town, village and city across America. Yet little support was being provided at the federal level for those brave citizens who risked their lives every day to guarantee the safety and well-being of friends, neighbors, and people whom they had never met.

Witnessing annual federal appropriations of $4 billion in support of local law enforcement and hundreds of billions for the nation's military—all of which was justified—I could not understand the total lack of support for our firefighters and EMS personnel—"America's Domestic Defenders," as I labeled them.

Was the life of a firefighter or someone working in EMS less valuable than the life of a police officer or soldier? Except in war, two hundred to three hundred soldiers die each year. That is too many, as are the 130 police and one hundred firefighters and EMS workers who die each year. And many of the firefighters and EMS personnel are volunteers and receive no compensation for their dedication.

I asked myself, "Why are firefighters and EMS personnel being ignored by the federal government and elected leaders of the US Congress, and what can I do to change that situation?" I knew full well that firefighters and EMS received universal respect from all citizens in every community in my home state of Pennsylvania and neighboring states of Delaware and New Jersey. But because firefighters and EMS personnel, by their very nature, are doers who rarely complain, I concluded that their story was just not being told to those who represented them in the halls of Congress.

As an educator and local activist, I began to realize that my job was to awaken this sleeping giant of local responders nationwide and help empower them to receive the recognition and support of their elected leaders in Washington, DC, as well as in the state capitals.

As a firefighter I knew the power and respect of firefighters and EMS personnel in every community in every state and congressional district in America. If we could organize and empower these local leaders, I knew we could achieve success in Washington, DC.

During my first term in Congress, I got to know a group of like-minded members of the House of Representatives, including Democrat Doug Walgren (Pennsylvania) and Republican Sherry Boehlert (New York) and Democratic Senator Al Gore (Tennessee) and Republican Senator John McCain (Arizona). Working together as a bipartisan coalition, we conceived and organized the Congressional Fire & Emergency Services Caucus with the support of Speaker Jim Wright and Minority Leader Bob Michel. The caucus and nonprofit Congressional Fire Services Institute (CFSI) became, and remains, the largest bipartisan caucus in the Congress, with more than three hundred members from both the House and Senate.

In my first term, something very unusual occurred. Working late in my second-floor office in the Longworth Building, directly across the street from the US Capitol, I smelled smoke and asked a staffer also working late to check the office for something smoldering. As the smell of smoke became stronger, I opened my office door and was immediately blunted by thick smoke billowing down the upper level of the hallway. Then I realized that it was emanating from Speaker Jim Wright's District Office, two doors down from my office in the corner suite of the Longworth Building.

While telling my staffer to call in the alarm and close all windows in the office, I ran down the hall to the Speaker's office, eventually kicking open the door to verify that all staff had left the suite. Once open, I crawled along the floor to search for staffers who may have been overcome from the smoke and toxic gases. I observed the entire kitchen area engulfed in flames licking out into the neighboring rooms within the Speaker's suite. I yelled to my staffer John McNichol to bring me the portable fire extinguishers that are located in hose stations on every floor of every high-rise office building. John quickly brought five portable extinguishers to the front of the Speaker's office. Unfortunately, three of them were not charged so they could not be used. I sent John back to the hose station telling him to bring me the preconnected hose and stand by to turn on the water spigot when I was prepared to use it. As I discharged the two portable extinguishers that were usable, I could hear John yelling to me that "there was no hose in the hose station."

Confirming that no staffers remained in the Speaker's office and realizing that there was nothing more that I could do to control the fire, I left the office and closed the door, and witnessed the panic and chaos in the hallways of the Longworth Office Building. Members of Congress and staffers were coughing and choking as they scurried down the marble stairways seeking an exit—not realizing what was occurring.

Observing Capitol Hill police officers yelling, "Fire—get out of the building," as they ran through the hallway pounding on office doors, I yelled, "Why is the fire alarm not sounding?" To which one officer yelled back, "There is no alarm system in this building."

No alarm system, no smoke detectors, no automatic sprinkler system, no automatic recall of elevators to the ground floor resulting in elevators stopping on the fire floor exposing occupants to massive smoke and toxic gases! It was then that I realized that this seven-story office building with four basement floors housing one-third of the members of the United States House of Representatives, hundreds of staff, thousands of daily visitors, some of whom had physical challenges, was in violation of every fire and life safety code in place in every city in the United States.

As a former fire chief and risk management officer for Insurance Company of North America (INA), I was fully versed on the NFPA Life Safety Code 101 and realized that my House office building in DC was in full violation of this national standard.

Washington, DC, Fire Chief Ray Alfred and his capable firefighters arrived within minutes. Thinking like a fire chief as well as House member, I encountered the chief and quickly explained that he had a "working fire in the corner office suite on the second floor that was vacant of any persons" and explained that the kitchen was fully involved requiring his firefighters to "lay lines" from his DCFD engines that had lined up immediately outside of the exits. As I briefed the chief, I added appropriate details stating, "I'm sure that you've pre-planned your response, rescue and plan of attack for this building," to which DC Fire Chief Ray Alfred responded, "We've never been permitted to preplan these office buildings!"

Standing outside of the building, observing DC firefighters as they efficiently began to attack and eventually control and extinguish the fire, I was confused and angry. With the media now assembled and documenting the incident, I recall one reporter sticking a microphone in my dirty face (realizing that I was a member of Congress) and asking me for my response. Irritated and frustrated, I responded that the Longworth House Office Building was a "fire trap" in violation of all applicable standards for a high-rise office building and should be closed until properly protected!

Significant damage had been done to the Speaker's office suite, but no injuries had occurred. Admiring the professional work of the DC Fire Department, I was angered by what had occurred and determined to initiate corrective change.

That night, Speaker Wright's chief of staff, Marshall Lynam, called me on my mobile phone to thank me. During our conversation, when he learned that I had been a volunteer firefighter and fire chief, he asked what actions I thought necessary for consideration by the Speaker.

When I arrived at the House Chamber the next morning, members from both parties inquired about the incident, my media comments, and my reaction. Jokingly, my Democratic friends asked if I had "started the fire in the Speakers office?" My Republican friends asked, "Why'd you try to put it out?"

At the opening bell of the House that day, I offered a privileged resolution regarding the health, safety, and welfare of members of the House. Speaker Wright recognized "the gentleman from Pennsylvania" and accepted the resolution after publicly thanking me for my response to the fire. As a result of the resolution, Speaker Wright appointed a four-member bipartisan panel to make recommendations regarding fire and life safety in all US House office buildings and the Capitol itself. Recommendations from that bipartisan panel resulted in all buildings on Capitol Hill being retrofitted with smoke detectors, alarm systems, automatic sprinklers, and other life safety measures. Speaker Wright presented me with an engraved crystal vase with his signature and the Architect of the Capitol presented me with the last "Manual Pull Fire Alarm Box" that had been located in the basement of the Capitol Building—both of which are in my Archives.

The Congressional Fire Services Caucus was now "on fire" as members from both parties rushed to join the effort. As the Fire Services Caucus grew in size, we realized that it was necessary to establish a separate organization of Fire Service Stakeholder Groups to act as the advocacy group working with staffers assigned by members of Congress.

Original cochairs of the caucus included Al Gore, John McCain, Doug Walgren, and Sherry Boehlert. During the first few years, Senator Joe Biden and Congressman Steny Hoyer also became cochairs and remained leading advocates throughout their entire tenure. Hoyer remains a cochair of the Caucus to this day. Biden remained active in all aspects of leadership of the Fire Caucus and attended (and keynoted) thirty of the thirty-three National Fire and Emergency Services Dinners held in DC each year. Other keynote speakers included Presidents Bush and Clinton, Vice Presidents Al Gore and Dan Quayle, Speakers Wright, Foley, and Gingrich, and national leaders Colin Powell, Janet Reno, Tom Ridge, Janet Napolitano, Jeh Johnson, and Michael Chertoff, as well as Hollywood stars Kurt Russell, Billy Baldwin, Charlton Heston, and Ron Howard.

Ron Howard, Kurt Russell, and Billy Baldwin also unveiled the film *Backdraft* at the dinner they attended, and Charlton Heston unveiled the film *A Thousand Heroes (Crash Landing: The Rescue of Flight 232)* when he attended and spoke. I escorted Ron Howard to the White House to meet President George H. W. Bush the day after our dinner. The ambassador to the United States from Kuwait, Sheikh Saud Al Sabah, appeared and spoke at one dinner, thanking American firefighters for responding and extinguishing the devastating oil well fires ignited by Saddam Hussein's retreating army in Kuwait. We honored American oil well–firefighting heroes "Red" Adair and Asger "Boots" Hansen and Ed "Coots" Matthews for their heroic work in Kuwait.

From the outset, the Fire Services Caucus was mandated to be bipartisan and nonpartisan. Cochairs would include two Republicans and two Democrats from the House and two Republicans and two Democrats from the Senate, with the chair rotating each session from one body to the other and one party to the other.

Fire Caucus growth was rapid and massive, and it was fun! Member "ride alongs" were organized with Washington, DC, Fire Department Chief Ray Alfred and his officers. Members from both parties were assigned to the busiest DC fire stations to meet and interact with firefighters and ride along to any and every call for assistance ranging from fires to accidents, shootings to drug overdoses, and every other imaginable emergency. Members of Congress could even be observed "packing hose" on DC fire trucks alongside DC firefighters after a fire in the DC prison.

Every member of the Fire Caucus assigned a staff member to liaison and interact on all issues involving firefighting and emergency medical service issues across the nation. One year after creating the caucus we created a 501(c)(3) Congressional Fire Services Institute organized to act as the intermediary between members of Congress and the more than forty national fire and EMS stakeholder groups.

The National Fire and Emergency Services Dinner was organized and is held in the largest ballroom in Washington, DC, and each year thousands of firefighting and EMS leaders from across the nation attend and interact with their members of the House and Senate. Workshops and a "Day on the Hill" are held prior to the dinner, providing the opportunity for leaders to interact directly with their representatives and senators.

Proceeds from the Annual National Fire Services Dinner are used to fund the Institute. Attendance at the annual dinner has averaged two thousand national leaders, with presidents, cabinet members and administration officials providing keynote speeches.

The Fire Services Caucus has brought out the best in our nation's leaders. Members and staffers have participated in fire and EMS training workshops as well as sprinkler and portable fire extinguisher training sessions. And, following a very impressive "rally" with more than three hundred fire and rescue vehicles from all over the East Coast, these brave firefighters and emergency rescue professionals from the rally joined cochairs Hoyer and me in a press conference held on a flatbed truck trailer that had been strategically placed in the US Capitol parking lot, surrounded by DC and neighboring fire/EMS department vehicles and dwarfed by two large aerial trucks with their ladders extended in an arch joined together with a huge American flag. One never forgets the amazing work of firefighters and EMS personnel after witnessing such a parade surrounding the US Capitol grounds.

This was not entertainment, but a serious effort that led to the creation of a national interoperable communication system. As members and staffers came out of their offices to see what all the noise and commotion were about, they walked over to the activity in the Capitol parking lot and then joined Steny Hoyer and me in a bipartisan press event. In our remarks, we made the case for immediate availability of a national interoperable communication system for firefighters/EMS nationwide—and that system was delivered!

During my twenty-year tenure in the House, Democrats joined me in visiting every state as I keynoted firefighting and EMS events and conferences. In most instances we were fortunate to have local members joining as well. We also organized bipartisan delegations to fly on-site within hours after every major disaster in the country, including Hurricanes Andrew, Hugo, and Katrina; Midwest floods; forest and wildfires in California, Oregon, Washington, Wyoming, Montana, Idaho, and Utah; earthquakes in California; the bombing in Oklahoma City; and terrorist attacks on New York City's World Trade Center in 1993 and 2001.

Maryland Democrat Roy Dyson and I traveled to California following the Loma Prieta earthquake in 1989, where we joined Democrat Sam Farr and Republican Elton Gallegly in expediting awareness and federal response to the devasted San Francisco region.

New Jersey Democrat Rob Andrews and I arranged a United Parcel Service planeload of supplies and electric generators that we delivered to the Metro Dade Fire Department immediately after Hurricane Andrew devastated southern Florida in 1992. We stayed in a tent city in Homestead, where we helped provide meals to families who were staying in shelters following the devastating storm.

Democrats joined me as we raised almost $500,000 to assist local New Orleans fire departments after our visit to witness the devastation caused by Hurricane Katrina. Congressman Steve Scalise (then a state senator) received the donations on behalf of the fire departments of the city and greater New Orleans region.

To achieve success in empowering America's firefighters/EMS, I delivered a five-part challenge to volunteer and paid firefighters/EMS at every Congressional Fire Services Caucus event in DC and at events across the country. It was simple and straightforward.

Awareness—Every firefighter/EMS individual and organization nationwide had to "tell the story" of the fire service! The story of men and women from all walks of life who don't just fight fires and respond to disasters—but who are dedicated and committed men and women who form the backbone of every community as well as the heart and soul of our nation. Older than America itself, firefighters/EMS pump out the flooded basements, rescue the cat in the tree, search for the lost child, organize the parades and community celebrations, host the local Scout groups, wedding receptions and polling places in the local fire halls, and provide the civic leaders that make our communities vibrant.

Unity—There is strength in numbers and firefighters had to develop and deliver a common message of needs and demands. For decades, Firefighters/EMS had been taken for granted by citizens in our towns and cities. Seeking neither fame nor glory, firefighters/EMS faithfully delivered emergency and community services, often raising their own funds to purchase equipment, operate the station, and maintain a healthy organization. No longer could individual associations and organizations act only for their own specific needs and agendas. For ultimate success, a common *unified* agenda would have every member of every stakeholder group agree on a common platform of needs and then add priorities specific to their status to the common agenda. In this way, volunteer firefighters/EMS, paid firefighters/EMS, fire chiefs, fire/EMS instructors, women firefighters/EMS, fire marshals, industry groups, and fire service media all agreed on a common message.

Proactive—America's two million active firefighters/EMS and various stakeholder group members could no longer lay back and accept whatever benefits and funding decisions made by elected officials and bureaucrats at all levels. Once an agenda was developed, proactive strategies for implementation had to be activated.

Work within the System—Firefighters/EMS are typically not people who yell and scream at public meetings or picket and stage protests. But to achieve ultimate success, firefighters/EMS had to fully understand how government worked at all levels and then work within the system. Priorities could not wait until after municipal budgets were adopted, but rather, firefighters/EMS had to learn to help shape the budget process working within the governmental process.

Political but Not Partisan—In a representative democracy like ours, people and organizations must be involved and respectfully demand positive response and actions to meet needs to better serve the public and protect the health and safety of emergency workers. Through the Fire Services Caucus and its activities and initiatives, firefighters/EMS were motivated to get involved in the local, state, and national political process, advocating and supporting fire/EMS agendas—and respectfully demand results. But being political was always coupled with an admonition to *never* be so partisan as to always support candidates and leaders of one specific political party. Interaction, collaboration, and strategies needed to be developed and implemented with candidates and office holders from all political parties to achieve success.

Following these five basic admonitions to engage and benefit from the political process became the hallmark for success nationally. In addition, many individual state and regional fire/EMS stakeholder groups established state and regional fire/EMS caucuses using the same model.

Time and again, the model and strategy worked, and the "awakening of this sleeping giant" in America occurred.

In 2000, Hoyer, Pascrell, and I authored the Assistance to Firefighter Grants (AFG) Program, initially getting no support from the outgoing Clinton nor incoming Bush White Houses. As a senior member/vice chair of the House Armed Services Committee, I attached the authorization for the AFG Grant Program to the Defense authorization legislation. When President Clinton signed the 2001 Defense authorization legislation, the AFG Program became law.

But authorization meant nothing without actual appropriations and President George W. Bush's first budget request had zero funding for the new grant program. I summoned the Director of the Office of Management and Budget Mitch Daniels to my office in the Rayburn building to discuss the lack of funding request where dozens of Democratic and Republican members waited like vultures for his arrival. Obviously warned by staff, Mitch grabbed a portable fire extinguisher from a hallway cabinet and carried the extinguisher into my office telling us, "I think I'm going to need this!"

Without the initial support of President Clinton or Bush, we were able to appropriate the first $100 million in funding the Assistance to Firefighter Grant Program in 2001. In subsequent years, bipartisan support appropriated more than $15 billion for the AFG Program and the SAFER Program, totaling over $16 billion. The AFG and SAFER Programs are two of the most popular programs with members from both parties to this day.

Through these two historic programs, because of overwhelming bipartisan efforts, thousands of small town and big city fire departments have been able to purchase new equipment, enhance training, and better serve their communities.

Thirty-six years later, the Congressional Fire/EMS/Disaster Caucus remains one of—if not the—largest bipartisan caucuses in the Congress. The Annual National Fire and EMS Dinner in DC attracts thousands of attendees and has been addressed by numerous members of the House and Senate as well as presidents and cabinet members.

Having organized the Fire Caucus and traveled to all fifty states visiting local fire departments and association meetings and conventions, I noted that the response to disasters across the United States and worldwide was the same: respond, mitigate, and recover. Serving as oversight chair of all military research and technology during my twenty-year tenure as a member and vice chair of the House Armed Services Committee, I couldn't help but notice that much of our technology achievements being used by our military also had dual use applications for firefighters and first responders. Working with colleagues in both parties, we enacted my amendment to the annual Defense authorization legislation that mandated efforts by the Department of Defense to share technology with fire departments that could help predict and prevent disasters. That effort continues to this day.

Having chaired bipartisan congressional delegations (co-dels) to 104 nations during my twenty-year tenure in the House, I frequently visited overseas disaster areas within days of an incident to assist and learn lessons that could be applicable to future similar incidents. In our co-dels across the United States and worldwide (often witnessing traumatic incidents) we were struck by the unique nature of the firefighters and rescue workers (first responders) whom we encountered.

Not driven by power nor money, and often speaking different languages, the one constant that we observed were the characteristics of the first responders. Risking their lives for people whom they had never met (from all backgrounds and socioeconomic statuses) these unsung heroes were the same worldwide.

As a result, it became apparent that we needed to conceive and create a new international nongovernmental organization (NGO) that would forever empower firefighters/EMS worldwide and alter disaster preparedness and response in every region of the world. At the 2014 World Economic Forum in Astana, Kazakhstan, I led a twenty-member bipartisan delegation that delivered the challenge to change the international disaster paradigm worldwide forever.

One World for Life was organized and incorporated with two fundamental purposes:

- Identify, organize, and empower the estimated 25+ million firefighters/EMS worldwide in every country regardless of political or governmental systems;
- Identify and use new and existing technology that, in many cases was largely designed for military use to *predict* and *prevent* disasters, thus fundamentally change the disaster paradigm worldwide.

Initiatives are now underway to fully implement One World for Life, including:

- Capitol Hill thirteen-story Firefighter/EMS First Responder Center, including:
  - National fire/EMS first responder museum,
  - Historically renovated DC fire station reopened as "America's Firehouse,"
  - Offices and recording studio for fire/rescue TV network nationwide;
- Linking a fire/rescue TV network to all of the more than fifty thousand fire/EMS stations nationwide;
- Next generation firefighter/EMS K–12 education civic engagement program through the Rendell Center for Civics and Civic Engagement;
- Responder Lifeline mortgage and financial services platform for fire/EMS/first responders;
- *Firefight* documentary film, followed by one hundred UN-endorsed climate and disaster films over ten years;
- HEROES Firefighter/EMS First Responders Mental Health Podcast Initiative;
- OWFL international private browser benefiting first responders worldwide;
- International fire/EMS/disaster training center;
- Firefighter/EMS first responder technology directorate;
- Worldwide communication network for first responders.

To announce and support the OWFL agenda, Congressman Bob Brady (D-PA) and I have secured the support of President Joe Biden for the first-ever White House Conference on Firefighters/EMS now being planned.

America has always succeeded as a nation because of our common values, desire to assist others in need, and determination to work together. Through the Congressional Fire/EMS/Disaster Caucus, hundreds of members of the House and Senate from both parties have come together over the last three decades to assist and empower our communities in support of firefighters and EMS first responders.

The Congressional Fire/EMS/Disaster Caucus has not only succeeded and excelled, it has created a template for success for any challenge facing our nation.

CURT WELDON *is a former Republican member of the US House of Representatives from Pennsylvania.*

TEN

—ᴡ—

BIPARTISANSHIP NEEDED TO REDUCE GUN VIOLENCE

PAUL HELMKE

COLUMBINE, VIRGINIA TECH, AURORA, Sandy Hook, Las Vegas, Parkland, Uvalde . . . the places associated with mass shootings over the past twenty-five years still bring back painful memories of the continuing tide of gun violence in our country, but the daily notices and local or "minor" headlines of deaths ("Nine Injured in Denver Shooting after Nuggets Win NBA Title"; "2 Killed in Mass Shooting after Virginia High School Graduation Ceremony"; "8 Killed, 71 Injured in Mass shootings over Long Holiday Weekend") along with unintentional shootings ("Woman, Unborn Child Die after Shooting"),[1] and the often unreported deaths by suicide using a gun, are what contribute even more to the nearly 120 killed and 200 shot and wounded, by guns every day in the United States.

While we often read about the ages, races, genders, sexual orientation, and religions of the victims, I don't recall ever seeing much about their political affiliations. Sometimes I'll see stories blaming Democratic mayors for violence in their cities (even if there are Republican governors and/or preemption policies passed by predominately Republican legislatures), but presumably, Republicans, Democrats, Independents, or politically unaffiliated individuals are just as likely to be injured by bullets as anyone else. If this is the case, then the question arises why there often seems to be such a partisan split by our elected representatives in their support for efforts to reduce gun violence. To make progress on this issue, we need bipartisan approaches.

I was elected, as a Republican, to three terms as mayor of Fort Wayne, the second largest city in Indiana. During my service from 1988 to 2000, I joined Democratic and Republican mayors in supporting the Brady Bill and the so-called Assault Weapons Ban, both of which were signed into law during President Clinton's first term. A few years after deciding not to run for a fourth term, I was selected to lead the national Brady Campaign and Center to Prevent Gun Violence, serving as president and CEO from July 2006 to July 2011. In both roles, I interacted frequently with the public, the media, gun rights supporters and organizations, appointed officials, and elected representatives at all levels from both major parties.

Taking common sense steps to try to reduce gun violence should not be a partisan issue. James Brady, who was seriously injured during the assassination attempt on President Ronald Reagan on March 30, 1981, and his wife, Sarah, were prominent and active Republicans. Presidents Reagan, G. H. W. Bush, and G. W. Bush all supported measures to reduce gun violence. The divide on gun issues in the past was often more of an urban-rural split than a partisan one, but over the past twenty years, bipartisanship on gun issues has been hard to find.

Some of the lessons I've learned over many years dealing with this issue may be helpful as new groups and individuals take up the cause.

STORIES

While research and statistics should always have a major role in policy discussions like those involved in how best to reduce gun violence, the personal experiences of both Republicans and Democrats with guns, and the stories of the individuals involved in pushing for or resisting change, may play an even more important role. As a result, those who have been personally impacted by gun violence, or who have been trained to use guns as members of law enforcement or in the military, often tell the most compelling stories. But still, all of us are likely to have some direct experiences that lead to our attitudes toward guns.

My personal experiences with guns were very limited. My maternal grandfather, a Democrat, who died when I was five, occasionally went hunting, but neither my paternal grandfather nor my father was a hunter. Both, however, had been elected on the Republican ticket as county prosecuting attorneys and would tell stories at home about "bad guys" who had used guns in serious crimes, including murder. I took riflery classes at YMCA camp during the summer, learning the risks and responsibilities of handling guns along with how to shoot. I kept the National Rifle Association (NRA) Marksmanship and Pro-Marksmanship badges that I earned with my other prized possessions from childhood. Shortly before starting high school, I learned from the evening local news that one of my best friends from grade school had been shot and seriously injured when visiting someone's house. A friend of a friend found an older brother's gun and decided they would try to "scare Scott" by pointing the gun at him and pulling the trigger. Scott still has the bullet in his back—an eighth of an inch either way would have left him dead or paralyzed. It became obvious to me then that not everyone took the gun safety rules I had learned to heart.

The assassinations and gun violence of the 1960s led me to write a couple major papers in college on the issue, but I really didn't get directly involved till I was elected mayor in 1987. Our city, like many in the late 1980s and early 1990s, was experiencing a rise in crime and violence because of gangs and drugs—and guns. I raised taxes to hire more police officers, worked with neighborhoods and faith-communities on crime-prevention and crime-fighting initiatives, and looked at cities across the country for any ideas on how to make my community safer. One of the things I learned from my police chief and other officers was how few laws there were at the state and national level to make it harder for dangerous people to get particularly dangerous weapons. As a result, I started advocating for Brady background checks and restrictions on "assault rifles" and other proposals at the national and state level. From my perspective as mayor, I saw these measures as "law and order" proposals that might help make my community safer. As head of the US Conference of Mayors, and previously head of the Indiana Association of Cities and Towns (now, Advancing Indiana Municipalities), and public safety chair for the National League of Cities, I was able to speak not only for myself and my city but also for communities of all sizes and political persuasions across Indiana and the nation. During the 1990s, these efforts were supported by bipartisan groups of mayors and city officials as well as our local law enforcement officers and partners.

While my experience as mayor gave me some credibility in talking about the gun violence issue, the strongest emotional impact came from those who had been victims. While the Bradys were the signature names for our organization, I also hired a young man to work for us who had survived being shot four times on April 16, 2007, at Virginia Tech. I got to know Colin Goddard's family after the killings. After Colin finished his schooling in Blacksburg and then in France, he expressed an interest in doing advocacy work for the Brady organization. One of his projects was traveling to gun shows around the country to document on camera how easy it was to buy the same type of gun used against him from so-called private sellers without any background checks. When we would visit the Hill, his experiences gave him additional credibility and access to elected officials and staff from both parties—after all, electeds (and their handlers) don't want to see stories that they refused to meet with or slammed the door on a victim of a recent, well-known mass shooting. Even if we couldn't pick up their support or get their vote, at least we were able to make our case face-to-face.

Obviously, there are many different types of experiences individuals have had with guns. Many have been victims, but there are others who feel that they might have been able to stop some violence if only they had not been barred from having a gun to use in certain situations. Many have experience from the military or from law enforcement—for some, this reinforces the importance of training as well as the risks and responsibilities of owning a gun; for others, this leads to a distrust of any government restrictions on the use of guns. Many who grew up hunting feel that everyone who wants a gun must have the same level of expertise that they have. Many who are concerned with their personal safety feel that they could handle an encounter with a "bad guy" in a success-ful manner, whether or not they have been trained or tested. Some feel they could handle pressure situations like characters they have seen in movies, on television, or in video games. Some buy into myths about the "Wild West" or past American wars to buttress their confidence with weapons. Some actually could handle their weapons properly and effectively to protect themselves and their family—but others might shoot the stranger who accidentally knocks on the wrong door. The bottom line is that everyone, regardless of political party, brings a different set of experiences and preconceptions or misconceptions to the gun issue—knowing what these are and exploring them openly is a crucial step in trying to find common ground.

STATISTICS

Policy arguments and decisions need to be based on more than just stories and anecdotal evidence, but good statistics on gun violence are difficult to obtain. Different jurisdictions often report shooting incidents and gun deaths in dif-ferent ways, making the information collected at the federal level incomplete. Many jurisdictions are reluctant to provide detailed information, particularly if criminal investigations or charges are pending, or appeals are being considered. Causing additional problems are restrictions imposed by the US Congress on data showing where guns used in crimes come from (the Tiahrt Amendment) and, particularly between 1997 and 2018, on research by the Centers for Disease Control and Prevention (CDC) that might be used to "advocate or promote gun control" (Dickey Amendment). Similarly, Congress has made it very dif-ficult even to initiate and file lawsuits against gun manufacturers, distributors, and dealers, thus taking away the opportunity to gather crucial information through legal discovery efforts.

It is also difficult to assess the effectiveness of measures to reduce gun vio-lence since different laws and policies may be in place at different times in different places. The ease of personal movement, and transport of guns, between jurisdictions also makes conclusions about the efficacy of local or state laws problematic. The "grandfathering" of restricted weapons adds further to the difficulty of making sound conclusions.

Advocates for gun restrictions do their best to collect statistics on deaths and injuries from guns to highlight the scope of the problem. They also categorize and rank the states with few gun restrictions and those with more restrictions, and then map that with the levels of gun violence in those states (while also noting the flow of guns from the states with few restrictions to those with more). Advocates for less gun restrictions often focus on defensive gun uses and the impact of "gun free zones" imposed by governmental units of private property owners on shootings initiated or stopped. Collecting good information on these issues can be very difficult. Surveys are used but these have margins of error and statistical challenges. Definitions of things like "defensive gun uses" can skew the results ("brandishing" a weapon to scare off a "bad guy" who may or may not be present? Shooting at a threatening animal? Just saying "leave or I'll shoot" or "I've got a gun"?). Similarly, is a place a "gun free zone" if the property owner posts a sign, but does not enforce it? How do we count shootings of multiple individuals in someone's home (including domestic quarrels and family murder-suicides)? These are where many shootings occur but are often left out of statistical compilations by gun rights advocates. How about shootings on public streets in communities or states that do not restrict guns?

Forging a bipartisan consensus to fund better research would be great regardless of one's position on these issues. A Republican-controlled Congress started allowing the CDC to do some research in 2018 and subsequently allocated some funding for gun violence research for the first time since 1996. This showed that bipartisan efforts are possible. More academics are beginning to focus on these issues as well. It would be useful if there could be some basic information on what generally helps reduce gun violence and what doesn't. Maybe there are some proposals from both the "gun rights" and the "gun control" sides that make sense, and others that don't. Good data and research should be something that everyone who wants to find solutions should agree to support.

POLITICIANS

Even the best statistics and stories aren't of much value unless you are able to present them to elected officials who will have the chance to vote for or against changes to the law, and/or their staff members on whom the elected officials

rely. Best practices here probably aren't much different for the gun issue than
for others, but a few points are good to remember.

When requesting to meet with an elected official, make sure to include (and
highlight) a constituent if possible. It is often hard to get much time on the
calendars of the elected officials and their staff, regardless of party, but one of
their top priorities is to be responsive to the people they represent and who can
theoretically vote them in or out of office. Someone who has a direct connec-
tion to the issue (who has a story to tell) as well as a subject matter expert (who
can talk about the statistics) are also important. If you can't get in to see the
elected official, be sure to take a meeting with the staff person. Have copies of
the materials you want them to read. If you are focusing on a specific bill you
support or oppose, make sure to know where the bill stands in the legislative
process and what position, if any, the legislator has taken on the specific piece
of legislation. I would avoid mentioning financial support, if any, that you've
given to the legislator—you don't want to look like you're asking for a quid
pro quo, and they can check their records on this easily enough if they think it
might be relevant.

Ask for a meeting even if the legislator has been unfriendly to your position
on the gun issue in the past. You can bring up recent shootings, particularly if
they are from your district or state, and make the point that what we've been
doing as a country to reduce gun violence is not working and that maybe the
legislator should consider a new approach. If nothing else, your advocacy may
contribute to an increased sensitivity to the importance of the issue. I remember conversations with top staff members for some of the Republicans representing Fort Wayne in DC when I was mayor and was making the case for
certain bills. They would mention the pressure they were receiving from the
other side and wouldn't make any commitments. When the legislators ended
up voting the way I hoped, I felt that my comments—along with others on my
side—helped balance and finally outweigh the calls of our opponents.

Make sure to introduce yourself and your issue every chance you get. If the
elected official conducts town halls or district office hours, make sure you or
one of your supporters show up and stress the importance of the gun violence
prevention issues every chance you get. One of the longtime champions of
sensible gun restrictions in both the US House and US Senate, Chuck Schumer
from New York, met with my Brady Board Chair and me in his private office
during one legislative battle and mentioned that he rarely heard people bring
up the gun issue when he was participating in community parades or events. I
often had the same perspective when I was active in politics—if I didn't hear
about some issues when I was out in public, or if I heard about them less than

I used to, it made me question if support had decreased or the controversy had disappeared.

Don't treat your allies worse than your opponents. There were occasions when we would criticize a generally friendly legislator for not supporting one of our new initiatives. There is nothing wrong with trying to get friends on board with our plans, but I'd often have to point out that we rarely focused as much criticism on those who never supported us. It is easy to say that the opposition doesn't pay attention to the criticism. But if a friendly legislator senses they're being treated more harshly than someone who is unfriendly, it might make them wonder whether it is "worth it" to be with us at all.

One of the most sensitive times this issue arose when I headed Brady was after President Obama's first year or two in office. We did a "report card" on the administration's work on preventing gun violence and, after some back-and-forth internal discussions, including whether to give an "Incomplete," ended up assigning a "failing" grade. We knew the Obama administration was supportive of our positions, but we were very disappointed that they hadn't pushed for more when they first took office. This "grade" got thrown back at us when we had subsequent meetings with Attorney General Eric Holder and brought a little chill to a meeting we had with President Obama, the Bradys, and me on the thirtieth anniversary of James Brady being shot and injured. Our goal, though, was to push for quick action—so sometimes these critical evaluations are necessary.

One of my biggest disappointments from my time at Brady was that President Obama didn't mention guns once at the State of the Union address just a couple weeks after the Tucson shooting of Gabby Giffords and others. There were many early references to her absence, and recognition of families of those who were killed, but no mention of guns—a visitor from another planet might have thought that folks had been touched by a plague rather than another episode of gun violence. Of course, this was just a year before the reelection campaign, and I'm sure there were voices inside the administration wanting to avoid the issue. After the December 2012 Sandy Hook massacre, and other subsequent shootings, President Obama brought the full power of his eloquence and office to the issue and his administration pushed as hard as it could for legislation and regulations. I keep wondering, however, if he had pushed harder after the Tucson killings, whether the Congress and the country might have been more supportive of the policies he advanced after Sandy Hook.

All politicians are nearly always evaluating issues under multiple prisms— good/bad, right/wrong, now/later, high priority/low priority, high salience/ low interest, helpful/damaging, controversial/bland. The job of advocates is to help push and encourage, respectfully but forcefully, the politician to adopt the "right" decision, and provide the necessary backing when the opposition kicks in. Legislators—on all sides of the issue, both Democrats and Republicans—need our help in getting this right.

MEDIA

In addition to direct contacts with legislators, advocates need to know how to use the media to reinforce their message. Different methods work best in different situations—social media plays a much more important role today than when I was at Brady, and barely existed when I was mayor. The bottom line, though, is still the same—you want your message to be heard by those who can vote on legislation, and by the voters who choose those legislators.

While at Brady, I felt it was important to get on as many media outlets as possible to tell our story. Some of my staff and board members would often question why I would go on Fox News and similar channels. They were concerned that our position would be criticized before I spoke, challenged when I spoke, and trashed afterward. While these were legitimate points, my response was that this could happen even if I did not appear and that I could at least get some of our points out to the viewers. If we weren't using a bipartisan strategy, trying to reach Fox viewers as well those who watched channels like MSNBC, then we would never have a chance of getting enough public support to get our proposals adopted.

Sometimes this strategy worked better than others. I remember one appearance on Fox News where I was paired with a gun dealer (appearing remotely) who had sold guns to two different individuals involved in two different mass shootings. During an ad, the host complained to me that I was being "too reasonable" in criticizing the gun dealer—she would have preferred that I be more extreme in my comments.

Regardless of the show, sometimes there is just a limited amount of solid information in the immediate aftermath of a shooting. I felt that it was still important to appear and comment on the facts that were known. The evening following the Virginia Tech shooting, for example, there was still a lot we didn't know. We didn't discover until a few days later that the shooter previously had been found to be a "danger to himself and others" by a Virginia court and that this should have kept him from buying the guns he purchased at a Virginia gun store if only the courts had submitted that information to the national background check database. That first night I was able to make the point that the shooter's roommates and a teacher were being quoted as saying he was someone too dangerous to have a gun and that this was information that should be relevant to a store before selling someone a gun. I also made the point that what we're doing to prevent gun violence as a nation was clearly not working and that new options should be explored. This bipartisan, common sense approach got both the MSNBC host and my conservative counterpoint that evening, Pat Buchanan, to agree that my arguments made sense.

OPPONENTS

The gun rights lobby in this country is very powerful. The NRA has been around since 1871 and claims to have more than five million members. Its CEO and executive vice president, Wayne LaPierre, has held that position since 1991. None of the gun violence prevention (GVP) groups have anywhere near that lengthy history and few have anywhere close to that continuity in leadership. In addition to the NRA, there are a number of other smaller groups espousing gun rights such as the Gun Owners of America and Second Amendment Foundation. Groups like the Cato Institute as well as various lawyers, academics, and researchers also play an active role with the gun issue.

I felt it was important to debate and engage with these groups and individuals in public forums and on television and radio whenever I got the opportunity. When I started at Brady, I wrote LaPierre and suggested that we meet to discuss whether there was any possible common ground that we might be able to agree on regarding gun laws. The NRA in the past had supported reasonable gun restrictions, and while they had gotten increasingly more political and less open to new laws since 1977 as they moved away from a focus on hunting, conservation, and marksmanship, I still thought it was worth reaching out. I never heard back. When I occasionally debated NRA representatives, I would repeat this offer to no avail. LaPierre rarely did joint appearances, but we were on television shows together on two occasions, in June 2008 and June 2010, after major gun decisions by the US Supreme Court. On each occasion I said that since the NRA had finally gotten rulings finding that there was an individual right to gun ownership unconnected to a militia or collective purpose, we should sit down and talk about what "presumptively lawful" (to use Justice Scalia's words in the *Heller* case) restrictions might make sense. LaPierre refused to respond to this, even after *PBS Newshour* host Gwen Ifill repeated my suggestion and said it was something he should answer.

Since the NRA generally skipped joint television appearances, I frequently shared time with representatives from some of the other groups. They often staked out positions more extreme than the NRA ("why not allow people to carry guns on airplanes?") which made it even easier to stress the common sense nature of our proposals. My goal was not to change the opinions of those I was debating, but to get our positions explained in a calm and reasonable manner to the viewing public from both parties.

I also had the opportunity to debate lawyers who had done work for the NRA or who were handling the major cases initiated by the Cato Institute and Robert Levy, sometimes just on television but often in front of law-related groups. These discussions were always interesting and challenging—a lot more like a legal argument, but with strong policy considerations too. Even when the host group would be a law school's Federalist Society chapter (generally a conservative/ libertarian group), I always felt I had a fair chance to present my legal and community safety arguments in these debates, and maybe changed some minds.

Debating academics can be a little trickier. It is important to read the research that the academic has published and understand the methodology that underlies their conclusions. Oftentimes the strongest counter is to stress the limitations of the research, and then cite contradictory studies and ask the audience to apply some common sense. One of my regular debate opponents over the years, including since I left Brady, is particularly controversial in GVP circles because of questions about his research work and some self-promotion steps in the past. There are some who argue that debating only gives his research and him more attention. From my perspective, I felt that it was important to engage on the main issues and leave the past controversies behind. He is someone who has very little trouble getting quoted by gun rights advocates and politicians and finding a platform with the media. If he is going to be making his points regardless, I figure I should welcome the opportunity to make mine. It is possible to be civil and friendly with individuals you disagree with—even when you have to share a three-hour ride both ways in a rental car when flights to a debate site in Missouri are canceled because of weather.

LEGAL ISSUES

The current state of the law and understanding of the Constitution may not impact every controversial policy initiative, but this has certainly been a crucial part of the gun debate. Even though gun rights advocates have argued against restrictions for years because of their reading of the Second Amendment, it wasn't until the *District of Columbia v. Heller* decision in 2008 that the US Supreme Court first decided that it conferred an individual right unconnected to a collective purpose (basically saying that the first thirteen words of the amendment didn't really decide anything). Still, that decision also made it clear that this right, like others, was "not unlimited" and that a broad range of restrictions on who could have guns, how they were sold, how they were carried, where they could be taken, and what kind could be sold were "presumptively lawful."

Even with this fairly recent decision, many politicians would answer questions on whether they would support measures like "universal" background checks by saying "I support the Second Amendment"—which basically says nothing. Just as frustrating for those of us in the GVP movement were supportive politicians who before the *Heller* decision would concede that the Second Amendment did confer an "individual right." Disputed legal issues are tough enough to argue without individuals on both sides acting like the Constitution said something other than what it did.

It was also frustrating to have to fight over restrictions that were the hardest to defend such as the near total gun bans in Washington, DC, and Chicago. When asked what I thought about these measures, I would usually respond that these were not things I would have pushed for in my city when I was mayor, but that if people didn't like the restrictions they should run for office in those cities and try to change things at the local level. Once it looked like these cities who had adopted restrictions were going to lose, we also suggested that it might make sense to repeal or modify the restrictions rather than face a negative US Supreme Court ruling with nationwide implications. Neither of the two cities wanted to adjust its strategy based on these concerns, however.

The legal scene is even more complicated now with the June 2022 US Supreme Court decision in *New York State Rifle & Pistol Association, Inc. v. Bruen*. It will now be even harder for gun restrictions to pass constitutional muster unless some similar restriction can be shown to have been around near to 1791 (when the Bill of Rights was adopted) or 1868 (when the Fourteenth Amendment was adopted). It is still important for activists concerned about gun violence to push for a broad range of common sense, bipartisan, restrictions to help make us all safer, but now there has to be some concern with justifying these not only as good policy for today, but as something similar to historical restrictions. We need to remember that anything that gets passed is almost definitely going to be challenged in the courts, so supportive lawyers (and now historians) need to be involved from an early stage.

COMPROMISE

Finally, I want to make a pitch for the importance of bipartisan and ideological compromise in advancing a controversial agenda. This concept is usually looked on with disdain by all sides of an issue, but history shows that it is almost always needed to make any long-term progress. As mentioned above, if the cities of DC and Chicago had been willing to consider modifications in their city ordinances, we all might have been able to avoid or delay the critical losses in the *Heller* and *McDonald v. Chicago* cases.

To get anything done in Congress, compromise will almost always be required. Since the Columbine massacre in 1999, and the unsuccessful attempts afterward to require background checks on all gun sales, there had been no recorded vote on a gun measure until after the Sandy Hook murders. The vote to close the so-called gun show loophole passed in the US Senate (with Vice President Al Gore casting the tie-breaking vote) but failed in the US House of Representatives. Not until 2022, after a series of mass shootings, did Congress approve some important, but still relatively minor, gun restrictions in a recorded vote. The Bipartisan Safer Communities Act, which helps encourage states to adopt "red flag laws" and include disqualifying juvenile records in the background check database, as well as strengthen the definitions of gun sellers and domestic abusers, would not have been approved, however, without compromises.

I got very involved in helping get some national legislation approved after the Virginia Tech killings in 2007. There was a bill pending at that time authored by one of our strong allies, Representative Carolyn McCarthy from New York, to incentivize states to send more records of prohibited purchasers into the national background database. Once we learned that the Virginia Tech shooter had been found by a court to be disqualified from buying guns legally, but that Virginia had not submitted these records, the McCarthy bill became one of our top legislative priorities. While the NRA had not signaled any strong opposition previously, the bill wasn't going anywhere until the GVP groups started pushing for action in the media and on the Hill. The legislation passed the House a couple months after the massacre in Blacksburg, but the Senate looked more problematic. Behind the scenes, the NRA was telling its allies that it would oppose this effort to get more names added to the prohibited purchaser list unless there was also a streamlined procedure to get individuals off the list if they had been added because of the Veterans Administration—required conservatorships or other similar procedures.

As a result of this effort by the NRA, many of the GVP groups were threatening to oppose the bill if these new procedures were included. While we fought to keep these things out of the bill, it eventually looked like there would be no movement, no vote, and no legislation unless the NRA additions were included. Our champion, Representative McCarthy, was willing to make the trade-off. My sense was that if we did not support our friend and champion, Representative McCarthy, at this stage, I wasn't sure how we would ever get her or other allies to rely on us—one of the oldest axioms of politics is to "dance with the one that brought you"; in other words, to stick with your friends. I was also sensitive to the issue of how we deal with mental illness—if someone was disqualified from purchasing guns today because they were a danger to themselves or others, we should still realize that a doctor could find them with no disqualifying condition sometime in the future.

Things stayed stuck until the congressional session was winding down in December 2007. I got a call one evening that month from Senator Ted Kennedy, one of our movement's longtime strongest allies, indicating that he'd been getting conflicting advice and signals from GVP advocates but that a decision had to be made right away whether to let the bill die or go ahead with the NRA additions. I told him that while there were legitimate concerns, I felt it was still important to get something positive passed. If a million names of prohibited purchasers were added to the database, that outweighed the possibility of one hundred thousand other names being removed through the NRA process. I also felt that if we weren't going to be able to get something passed after the largest mass school shooting ever, when would we be able to see something done? After I expressed my opinion, Senator Kennedy said he was going to tell Senator Tom Corbin, a Republican from Oklahoma who was advocating for the gun rights position, and Senate Majority Leader Chuck Schumer that he was going to support the compromise. The bipartisan legislation then passed on a voice vote and was signed by President George W. Bush in January 2008, although without any fanfare or ceremony.

The difficulty in getting anything done in the years since Virginia Tech makes me more confident that bipartisan compromise was the right call with the McCarthy bill. Not only did we show that something positive could be done, with bipartisan support, but the provisions in this bill have helped increase the value of the prohibited purchaser list and the legislation has been an underlying basis for new proposals to reduce gun violence following more recent mass shootings, such as the 2022 legislation. Nothing is easy, and we should always push for what we feel is needed, but we also need to know when compromise is required to achieve at least some progress.

CONCLUSION

While views on guns have long been polarized, it really is an issue where bipartisan common ground should not be that hard to find if folks are willing to set aside preconceptions and focus on facts. No one wants gun violence to continue, even if there are different positions on how best to reduce it. Unless someone wants to ban all guns (which would be impossible given that there are more than four hundred million in circulation already), or feels that anyone should be able to take any gun anywhere they want, there should be some areas of agreement.

Justice Scalia's list of possible restrictions from the *Heller* case provides a good framework. Are there some individuals we can identify in advance who nearly all of us can agree should not be able to buy guns? Maybe we can add those who have committed violent misdemeanors to the "prohibited purchaser" list, but take off those who have been found guilty of nonviolent felonies? Are there some places where it is clearly too dangerous to allow loaded guns? What information do gun sellers need to make sure they don't sell to clearly dangerous individuals? Should there be storage requirements when young children are nearby? Should we treat semiautomatic weapons differently from revolvers and hunting rifles, maybe the same as machine guns and other fully automatic weapons, or perhaps in a new category? What are we going to do about "ghost guns" and devices that convert semiautomatics into something close to a fully automatic weapon? There are a variety of ways to answer these questions, and legitimate positions along the policy spectrum for each of them.

To make our communities safer, we need to find bipartisan common ground. Gun violence is a public health issue as well as a public safety issue. Let's focus on the common goals and figure out what steps we need to take to get there. This is an issue where we should be able to make progress, not something that is unsolvable and beyond our control.

NOTE

1. "Nine Injured in Denver Shooting after Nuggets Win NBA Title," *Guardian*, June 13, 2023, https://www.theguardian.com/us-news/2023/jun/13/nba -shooting-denver-nuggets-win-title; Nouran Salahieh and Lauren Mascarenhas, "2 Killed in Mass Shooting after Virginia High School Graduation Ceremony," *CNN*, June 7, 2023, https://www.cnn.com/2023/06/07/us/richmond-shooting -virginia-wednesday/index.html; Jared Gans, "8 Killed, 71 Injured in Mass shootings over Long Holiday Weekend," *The Hill*, May 30, 2023, https://thehill .com/blogs/blog-briefing-room/4025816-8-killed-71-injured-in-mass-shootings -over-long-holiday-weekend; Joe Centers, "Woman, Unborn Child Die after Shooting," June 16, 2023, https://norwalkreflector.com/news/465284/woman -unborn-child-die-after-shooting/.

PAUL HELMKE *is a Professor of Practice and Director of the Civic Leaders Center at the Paul O'Neill School of Public and Environmental Affairs at Indiana University Bloomington. He served three terms as Mayor of Fort Wayne, Indiana and as President and CEO of the Brady Center/Brady Campaign to Prevent Gun Violence.*

ELEVEN

WORKING TOGETHER FOR A HEALTHIER ENVIRONMENT

DON BONKER

PREFACE

During my years in Congress, I felt blessed to represent an area encompassing some of the most pristine natural resources in the country. It started with the magnificent Columbia River Gorge in southwest Washington State and proceeded northward through the Mount St. Helens volcanic area, then pivoted west along the Pacific Ocean (shorebird refuge), then upward to the Olympic Peninsula. For many, viewing these sites it is a breathtaking scenic beauty, what I often call the planet's natural cathedral.

For me, reverence of nature has been kin to the holiness of wonder and mystery, and the spirituality and glorious beauty of life itself. I felt a deep commitment to do whatever I could to preserve the state's rich natural heritage as an enduring legacy for others to experience and appreciate.

Much of this wilderness treasure was under assault as development and extractive industries ramped up in the Northwest, creating scarred hillsides, fouled streams, and places where the beauty of yesteryear had fled. We faced the challenge of balancing the economic well-being of a congressional district's rural communities that were heavily dependent on sustainable harvesting and processing of timber and fish, with the value of preserving the remaining wild lands to be forever cherished. While balance can lead to harmony, it was also a daunting task politically.

During the 1970s and 80s, most of the counties in southwest Washington State were struggling economically, as evidenced by the shutdown of lumber mills that had for decades fueled economic growth in local communities. It was disheartening to drive through my expansive district to see these cities looking like ghost towns. For me, a newly elected congressman, it was all about saving jobs and growing the economy.

Yet at that time, the environmental groups pressed hard for their congressman to sponsor legislation that would federally designate wilderness and refuge areas. It would come at an economic as well as a political cost. And without a local congressman's sponsorship, it would likely not happen. The task was daunting, and bipartisan support would be essential.

Another challenge would be the workload of Congress. Thousands of bills and resolutions are introduced in every congressional session, yet only a few will make it to the president's desk for signature. The committees of jurisdiction are often on overload, with both chambers having to take action and reconcile their differences before a final vote and before the final version of the bill is sent to the White House for the president to sign.

The good fortune was our state's congressional delegation, noted for its bipartisanship and for placing the common good above self-interest. During the 1970s and 80s, Washington's two seats in the US Senate transitioned from powerful Democrats, Warren Magnuson and Henry Jackson, to highly respected Republicans, Dan Evans and Slade Gorton, who upheld the tradition of working across the aisle. Senator Evans, who had previously served as governor, became the champion of preserving the state's natural resources.

Protecting our natural resources is a highly politicized issue. Democrats are more likely to support regulations for protecting the environment and Republicans generally oppose legislation that designates wilderness and refuge areas or creates federal mandates restricting the rights of property owners.

What's portrayed here are four landmark bills that passed the Congress and were signed into law by President Ronald Reagan. The fortieth president of the United States was known for opposing environmental regulation, so how did this happen?

It was the exceptional bipartisanship in the Senate and House chambers that allowed it to happen.

The legendary Winston Churchill's feisty words "democracy is the worst form of government except for all the others" are an incredibly astute characterization of our system of governance. His words were insightful of how our Founding Fathers struggled to adopt the Constitution, coping with multiple conflicting interests at the time. But they ultimately found common ground on the fundamentals of our democracy.

That common ground is what allows us to make deals. As former US representative Jill Long Thompson shares in her book, *The Character of American*

Democracy, "In a democratic society, how we make deals is as important as the deals we make." She elaborates that "we must be forthright and equitable in the creation and adoption of laws, not just in their content. All of us, leaders and citizens alike, have a responsibility to play fairly and equitably in the governing process."

Bipartisanship that rises above the political interests to achieve the common good is democracy at its "best" not its "worst," especially in preserving the nation's precious natural resources.

COLUMBIA GORGE NSA

An early challenge in my congressional career involved the eighty-mile Columbia River Gorge, carved through the Cascade Mountains by repeated catastrophic breakouts of mammoth glacial lakes at the end of the late Ice Age. It is one of the most dramatic landscapes—and geologic stories—anywhere. In the early 1920s, Samuel Lancaster, noted for his elegant design of the highway paralleling the Columbia River, captured the exquisiteness of the Columbia River Gorge this way: "God shaped these great mountains round about us, and lifted up these mighty domes. He fashioned the Gorge of the Columbia, fixed the course of the broad river, and caused the crystal streams both small and great, to leap down from the crags and sing their never-ending songs of joy."

This description of the gorge continues to speak for all who cherish the awesome beauty and wonder of three thousand basalt cliffs scoured out by the ancient Missoula floods—from the early preservationists a century ago to our present and future generations. The gorge sheltered for eons our Native American peoples, provided the gateway to the Pacific for the Lewis and Clark expedition, and today continues to provide us with abundant natural resources, ranging from deep verdant forests in the west to the Columbia Plateau Desert in the east. The gorge spans nine distinct ecosystems with sixteen species of wildflowers found nowhere else in the world and it boasts the largest waterfalls in all of North America.

Back in the mid-1990s, driving along the scenic Columbia River Highway, now called the Samuel Lancaster Highway, one could experience the magnificence of this treasured natural resource. On the Oregon side, people could appreciate Samuel Lancaster's description of its natural beauty, but as they glanced across the river to the Washington side, they saw something different. The view to the west was tarnished by large bare patches where timber had been clear-cut, by lumber mills with their wigwam burners filling the air with smoke, and by the pulp and paper mills. And to the east were aluminum smelters.

While both Washington and Oregon states shared the Columbia River Gorge, their perspectives were quite different. For Oregonians, it only took a short drive from downtown Portland to enter the majestic gorge. What pride there was in showing visitors the natural splendor of Multnomah Falls and the idyllic Hood River. The Oregon side had multiple locations for parks, campgrounds, hiking, bike paths, and boat landings. Portland's preservationists, led by the Friends of the Columbia Gorge, mounted a formidable campaign to save the gorge.

On the Washington side, a drive up the gorge river was something different. While there was natural beauty along the way, it was more revealing of the scars of logging, the lumber and paper mill smoke stacks, and aluminum plants. Essentially, the once pristine landscapes had been transformed into industrial sites that provided the needed jobs and economic well-being to the local communities. It would be political suicide for a local congressman to support a federal law that would essentially shut down much of the local economy. At that time, the idea of replacing lumber mill jobs with tourism was seen as ridiculous and unrealistic. Nonetheless, there were legislative proposals for promoting tourism, including to provide $10 million to build the Skamania Lodge.

The politics of preserving this precious eighty-mile Columbia River Gorge for future generations would be a challenge for the two states. It would take federal legislation to define the boundary of a scenic area and to establish a management entity empowered to restrict development and overlay protective guidelines on the six counties and many localities on both sides of the Columbia River. On the Oregon side, there was popular support on the west side and the Portland metro area. But that support did not extend to the rural east part of the state that was represented by two conservative Republicans who were dead set against federal land use controls and restrictions of private property rights.

Opposition quickly formed on the Washington side, headed by a four-hundred-strong organization called the Columbia Gorge United. There was also strong protest among local officials that had shared concerns over having a federal regime with mandates to control property rights in the three counties along the Columbia River. A local newspaper editor stated that "the gorge-for-lunch bunch is threatening our way of life here. We are an endangered species, little counties like ours." In a memorable display of political courage, Senator Dan Evans and the local Republican congressman, Sid Morrison, got an earful from furious constituents at a number of local public hearings.

Despite the growing opposition, Senators Mark Hatfield and Dan Evans proceeded to craft a proposal, striking the delicate balance of preserving the eighty-mile Columbia River Gorge while attempting to minimize the impact on local economies. Its main features were designating the boundaries of the scenic area and establishing a Gorge Commission of twelve local citizens, half appointed by the two governors and one from each of the six counties bordering the river. This, in effect, gave the federal government a huge mandate to oversee and restrict private property rights, no doubt, at high political risk.

Navigating a bill through both the US Senate and House of Representative is a formidable task. In mid-October 1986, the 99th Congress was about to adjourn when the Hatfield-Evans proposal was stalled by a procedural issue that made its passage unlikely. That's when Representative Tom Foley, the majority whip (and future Speaker), got personally involved to ensure the Rules Committee would approve the measure for a House vote, permitting several amendments. His strategy was successful and the House passed the Columbia Gorge National Scenic Area Act by a vote of 290 to 91.

On the Senate side, Senator Hatfield, chairman of the powerful Senate Appropriations Committee, got the bill onto the Senate floor and it eventually received a favorable vote. It passed both the Senate and the House in the final hours of the 99th Congress and President Reagan signed into law the Columbia Gorge National Scenic Area Act on November 17, 1986.

How these Pacific Northwest leaders gathered bipartisan support among House members in both states, and overcame insurmountable odds to persuade a reluctant president to sign this bill that was contrary to his personal beliefs, made this a landmark achievement.

In December 2009, *National Geographic* magazine rated the Columbia River Gorge and Scenic Area as number six of 133 of the world's Great Places to visit. It noted "the incredible job of protecting the views and many towns with considerable charm," but also recognized that "this is a federally managed scenic area that benefits from some of the best land-preservation programs in the nation."

VOLCANIC FURY

On May 18, 1980, Mount St. Helens belched out a dense cloud of smoke and debris in an eruption that intensified with drumbeat of explosions, blowing foul-smelling columns of steam, ash, and boulders high into the air as molten lava continued to breach fire into the snow-covered volcano.

Mount St. Helens, named for an eighteenth-century nobleman, was the most photographic of the dozen or so active volcanoes in the Cascade Range. The 1980 eruption was a catastrophic moment that plagued the area for several years. The eruption blew down two billion board feet of lumber and had devastating impact on wildlife, the victims a result of the ash, mud, and fumes. The local communities suffered the abrupt fear, short-term stress, and long-term impacts that would require federal assistance.

As the congressman who represented this area, I was struck with the huge impact it had on my constituency and how quickly it drew national attention. The daily reports were alarming: ultimately fifty-seven local citizens were killed, the eruption created a three-billion-cubic-yard debris flow, filling the Toutle River valley, choking the other rivers that fed into the Columbia River, which shut down shipping to Portland. The multimegaton blast flattened thousands of acres of trees up to fifteen miles north of the mountain. And it spewed a 65,000-foot high cloud of hot ash that would spread eastward. The volcanic debris avalanche was an unstoppable flow of destruction that paralyzed traffic across the state, sweeping away twenty-seven bridges and burying 185 miles of road.

Such a natural catastrophe raised urgent questions beyond what state and local governments could address. All the attention turned to the federal government. So many questions. The immediate impact, the devastation to local communities. Would the ash particles in the air damage lungs and human health? And what would be the fate of the once-vibrant forestry? Would the fish population return? The human agony of lost lives, personal injuries, and destroyed homes was intense. How were we to respond to these urgent needs that demanded priority attention of federal departments and agencies, plus legislation and funding. The challenge was not partisan at the moment, given the national attention and how everyone was rallying around relief and sympathy to those directly affected.

The cost of the Mount St. Helens volcanic eruption was best described in a local newspaper headliner simply as an "avalanche of dollars." Fortunately, Washington's US senator, Warren Magnuson, was chair of the Senate Appropriations Committee. He had no clue of the cost but held the gavel, so he proposed $1.06 billion to fund various projects, including the building of tunnels and sediment dams, the US Army Corps of Engineers dredging the Cowlitz, Toutle, and Columbia rivers, reforestation, highway, and roadway repair, plus whatever was left for small businesses. For my DC and local congressional offices, it required outreach to the two principal federal agencies, US Forest Service and the Corps of Engineers, plus coordination with local county and city officials. This occurred during the Ronald Reagan administration's "no increased spending" era. There was tightening of federal budget screws under the Gramm-Rudman-Hollings Balanced Budget and Emergency Deficit Control Act of 1985, demanding state and local governments put up a quarter of the cost.

Coping with the immediate impacts of the volcanic eruption was just the start. Securing federal funding for relief and continuing needs, especially dredging of rivers, was an ongoing priority. My multiple appearances before committees of jurisdiction, plus the subsequent minor volcanic eruptions (full media coverage), guaranteed the priority attention and full bipartisan support diligently needed at the time. The political challenge would come later.

The year following the eruption, various government agencies and private entities were rushing to advance proposals to create a monument area. Of course, each was designed to serve their own interests and secure my early support. This is where political divisions started to appear, with the divide between environmentalists and the timber and mineral sectors, and government agencies caught in between.

The environmentalists announced their ambitious proposal to create a 21,000-acre monument area that would protect everything of geological, scenic, recreational, and ecological interest around the historic mountain. A second proposal was taking shape, this one drafted by state agencies and representatives of the timber companies. It was predictably modest, recommending about 50,000 acres be set aside for scientific study. The US Forest Service had its own proposal, offering a compromise, calling for an "interpretive area" of about 85,000 acres. Not surprisingly it was tilted in favor of the timber industry, allowing for downed timber to be salvaged, permitted geothermal leasing and mineral protecting, and favorable to open-pit mining operations.

There was much to review in crafting legislation that would be the Mount St. Helens National Volcanic Monument. Six months later, the newly elected Republican governor would oversee the drafting of another proposal ingeniously combining elements from the United States Forest Service (USFS) proposal with those from the environmentalists into a consensus package. It was to my liking but there remained one contentious issue—which federal agency would manage the designated area.

That spring I introduced the Mount St. Helens Volcanic Area Act, proposing a land mass of 110,000 acres, similar to Governor Spellman's proposal. I added a provision that created the Mount St. Helens Visitor Center. We were on the path to getting it signed into law. In July 1982, my proposal to protect 115,000 acres of protected land passed the House of Representatives. A few days later, the US Senate's approval of a bill that protected 105,000 acres had differences that needed to be resolved. What finally emerged called for a monument area of 110,000 acres, which passed the House of Representatives with a vote of 393 to 8. The Senate passed it without dissent.

Obviously, there was full bipartisan support of this landmark legislation. What was the political problem? It was the designation of the federal government department or agency that would have jurisdiction and essentially manage the newly created monument area. The US Forest Service (USFS) was obviously more friendly to the timber industry, which alarmed the environmentalists, who favored the US Park Service.

The USFS was the federal designated agency before the eruption, but the environmentalists demanded that it be the US National Park Service. Their concern was that the Gifford Pinchot National Forest would be overly appealing to the private sectors that would be building roads and promoting logging and mining expeditions, and the United States Forest Service would have little interest in preservation. The compromise language in the final bill established a separate entity within the USFS with its own supervisor and planners. The new law specified that "it shall manage the Monument to protect the geological, ecologic, and cultural resources to carry out the mandates in the bill." Forty years later this remains a controversial issue.

The bipartisan support was essential to get it signed into law. After passing Congress, the legislation was headed to a less-than-friendly Ronald Reagan White House. President Reagan remained faithful (earlier promises) to the so-called Sagebrush Rebellion, a movement driven by supporters who wanted more state and local control over federal lands in thirteen Western states. The rebellion took its name from the rampant desert plant of the same name that covers large patches of steppe in Western American states. Ronald Reagan himself caused some stir by declaring himself a sagebrush rebel in a 1980 campaign speech in Salt Lake City. His pick to head the Department of Interior, James Watt, was dead set against any expansion of federal power over Western lands. The president's head of the US Forest Service, John Crowell, who was a former lobbyist for the timber industry, urged the president to veto the Mount St. Helens Volcanic Monument Act. This is why congressional bipartisanship can make a difference. Ronald Reagan believed that a veto of the bill would be overridden by the Congress.

During my tenure in the House of Representatives, it was surprising to observe a Republican president sign into law two landmark environmental measures. For those keeping score, a Republican president not only approved these government mandates to protect wilderness areas, but he did so despite fierce opposition across America's heartland to any federal agency that would oversee and restrict private property rights within these designated zones. James Watt proudly wore the label of "anti-environment." During his tenure as secretary, he actively campaigned to open the country's eighty million acres of undeveloped land to mining and drilling by 2000.

Even a powerful president and cabinet officials fully committed to block all environmental measures cannot have the final say when you have full bipartisan support in the US Congress.

HISTORIC OLYMPIC AND POINT OF ARCHES

The Olympic National Park is a precious natural resource with a rich history. It dates back to 1897, when President Grover Cleveland officially established its designation as Olympic Forest Monument. Twelve years later, in 1909, President Theodore Roosevelt set aside a part of the reserve as Mount Olympic National Monument to protect the habitat of the endemic Olympic elk that was in sharp decline at the time. This species was subsequently renamed the Roosevelt elk, the largest of the rare species of elk found in North America.

Then in 1937, President Franklin Roosevelt personally visited the Olympic Peninsula, officially establishing the Olympic National Park. In 1988, Congress acted to further protect the remnant of wildlife in America by designating 95 percent of the park as the Olympic Wilderness. More recently, in 2016, Congress passed legislation to officially designate Olympic National Park as the Daniel J. Evans Wilderness Park.

This largest designated wilderness in the state of Washington encompasses the upper part of my congressional district. The park spans the rugged Olympic Mountains and pristine old-growth forests and makes up the third largest glacial system in the country. For beach lovers, it contains forty-eight miles of wilderness coast filled with beachheads, rugged headlands, tide pools and stacks, and coastal rainforests.

It was a treasured resource that was nationally recognized over one hundred years ago, but the national park became a source of intense local resentment, hostility, and indigenous fury. Most of the anger was directed at the National Park Service, which had been granted authority over local entities and the so-called in-holders. Essentially, property owners who resided inside the designated area were subject to the policies and regulations of the National Park Service. It was the federal government, not municipal or county officials, that had the final say if a so-called in-holder wanted to build a garage.

The public outrage was evident not only among the in-holders but throughout Clallam County and its principal city, Port Angeles. The county and local cities, plus organizations such as the Chamber of Commerce and organized labor entities, all had passed resolutions denouncing the Department of Interior, petitioning me to curb the department's interference with local planning matters.

As a newly elected congressman, I had no clue I'd be confronted with such a contentious issue. How should I respond? I certainly did not want to be non-responsive or, at worst, take the position of supporting the Department of Interior. Generally, there are two sides to a controversial issue, but not so this time.

Before my next visit to the Upper Peninsula, I contemplated how to respond in a favorable way to my constituency.

At the same time, Washington's Republican governor, Dan Evans, asked that I introduce legislation to add the Point of Arches to the Olympic National Park. This was prompted by the nonprofit Nature Conservancy's purchase of the Point of Arches and made it available to the federal government. This would be hugely beneficial to everyone, welcoming for hikers, beachcombers, and campers, surrounded by stunning vistas and amazing sunsets. The governor, sculptor Marie Louise Feldenheimer, and environmentalists were all anxious to have this happen.

However, such action would affirm the federal government's continued authority over the current and future in-holders. I was confronted with a political nightmare. I could not ignore the in-holders rightful concerns that had widespread support in Port Angeles and throughout Clallam County but, ultimately, I had to make the right decision regardless of the political fallout. I called Governor Evans and said, yes, I would introduce his Port of Arches proposal and work hard to get it enacted.

Yes, this was premium bipartisanship. After serving twelve years as governor, Dan Evans in 1983 was elected to serve in the US Senate. During our time serving in Congress together, we cooperated on a number of environmental issues, highlighting the importance of bipartisanship to make things happen.

In early 2016, two Democrats, Senator Maria Cantwell and Representative Derek Kilmer, drafted and sponsored legislation to honor Daniel Evans by officially designating the Olympic National Park as the Daniel J. Evans Wilderness. All of Washington's Democratic members of Congress showed their commitment to honoring a Republican for a lifetime of bipartisan accomplishments as the state's governor and US senator. On August 17, 2017, there was a dedication of the newly designated Daniel J. Evans Wilderness, with Mr. Evans and the state's congressional delegation attending, to pay tribute to this legendary leader for all his accomplishments as Washington's governor and US senator.

The *Seattle Times* reported on the event the next day, quoting Senator Cantwell, who said, "For many, Evans is that rare thing—a beloved political leader whose stature transcends party or generation. Naming the wilderness for Evans puts an iconic name next to an iconic place."

This is one of many quotes by Democrats praising this Republican icon. Here are what the other Democrats said at the dedication ceremony:

Senator Patty Murray: "Washington state is so lucky to have had an advocate for the great outdoors like former US Senator Dan Evans. It's only right to honor his legacy in our state by renaming one of the places he helped protect, the Olympic National Park Wilderness as the Daniel J. Evans Wilderness."

US Representative Suzan DelBene: "The Washington delegation has a long tradition of bipartisan support for responsible stewardship of the state's public lands. Renaming the Olympic National Park Wilderness honors Senator Evans's legacy and lifelong fight to protect the environment."

US Representative Rick Larsen: "Sen. Evans led with passion and commitment to preserve Washington state's natural resources. Renaming the Olympic National Park Wilderness honors Senator Evans's legacy and lifelong fight to protect the environment."

US Representative Derek Kilmer: "Throughout his life, the outdoors have been a special place for Senator Dan Evans. Through his leadership, he has embraced the power of the outdoors to bring people together while at the same time creating economic opportunities for communities in our state."

US Representative Adam Smith: "Sen. Evans worked throughout his distinguished career to preserve Washington's national parks and forests for future generations. I am pleased to see that the wilderness Sen. Evans worked so tirelessly to protect will bear his name and carry on his legacy."

ENDANGERED SHOREBIRD REFUGE

Nowhere in southwest Washington was there a greater balancing act between protecting our natural resources and the economic well-being of a local community than in Grays Harbor County. A place known as Bowerman Basin was a major migration refueling spot for shorebirds, unmatched by any other in the entire United States. In the spring, these mudflats become the feeding ground for more than a million shorebirds. Lying within the Grays Harbor National Refuge, Bowerman Basin's fifteen hundred acres of salt marsh and mudflats play host each year to the massive influx of shorebirds that stop to rest and feed—some doubling their body weight in ten days after a thousand mile nonstop leg of their seven-thousand-mile journey from South America to nesting grounds in the Arctic.

Flocks of migrating shorebirds and waterfowl are present in smaller numbers in the fall. This offers a rare opportunity to view shorebirds on their return migration. In the winter, flocks of Canada geese may be found on the mudflats, while the lagoons offer birders a chance to see many types of waterfowl in the spring. All the usual ducks are there as well as gulls and a few wintering shorebirds. It is quite a gathering, and no humane individual would ever want to see this lost.

Bowerman Basin was one of nature's crown jewels, especially for lovers and advocates of preserving estuaries. But in the mid-1970s, a threat evolved that seemed unimaginable—this precious resource was about to be replaced by an industrial and commercial center. That was the intention of the Grays Harbor Port District, the linchpin to the regional economy, whose ownership of the estuary gave it the final word, which set off alarms among environmental activists.

Like most of the counties in my district, timber harvesting and lumber mills were paramount to local economies. But the Grays Harbor Port District added much more. Due to the Columbus Day storm on October 12, 1962, the Northwest was left with with tens of thousands of blown down trees that prompted Japan and other countries to salvage and have them shipped off to their own lumber mills. That was hugely beneficial to the port district, which became a regional hub for shipping this prized Northwest resource off to other countries. Indeed Japan, now heavily dependent on Northwest timber, engaged in bidding up the price of timber—which had a punishing impact on domestic mills that could not compete with Japan, and thus had to shut down their operations with severe consequences on local communities.

That's why in the late 1970s, for local officials, it was a panic moment trying to address these economic problems. At the time, the man who was the local economic ruler was Henry "Hank" Soike, general manager of the Grays Harbor Port District. Soike also had political influence both statewide and nationally. The port required large-scale improvements, which included dredging channels—an expensive process that demanded huge federal funding. He cozied up to Senator Magnuson, chair of the Senate Appropriations Committee, and Representative Julia Butler Hansen, chair of the House Appropriations Subcommittee, enjoying the red-carpet treatment when he visited Washington, DC, with his portfolio of funding needs. That only lasted until my election in 1974, when I defeated his preferred candidate in the state's primary election, state senator Bob Bailey. Yet Hank Soike still found ways to get what he wanted.

Hank Soike's next ambitious initiative was to diversify and expand the area's industrial base. He was prepared to tap into the Industrial Development Districts that enabled the port to use its authority to lease land to industrial and commercial companies. That would attract more business and manufacturing jobs to a county that was in desperate need. Grays Harbor County was about to convert what was a coveted estuary into an industrial park, which threatened shorebirds and other migrating birds and triggered a high alert among state and local preservationists.

Nor surprisingly, Helen Engle, who served on the board of directors of the National Audubon Society, and other environmental activists, showed up on my doorstep, as they were anxious to enlist my help to protect this prime refuge area. Yes, they made a compelling case, yet I was struck again with the consequences such actions would have on the local economy.

First and foremost was meeting with county and city officials, adjacent property owners affected by such designation, and, yes, Hank Soike and businessmen worried about lost opportunities. There were contentious issues leading to months of negotiations, primarily about compensation to the port district and to the city of Hoquiam, which owned about sixty acres of the refuge area. My response was, yes, you have my commitment to insure proper federal compensation for acquisition of lands for preservation purposes. On May 4, 1987, *The Olympian* newspaper posted this headline, "Bonker Pushes for Wildlife Refuge," noting that I had multiple meetings with local officials and property owners.

Obviously, to fulfill such a commitment would be a bigger challenge in the other Washington. I was in my last year as congressman (now candidate for US Senate), so leveraging a quick and favorable action on the House side seemed unlikely, but it would be even more challenging to secure a Republican senator as a sponsor. My bill would be assigned to the House Committee on Merchant Marine and Fisheries (which has jurisdiction over the National Wildlife Refuge designations). As a member, I was in a position to get more favorable action.

Senator Dan Evans would be the most suitable sponsor. Initially he was open to the idea, but we had differences at the outset, mostly over federal funding of acquiring property to preserve the refuge.

Months of negotiations led to a final agreement. On December 10, 1987, the two Seattle newspapers carried these headlines: from the *Seattle Times*, "Evans and Bonker Resolve Wildlife-Refuge Dispute," and from the *Seattle Post Intelligencer*, "Evans and Bonker Compromise on Bird Refuge." It was signed into law by President Ronald Reagan on August 22, 1988. The following year, the Bowerman Basin was officially designated as the Grays Harbor Wildlife Refuge. Again, a prime example of bipartisanship, working out differences to achieve a landmark accomplishment.

On April 22, 1989, after I left Congress, the National Audubon Society scheduled the Grays Harbor National Wildlife Appreciation Day Ceremony. Helen Engle, representing the board of directors, announced, "Few sites compare to Bowerman Basin for its importance to shorebird migrations and no one compares to former congressman Don Bonker in having made the difference in protecting this jewel on the Washington coast."

Ms. Engle concluded, "We will always think of this Refuge as an ongoing sustainable resource, as a well-deserved tribute to Don Bonker—it couldn't have happened without him." I appreciated this recognition, but the Republican senator, Dan Evans, deserved equal, if not more, praise. Definitely the Grays Harbor Wildlife Refuge would not have happened without him.

DON BONKER *was a Democratic member of the US House of Representatives from Washington. He passed away in 2023, several months after writing this essay.*

TWELVE

—ᴦᴦ—

A BIPARTISAN AGENDA FOR
DEFENDING FREE ENTERPRISE,
ASSURING HONEST GOVERNMENT,
AND FIGHTING CLIMATE CHANGE

RICHARD W. PAINTER

THE UNITED STATES HAS A bright future if we adhere to our founding principles of representative democracy. From the Declaration of Independence through passage of the Fifteenth Amendment and the Voting Rights Act of 1965, we have expanded the franchise so every American, not just the privileged few, has a voice in choosing our government. From the Boston Tea Party of 1773, when patriots tossed East India Company tea into Boston Harbor, up through the Progressive Era when Congress passed antitrust laws and banned corporate money in federal elections, and then with the McCain-Feingold Bipartisan Campaign Reform Act of 2002, Americans have resisted consolidation of corporate power as well as collusion of politicians with those who would stifle competition in commerce and politics.

There are, however, serious threats to our Republic. One is the relentless attack on voting rights by those who would return our country to the days of limited franchise based on race and social class. This chapter will not delve further into that very serious threat to representative democracy, but we ignore it at our peril. A second threat is the relentless effort of highly concentrated business interests to control the halls of Congress, the presidency, and even the Supreme Court. Today, the domineering forces in our political life include the titans of Wall Street, high tech, and the oil industry, among others. These are the modern-day renditions of the East India Company and its bought Parliament that Bostonians rebelled against in 1773, and the threat to our self-governance is in some ways much the same.

In this chapter I examine one public policy problem, perhaps our most serious problem—climate change—and how corporate money in politics is making it extraordinarily difficult to find solutions. I also urge a bipartisan solution: a pro-free-enterprise and pro-environment approach to growing our economy while protecting our planet.

Climate change is a problem that can be solved, not by government alone but by government taking swift action to correct market inefficiencies that reinforce monopoly power of fossil fuel companies at the expense of entrepreneurs working to produce and use clean energy. As I discuss here, if we remain true to our founding principles of representative democracy, we can solve climate change. If we revert to the days of corporate control of government, with Chevron and ConocoPhillips and other monopolies controlling the legislative process, federal legislation and rulemaking will fail. The choice is ours, but time is short and now is the moment to decide.

FREE ENTERPRISE CAN SOLVE CLIMATE CHANGE

A free market can solve problems such as climate change. This assumes that the market really works because people are charged the actual cost of producing and consuming the energy they use. If a substantial portion of that cost—here, the impact of CO_2 emissions on the planet—is excluded from the price people pay to produce and consume energy, we will produce and use more fossil fuel than we should and will not acquire technical know-how to produce the clean energy we need.

The externalities in the energy sector are enormous. Climate change destroys the economy, and investors' wealth, in addition to the planet. That's one reason so many institutional investors care about CO_2 emissions. Having profitable fossil fuel companies in a portfolio does an investor little good if environmental externalities destroy economic wealth overall and harm the value of other investments in a portfolio.[1] The entire point of a free-market economy is to grow the entire economy, not just one industry at the expense of all the rest.

Furthermore, countries that internalize the external costs of fossil fuels will move more quickly toward cleaner, more efficient fuels, giving those countries a competitive advantage over countries that do not. Clean energy production is a business that requires investment, technological know-how, and a market for its products; entrepreneurs who start early are more likely to do well. Indeed, one hundred years from now, the more economically advanced countries may be those that moved more quickly now to adapt to clean energy just as the first countries to introduce electricity in the late nineteenth century had a competitive advantage for decades to come.

There are two ways governments can internalize the external societal costs of fuels. One way is to impose taxes and/or regulatory restrictions on fuels that are inefficient because they impose high externalities, namely CO_2 emissions. The second approach is to give tax breaks, subsidies, and regulatory relief for production and consumption of fuels that have positive externalities because the positive benefits to the overall economy from clean energy production exceed the benefits to individual consumers who pay for it. A country that wants to be a leader in production and consumption of clean energy will focus on the second approach.

Unfortunately, the United States and many other countries around the world are doing just the opposite—they are subsidizing the fossil fuel industry. According to the International Monetary Fund, "Globally, fossil fuel subsidies were $5.9 trillion or 6.8 percent of GDP in 2020 and are expected to increase to 7.4 percent of GDP in 2025 as the share of fuel consumption in emerging markets (where price gaps are generally larger) continues to climb. Just 8 percent of the 2020 subsidy reflects undercharging for supply costs (explicit subsidies) and 92 percent for undercharging for environmental costs and foregone consumption taxes (implicit subsidies)."[2] These subsidies come in the form of both production subsidies and consumption subsidies.[3] In short, governments using taxpayer money are paying businesses and consumers to destroy the planet even though in a free market without subsidies they would probably make a very different choice.

Finally, government will not solve this problem alone, and likely will fail if energy policy relies on heavy layers of regulation and keeping clean energy production tightly controlled by government as a quasi-state-owned enterprise. Clean energy is ideally and most efficiently produced in a competitive market broadly supported by government tax and regulatory policy. Furthermore, when regulatory burdens stifle free enterprise, it is newer more innovative companies that probably will suffer the most, advantaging older more established energy companies that know how to work around government regulation to their competitive advantage. And those of course are most likely to be the companies that produce and use fossil fuels.

Monopoly power hates competition. For the fossil fuel industry, clean energy is competition. It's better, cleaner, and ultimately will be a lot cheaper than fossil fuels, assuming clean energy is allowed a fair chance to compete. But fossil fuel companies have a century-long head start going back to the days of the oil monopolies that Congress and Theodore Roosevelt waged war with during the Progressive Era. If we do not confront the problem of money in politics, the fossil fuel monopoly will prevail, although theirs would be a Pyrrhic victory. Will our representative democracy, our system of free enterprise, and our planet survive this challenge? The choice is ours.

1773 TO 2023: AMERICAN'S 250-YEAR REVOLUTION AGAINST CORRUPT GOVERNMENT, REINFORCED MONOPOLY, AND STIFLED ENTERPRISE

Corruption of government officials is an old problem.[4] Edmund Burke, as a member of Parliament denounced the corrupt influence on government of corporations, particularly the East India Company.[5] After the Tea Act in 1773 granted that company a monopoly on sale of tea in America, Tea Party patriots dumped the tea into Boston Harbor. Americans then and now are fed up with corporate money buying legislatures and making law.

Adam Smith also detested the way corrupt politicians supported inefficient companies that amassed monopoly power and political power at the same time.[6] Free enterprise and government sanctioned monopolies cannot coexist. Smith's *The Wealth of Nations*, published in 1776, may have fallen on deaf ears among the mercantilists in Parliament, but two principles—free enterprise and representative democracy—were soon to become the guiding spirit of the new Republic across the Atlantic.

But concentrated wealth does not go quietly. From the earliest days of the Republic, commercial interests have tried to corrupt our government, with mixed success, and Americans loyal to our founding principles have fought back.[7]

In 1907, Congress passed the Tillman Act,[8] which prohibits donations from corporate treasuries to federal political campaigns. *Repeat: More than a century ago, Congress banned corporate money in politics.* That is the law and it's never been repealed nor explicitly overturned by the Supreme Court. That law has just been avoided and evaded until today, a century later, the law is virtually meaningless.

Like manipulators who exploit loopholes to get around taxation and environmental regulation, campaign operatives and donors combine barely legal law avoidance with illegal law evasion—a practice known as *law avoision*. This term, introduced by London School of Economics professors in a 1979 book, *Tax Avoision*,[9] was popularized on the television show *The Simpsons*.[10] Avoision is all too common in many areas of the law, including campaign finance. Lawyers, for a fee, often lend a helping hand.[11]

So do the federal courts. The Supreme Court in *Citizens United v. Federal Election Commission* struck down a key provision of a law cosponsored by

Senator John McCain and signed into law by President George W. Bush. The Court ruled that unlimited expenditures from corporate treasuries on election-eering communications were constitutionally protected speech because corpo-rations are "people" like the rest of us. The Court has not yet struck down the Tillman Act prohibition on direct corporate contributions to campaigns, but corporate funded political action committees (PACs)and Super PACs presum-ably have First Amendment protection to say whatever they want.[12] The current state of the law is that, while some restrictions on direct contributions to cam-paigns and political parties are upheld,[13] unlimited spending by campaigns and by dark money organizations is constitutionally protected. As Justices Sandra Day O'Connor and John Paul Stevens famously wrote in *McConnell v. Federal Election Commission*, one of the few cases upholding campaign finance laws, "money, like water, will always find an outlet."[14] And so it does.

In early 2016, I authored a book explaining why political conservatives should support campaign finance reform.[15] Almost nobody—except a faction of the extremely wealthy and the politicians they own—likes the Supreme Court's decision in *Citizens United v. Federal Election Commission*.[16]

Many industries use money to tilt the playing field in their favor. The finan-cial services industry used its influence in Washington, DC, to buy deregu-lation during the Clinton[17] and Bush administrations, setting the stage for the economic calamity of 2008.[18] Convicted cryptocurrency fraudster Sam Bankman-Fried, with the help of his politically connected parents, bought influence in both political parties and even testified as an expert for Congress before he was indicted. In my own field of work, higher education, some uni-versity presidents are like corporate CEOs, making as much as $4 million a year plus deferred compensation.[19] They expand their influence by setting up academic centers named after their favorite presidential candidate or centers that shill for corporate donors, including the fossil fuel industry.[20]

FOSSIL FUEL INDUSTRY MONEY IN POLITICS

As this author discussed in recent testimony before the US Senate Budget Committee,[21] fossil fuel money in politics is a significant cause of our inability to address climate change. Unregulated corporate political spending advan-tages big corporations with concentrated market power in established indus-tries to the disadvantage of competitors in new industries more likely to grow the economy, and in the energy sector, produce cleaner more efficient fuels.

The Tillman Act banning corporate money from federal election campaigns was passed in 1907, at the same time Theodore Roosevelt's administration was doing battle with the Standard Oil Company. Standard Oil eventually was broken up under the Sherman Antitrust Act[22] after the Supreme Court ruled against Standard Oil in 1911.[23] Fossil fuel companies' monopoly power was a grave concern then, and it is now. The concern both then and now isn't just monopoly pricing but use of the political power that comes with corporate wealth to suffocate competition. The competition for Standard Oil in 1911 was other smaller oil companies; today the competition for big oil is clean energy. The battle lines are much the same, only this time the future of the planet hangs in the balance.

Today, the fossil fuel industry's political spending is massive. According to Open Secrets, the fossil fuel industry spent $124 million on lobbying in 2022.[24] In the 2022 election cycle alone many companies in the oil and gas industry spent millions of dollars each on political campaigns. A single company, Koch Industries, spent $27,317,934 in 2021–22. Next comes Occidental Petroleum at $8,052,913; Chevron Corp at $7,587,934; the American Petroleum Institute at $7,183,300; and Energy Transfer LP at $5,206,768, followed by Samson Energy at $4,314,555; Devon Energy at $3,908,127; ConocoPhillips at $3,605,546, and so on.[25] Almost all this political money is spent without the consent of shareholders, who find out about it belatedly if it becomes public.

In addition to greasing the skids of politics, many companies excel at window dressing or "greenwashing," spending a small portion of their profits on green energy initiatives and paying public relations firms to design "green" websites and other promotional materials. ConocoPhillips even appointed as one of its directors a law professor who directs Harvard Law School's environmental law center, and who now says she's on ConocoPhillips board to make "a positive difference,"[26] plus of course, the $350,000 annual board member compensation.

Fossil fuel companies also take advantage of the revolving door in and out of government, when the president appoints their former officers, directors, lobbyists, or lawyers to high-level posts in the Interior Department, Department of Energy, and Environmental Protection Agency (EPA). There they are allowed to participate in regulatory matters that affect their former employers' industry. Existing ethics rules for the most part only limit participation in matters in which a former employer is an identifiable party; for example, an oil drilling permit or a lease of federal land.[27] Their ethics rules do not prevent participation in industry-wide regulations that affect a former employer.

Ethics rules are even looser in the legislative branch where members of Congress are allowed to participate in congressional investigations, hearings, and lawmaking that affect companies in which they own stock or have a similar financial interest. Several bills have been introduced that would limit congressional stock trading and investments in individual companies, but so far none of those bills have passed.[28]

Academia is playing along too. According to a recent study, the fossil fuel industry has provided more than $675 million in funding to twenty-seven top research universities: "Many of the nation's most prominent universities, including Harvard, MIT, and George Washington, are awash with fossil fuel funding, and scientists are ringing the alarm about the effects this money has on climate research. A new study revealed that favorability toward natural gas in research is directly related to a university's funding sources. Just as campaign donations are used to buy votes against climate action in Congress, research funding can be leveraged as an attempt to buy results or influence research priorities that benefit the fossil fuel industry's bottom line."[29] Universities that receive this funding, of course, say that it does not influence their research and that some of that research advances clean energy. The funding source, however, is suspect, a problem complicated by the fact that many universities don't publicly disclose funding from fossil fuel companies or from other sources.

Law enforcement is not immune from the influence of the fossil fuel industry. Most state attorneys general are elected, and corporate money may determine if they win or lose. As law professor and prosecutor Eli Savit pointed out in 2017, the fossil fuel industry pours "unprecedented sums of money into AG races throughout the country. That spending has apparently paid off . . . this regulatory capture of many AGs seems likely to impede environmental regulation for years to come."[30]

This fossil fuel industry money drenches American politics in an era in which objective truth is under attack. Advances in science provide new information, and our perceptions of objective truth will change accordingly, but only a fool would deny there is such a thing as objective truth. People used to think the world was flat; now we know it's round. No rational person can argue that the perspective of someone who sees the earth as flat is just as valid as the perspective of someone who knows it's round. Decades ago, perhaps there was debate about whether we are experiencing climate change, but today science has shown that the earth is warming, and that human activity is a substantial contributing factor.

Finally, much of the world's fossil fuel reserves are in countries under the control of dictators, including Russia, Saudi Arabia, and Marxist Venezuela. To access those reserves, fossil fuel companies for decades have coddled foreign dictators and encouraged the US government to do the same. Corporate interests, including some Americans with ties to industry,[31] encouraged Germany and the EU to build the Nord Stream 2 pipeline from Russia to Germany to import massive quantities of Russian natural gas, all while greenwashed German politicians lectured the rest of the world on climate change. Saudi Arabia uses proceeds from its oil exports to buy weapons from the United States, including a $110 billion arms deal spearheaded by Jared Kushner, who coincidentally closed a $2 billion business deal with the Saudi sovereign wealth fund months after leaving office.[32] Before Venezuela's economy collapsed from corruption and mismanagement, Venezuelan oil money subsidized the communist dictatorship in Cuba. In sum, the dictators who control much of the world's fossil fuel supply are not on the side of democracy, or of the United States.

WE CAN WORK TOGETHER TO FIX OUR POLITICAL SYSTEM AND FIGHT CLIMATE CHANGE

Congress can do something about the environmental crisis and the political crisis before us by addressing both crises at the same time.

First and foremost, we need to fix our campaign finance system so corporate profits, particularly from gigantic but outdated and dangerous industries, don't own our federal and state governments. Ideally Congress and state legislatures will use a three-pronged approach to even the playing field in elections: (1) prohibit corporate money from influencing elections to the extent constitutionally permissible, while advocating for a change in the jurisprudence of a Supreme Court that has struck down far too many campaign finance reform laws; (2) enhance disclosure requirements for corporations, nonprofits, and other entities that use corporate money to influence elections and public policy; and (3) give tax rebates to individual small donors whose contributions to candidates of their choice can help balance out corporate money and reduce elected officials' dependence on special interests.[33]

Corporations in all industries need to be more transparent about how they are spending money in the political arena, particularly when we consider that the Tillman Act ban on corporate contributions to federal election campaigns is still in effect. If corporations get around the Tillman Act through indirect funding of electioneering communications, they at least should have to do so in the open. Congress should require public companies to disclose in detail to shareholders their expenditures on electioneering communications, PACs, and Super PACs, as well as lobbying. The law should also require corporations to obtain prior shareholder approval for electioneering expenditures or lobbying over a certain threshold.

The revolving door from the fossil fuel industry and other special interests in and out of government needs to be shut. Congress should pass legislation limiting high ranking executive branch officials from participating in regulatory matters that affect industries in which they have been employed within the past two years or longer.

Members of Congress also need to stop owning and trading stocks in individual companies while in office. One in four US senators has investments in the fossil fuel industry.[34] At least one hundred members of the House are invested in fossil fuels.[35] As this author has urged repeatedly in letters to House and Senate leadership and in op-eds, members of Congress need to get out of the business of trading individual stocks—any stocks—and invest in broadly diversified mutual funds like most other Americans. Stockjobbing members of Congress are not unbiased or effective members of Congress.

Congress needs to put a stop to fossil fuel subsidies in the United States and insist that other countries end fossil fuel subsidies or face steep tariffs. Free enterprise is about free competitive markets, not markets rigged by government in favor of inefficient producers of energy that costs society a lot more than its sticker price. State subsidies for fossil fuels are a destructive form of state control, whether the government handing out subsidies is run by the Communist Party of China or the two major political parties in the United States.

Congress also should clarify that the Securities and Exchange Commission is authorized to proceed with rulemaking to require reporting companies to disclose material information about their carbon footprint—the impact of their business operations on CO_2 emissions.[36] Such disclosure requirements should be reasonable and not unduly burdensome, but the information is material to investors[37] and should be disclosed.

Moving on to laws that will help the clean energy competitors of big oil, Congress should provide generous tax breaks and regulatory relief for businesses that produce clean energy, including wind, solar, geothermal, and safe nuclear reactors. Just as the negative externalities from fossil fuel production are high, the positive externalities from clean energy are also high. Tax and regulatory policies should reflect that. Climate change is a problem the private sector can solve, but government taxation and regulation too often stand in the way. Congress must act now to encourage free enterprise in clean energy production, a sector of our economy that is critical for the survival of our planet.

CONCLUSION

Fighting climate change should be a bipartisan endeavor even if the parties disagree on how to accomplish that objective. For decades, from Teddy Roosevelt's protection of vast areas of federal land up through the creation of the

EPA, Republicans have historically championed environmental conservation. Democratic administrations have been responsible for some advances as well, for example, President Obama and President Biden bringing the United States into the Paris Accords on climate change.

Extremists on either side may seek to polarize the issue—far right anti-government nihilists see all environmental regulation as a manifestation of a pernicious "deep state," while extreme leftists mindlessly attack the capitalist system even though private industry is essential to successful implementation of scientific advances in clean energy. More sensible leaders in the two parties, however, should value the contributions of both government and private industry while recognizing that irresponsible use of power in either the public or private sector can make problems a lot worse. The two parties may differ in their assessment of the best mix between regulation and energy conservation on the one hand and private investment and energy production on the other, but we need both. After the usual partisan negotiation, the two political parties need to work together to solve the problem. Hopefully that is the direction of our future political engagement on climate change.

Of course, we can't stop candidates and political parties, in the context of elections, from accusing each other of being the sole source of the problem, with the usual hyperbole and loose relationship with the truth that goes along with campaign rhetoric and political advertising. But at some point, our government can't just be about winning elections. Governing itself is essential. And to govern, our elected leaders of both political parties must work together, and work with leaders in the private sector, to get the job done.

Political corruption and climate change have everything to do with each other. Governments bought by special interests will favor older established and concentrated industries over economic actors who invent new ways of producing things. In no sector is this more obvious than in energy. It is new economic actors—the clean energy sector—that could make the United States the world leader in energy production and help save our planet at the same time.

For too long—well over a century—oil companies and other fossil fuel conglomerates have dominated our economy and our politics. Profits earned from market power feed back into political power which is used to reinforce market power. The clean energy sector must break this cycle to compete on an equal playing field. Every step we take to free our government from the influence of concentrated corporate wealth will be a step in the right direction.

We will never solve climate change through government ownership or control of the clean energy sector; indeed, prior experiments with state-owned industry and socialism suggest that too much government control could kill clean energy, leaving fossil fuel companies even more powerful. Government can, however, even the playing field, assuring that what we pay for energy reflects its true cost, not just the cost to the producer and middleman seller. Conversely, government, through tax breaks and regulatory relief, can support innovative ways to produce, transmit, and consume clean energy.

Solving climate change will not stifle growth, rather, it will expand the economy, create jobs for Americans, and generate profits for new businesses. These are practical problems, and to solve them we must work together. Politics too often divides us, and dark money driving electioneering communications spent on attack ads divides us further. Restoring civility to discussions of public policy is critical to solving problems as difficult as climate change, and that will require us to fix a campaign finance system that spends billions in special interest money convincing Americans to distrust each other.

Now is the time for Americans to come together to support clean energy. Our partner in this endeavor should be a government that truly represents us, the people of the United States, not the special interests that for so long have been trying to take our government away from us.

NOTES

The text of this chapter is drawn in substantial part from written testimony submitted to the United States Senate Banking Committee on June 21, 2023. See Testimony of Richard W. Painter before the United States Senate, Committee on the Budget, Hearing "Democracy Distorted: Unraveling the Consequences of Fossil Fuel Dark Money in Politics," June 21, 2023, https://www.budget.senate.gov/imo/media/doc/Mr.%20Richard%20Painter%20-%20Testimony%20-%20Senate%20Budget%20Committee1.pdf.

1. "Due to the embrace of modern portfolio theory, most of the stock market is controlled by institutional investors holding broadly diversified economy-mirroring portfolios . . . [D]iversified investors should rationally be motivated to internalize intra-portfolio negative externalities." Madison Condon, "Externalities and the Common Owner," *Washington Law Review* 95, no. 1 (2020): 1. https://digitalcommons.law.uw.edu/wlr/vol95/iss1/4.

2. See International Monetary Fund, "Climate Change: Fossil Fuel Subsidies" (2022), https://www.imf.org/en/Topics/climate-change/energy-subsidies.

3. See Johannes Urpelainen and Elisha George, "Reforming Global Fossil Fuel Subsidies: How the United States Can Restart International Cooperation," Brookings Institution, July 14, 2021, https://www.brookings.edu/articles/reforming

-global-fossil-fuel-subsidies-how-the-united-states-can-restart-international
-cooperation/.

4. The late Judge John T. Noonan recorded the history of bribery over two thousand years in his seminal book *Bribes*, published shortly after President Reagan appointed him to the Ninth Circuit Court of Appeals. John T. Noonan, Jr., *Bribes: The Intellectual History of a Moral Idea* (Berkeley: University of California Press, 1986).

5. Edmund Burke, "Mr. Burke's Speech, On the 1st December 1783: Upon the Question for the Speaker's Leaving the Chair, in Order for the House to Resolve Itself into a Committee on Mr. Fox's East India Bill" (describing the East India Company's abuse of global monopoly powers bestowed on it by Parliament), https://quod.lib.umich.edu/e/ecco/004807298.0001.000/1:2?rgn=div1;view=fulltext.

6. Adam Smith, *Wealth of Nations* (1776).

7. See Richard W. Painter, "Ethics and Corruption in Business and Government: Lessons from the South Sea Bubble and the Bank of the United States" (Fulton Lectures 2006, University of Chicago Law School), https://chicagounbound.uchicago.edu/cgi/viewcontent.cgi?article=1003&context=fulton_lectures.

8. The Tillman Act of 1907 (34 Stat. 864).

9. Arthur Seldon, ed., *Tax Avoision: The Economic, Legal, and Moral Inter-Relationships Between Avoidance and Evasion* (London: Institute of Economic Affairs, 1979).

10. See *The Simpsons*, Season 7, episode 15, "Bart the Fink." Directed by Jim Reardon, aired February 11, 1996, on Fox, https://www.youtube.com/watch?v=wpEaFmK3lrY (Crusty the Clown arrested for tax avoision).

11. I have written about this problem for close to thirty years. See Richard W. Painter, "The Moral Interdependence of Corporate Lawyers and Their Clients," *Southern California Law Review* 67 (1994): 507–584.

12. See Lieu et al. v. FEC, No. 19–5072, (D.C. Cir., 2019), Order (dismissing suit brought against the FEC by Rep. Ted Lieu, Rep. Walter Jones, Senator Jeff Merkley, State Senator John Howe, Zephyr Teachout, and Michael Wager asking the Circuit Court to overturn its decision in SpeechNow.org v. FEC, 599 F.3d 686 (D.C. Cir. 2010) (en banc), *cert. denied*, 562 U.S. 1003 (2010) (interpreting the *Citizens United* holding to allow unlimited spending on Super PACs).

13. See Buckley v. Valeo, 424 U.S. 1 (1976) (holding that dollar limitations on contributions by individuals to campaigns do not violate the First Amendment but that limitations on spending by political campaigns do violate the first amendment); McConnell v. Federal Election Commission, 540 U.S. 93 (2003) (upholding limits on soft money contributions used to register voters and increase attendance at the polls); McCutcheon v. FEC, 572 U.S. 185 (2014) (striking down aggregate limits on donor contributions to multiple candidates).

14. McConnell v. Federal Election Commission, 540 U.S. 93 (2003).

15. See Richard W. Painter, *Taxation Only with Representation: The Conservative Conscience and Campaign Finance Reform* (Auburn, AL: Take Back Our Republic, 2016); Richard W. Painter, "The Conservative Case for Campaign Finance Reform," *New York Times*, February 3, 2016, https://www.nytimes.com/2016/02/03/opinion/the-conservative-case-forcampaign-finance-reform.html.

16. Citizens United v. FEC, 558 U.S. 310 (2010). See Peter Overby, "Presidential Candidates Pledge to Undo 'Citizens United.' But Can They?," NPR, February 14, 2016. https://www.npr.org/2016/02/14/466668949/presidential-candidates-pledge-to-undo-citizens-united-but-can-they.

17. See Richard W. Painter, "Standing Up to Wall Street (and Congress)," review of *Take on the Street*, by Arthur Levitt, *Michigan Law Review* 101, no. 6 (2003): 1512 (reviewing and discussing the role of financial services industry campaign contributions and lobbying in undermining the regulatory role of the SEC).

18. See Claire A. Hill and Richard W. Painter, *Better Bankers, Better Banks: Promoting Good Business Through Contractual Commitment* (Chicago: University of Chicago Press, 2015) (discussing the causes of the 2008 financial collapse and the need for personal accountability of senior bank executives).

19. See Susan Snyder, "Former Penn President Amy Gutmann Earned Nearly $23 Million in 2021, but Most of It Was Accrued over Her 18 Years as President," *Philadelphia Inquirer*, June 17, 2023, https://www.inquirer.com/news/amy-gutmann-university-of-pennsylvania-president-salary-20230617.html.

20. See Jack Stripling and Nell Gluckman, "To Court a Secretive Donor, Law Deans at George Mason Blasted Climate Scientists and Their Own Accreditor," *Chronicle of Higher Education*, December 18, 2019, https://www.chronicle.com/article/to-court-a-secretive-donor-law-deans-at-george-mason-blasted-climate-scientists-and-their-own-accreditor/.

21. See Testimony of Richard W. Painter before the US Senate, Committee on the Budget, June 21, 2023, *supra*, note 1.

22. The Sherman Act, codified in 15 U.S.C. §§ 1–38, was amended by the Clayton Antitrust Act in 1914.

23. Standard Oil Company of New Jersey v. United States, 221 US 1 (1911).

24. Inci Sayki and Jimmy Cloutier, "Oil and Gas Industry Spent $124.4 Million on Federal Lobbying amid Record Profits in 2022," Open Secrets, February 22, 2023, https://www.opensecrets.org/news/2023/02/oil-and-gas-industry-spent-124-4-million-on-federal-lobbying-amid-record-profits-in-2022/.

25. See "Summary: Energy and Natural Resources (Top Contributors, 2021–22)," Open Secrets, https://www.opensecrets.org/industries/indus.php?ind=e01.

26. Steven Mufson, "Fallout from Willow Oil Project Lands Hard on Harvard Climate Expert," *Washington Post*, April 22, 2023, https://www.washingtonpost.com/climate-environment/2023/04/22/willow-oil-alaska-conocophillips-harvard/.

27. See 5 C.F.R. 2635.502 (Office of Government Ethics impartiality rule, requiring prior authorization for an executive branch employee to participate in a particular party matter in which a former employer within the past year is a party or represents a party). Presidents Obama, Trump, and Biden each issued executive orders on ethics that lengthened this recusal period to two years or longer for appointees of the president. These ethics rules, however, do little to prevent federal officials from participating in regulatory matters that affect their previous employers' industry. The only legal requirement is that they divest their financial interest in the industry and sever employment with the former employer during their term in office. See 18 U.S.C. Section 208 (financial conflicts of interest for executive branch employees).

28. In several op-eds and letters to congressional leadership, I have urged passage of a law prohibiting stock trading by members of Congress. See, e.g., Richard W. Painter, "Why Members of Congress Should Not Trade Stocks," Bloomberg Law, January 25, 2022, https://news.bloomberglaw.com/white-collar-and -criminal-law/why-members-of-congress-should-not-trade-stocks; Donna Nagy and Richard W. Painter, "It's Time for Senators, House Members to Divest Stocks in Individual Publicly Traded Companies," Bloomberg Law, January 6, 2021, https://news.bloomberglaw.com/white-collar-and-criminal-law/its-time-for -senators-house-members-to-divest-stocks-in-individual-publicly-traded -companies.

29. Bella Kumar, "Accountable Allies: The Undue Influence of Fossil Fuel Money in Academia," Data for Progress, March 1, 2023, https://www .filesforprogress.org/memos/accountable-allies-fossil-fuels.pdf. This data was assembled by a progressive research group, with which many Americans may disagree on substantive political issues, but the data appears to be accurate, and in any event the influence of the fossil fuel industry in academia is common knowledge.

30. Eli Savit, "The New Front in the Clean Air Wars: Fossil-Fuel Influence Over State Attorneys General—And How It Might Be Checked," *Michigan Law Review* 115, no. 6 (2017): 839. Available at https://repository.law.umich.edu/mlr /vol115/iss6/5.

31. Americans with ties to German industry and fossil fuels promoted the Nord Stream 2 pipeline up until the eve of the Russian invasion of Ukraine. Daniel Benjamin, president of the American Academy in Berlin, which relies heavily on corporate donations, harshly criticized the Biden administration in March 2021 for not supporting the Nord Stream 2 pipeline. See Daniel Benjamin, "How One European Pipeline Is Derailing Biden's 'America Is Back' Promise," *Politico*, March 21, 2021, https://www.politico.com/news/magazine/2021/03/18/how-one-european -pipeline-is-derailing-bidens-america-is-back-promise-476901.

32. See David D. Kirkpatrick and Kate Kelly, "Before Giving Billions to Jared Kushner, Saudi Investment Fund Had Big Doubts," *New York Times*, April 10, 2022,

https://www.nytimes.com/2022/04/10/us/jared-kushner-saudi-investment-fund
.html. A panel that screens investments for the Saudi sovereign wealth fund had
serious doubts about the transaction with Kushner but "days later the full board of
the $620 billion Public Investment Fund—led by Crown Prince Mohammed bin
Salman, Saudi Arabia's de facto ruler and a beneficiary of Mr. Kushner's support
when he worked as a White House adviser—overruled the panel."

33. See Painter, *Taxation Only with Representation, supra,* note 16 (discussing
these three approaches to democratizing campaign finance).

34. "One in Four US Senators Still Hold Fossil Fuel Investments Even as
World Burns," Common Dreams, November 5, 2021, https://www.commondreams
.org/news/2021/11/05/one-four-us-senators-still-hold-fossil-fuel-investments
-even-world-burns.

35. David Moore, "At Least 100 House Members Are Invested in Fossil Fuels," Readsludge.com, December 29, 2021, https://readsludge.com/2021/12/29
/at-least-100-house-members-are-invested-in-fossil-fuels/.

36. See "The Enhancement and Standardization of Climate-Related Disclo-
sures for Investors," 87 FR 21334 (April 11, 2022) (proposing for public comment
amendments to rules under the Securities Act of 1933 and Securities Exchange Act
of 1934 that would require registrants to provide certain climate-related information
in their registration statements and annual reports). https://www.federalregister
.gov/documents/2022/04/11/2022-06342/the-enhancement-and-standardization
-of-climate-related-disclosures-for-investors.

37. See Condon, *supra,* note 2, discussing the impact of climate change on
portfolio values.

RICHARD W. PAINTER *is the S. Walter Richey Professor of Corporate Law at the University of Minnesota Law School. He served as chief ethics lawyer for President George W.
Bush.*

AFTERWORD

Bipartisanship Is Essential to Democracy

JILL LONG THOMPSON

WHY BIPARTISANSHIP IS NECESSARY

Great minds think alike.

That is a statement we often hear when people agree with one another. If it were a true statement, living in a democracy would be much easier because we would not have to spend time and energy dealing with all the disagreements that are part of a democratic decision-making process. We could simply elect one person with a great mind to make all our policy decisions. That brilliant person would know what is in the best interest of the country, what actually works to address the challenges we face, and how best to execute and enforce public law.

Research findings tell us, however, that great minds do not all think alike. Not only do we have varying experiences and knowledge that shape our beliefs and our understanding of the world, we also have varying ways of processing information. When we work with those who hold opinions different from our own, we often find that the differences can help us better understand the complexity of our challenges. And group decision-making can lead us to better outcomes.

We know from research that diversity improves performance, including the quality of decision-making. In a 2015 McKinsey Report on 366 companies, it was found that "those in the top quartile for ethnic and racial diversity in management were 35% more likely to have financial returns above the industry mean, and those in the top quartile for gender diversity were 15% more likely to have returns above the industry mean." Bringing people together and incorporating their input make us stronger.

Great minds do not all think alike.

Democracy is a form of government that recognizes we all have something to contribute to the governing process, as well as a right to participate in the process. In democracy, the government is "by the people," not "by the person," and none of us should expect to have the power of a dictator or an autocrat. We all have the right for our voices to be heard and incorporated into policy making and execution, and we all must recognize that compromise is essential to democracy. It is a shared experience and responsibility, and it is undemocratic to insist that "my way is the right way and no other way will do."

None of us gets our own individual representative, senator, or president. We share public officials with the rest of the population, and none of us should expect or demand that an elected official has political beliefs perfectly aligned with our own individual beliefs. Reasonableness, inclusivity, and respect for others are defining components of successful democratic governance.

Given that we know diversity can improve decision-making, a fairly elected legislative body that reflects the diversity of the population is not only essential to a fair democratic process, it is also essential to better policy making.

If we want our democracy to survive and thrive, then we must accept and even embrace the value of compromise. We must recognize that people who come from different backgrounds and experiences have different perspectives, and their perspectives have value. Disagreement, discussion, and debate can be very helpful to the democratic process because they can help us look more broadly and deeply as we seek solutions for addressing our challenges.

We must never confuse disagreement and debate with stubborn antagonism, however. A mulish unwillingness to compromise on matters of public policy, in most circumstances, is not patriotic. While one should never yield in ways that violate or sacrifice democratic principles encompassed in our Constitution, government by the people demands collaboration, cooperation, and compromise. In democracy "we are all in this together," and that means we must be willing to give and take in the best interests of all of us, in the best interests of our country.

As a Democrat who was privileged to serve three terms in the US House of Representatives, representing one of the most Republican districts in the country, I will always value bipartisanship. In the congressional district I represented, a candidate could not get elected without Republican support. I felt very honored to have bipartisan support and I thought it was good for our democracy that Democrats and Republicans were in agreement.

But even more, my life experiences have taught me that inclusivity leads to better decisions and outcomes. Our democracy is stronger when we collaborate, cooperate, and compromise. Respecting the rights of others and valuing the input of those with whom we disagree is essential to being a patriotic American, as well as to democracy's success. It is not patriotic to believe, "It must be my way or the highway."

It was at age six that I first began to understand how working together makes the democratic process function better. My dad was a Democratic precinct committeeman and my mother was a volunteer with the Democratic Party. When I would arrive home from school in the late afternoon, they would present me with two options: I could go to the barn and help Dad milk our cows or I could accompany Mom as she traveled throughout our rural precinct to register voters.

For me the choice was easy. It was fun to meet neighbors and listen to the conversations between them and my mother. Mom's engaging personality and sense of humor would almost always bring smiles to their faces. Because she was a volunteer with the Democratic Party, she would only register voters who identified as Democrats, but she was universally respectful, friendly, and polite to everyone we met. And regardless of an individual's political identification, she was always happy to provide information on how and where one could register to vote.

My parents were respectful toward all our neighbors and they taught us that everyone has a contribution to make to the community and our country. Dad was a US Army veteran who had served in the Philippines during World War II, and he fully believed that one's patriotism and loyalty are not determined by political affiliation. And no one person, regardless of how informed or experienced that person is, has all the answers.

I personally believe it is impossible to be an effective leader without the input of those with whom we disagree. Growing up in a rural community in the 1950s and 1960s, I had the opportunity to get to know families of varying income and education levels, as well as varying political beliefs. As an example, our family doctor lived on a farm just a few miles from our farm and he was very respectful of my grandparents whose formal education ended with their eighth-grade graduation. And he always seemed genuinely interested in talking with them about the latest approaches to crop and livestock production. There was a real sense of community, and neighbors helped their neighbors, regardless of political beliefs.

Democracy, by definition, exists only to the extent that the citizenry can work together to adopt, execute, and enforce laws. In democracy, political power is vested in the people. The first democratic government was formed in Athens, Greece. The word *democracy* comes from the Greek words *demos,* meaning the people, and *kratos*, meaning power. We must always remember that democracy means "power of the people," not power of the person.

British philosopher John Stuart Mill argued that giving political power to the masses requires those in decision-making or leadership positions to consider the varied interests of all, which leads to more balanced policy making. Anything less is not democratic. I also believe it is unpatriotic for those in leadership positions not to give serious consideration to varied interests.

I am personally concerned about how politically divided we have become in the United States, and I believe we all share the responsibility of making democracy work. It is our patriotic duty to participate in finding solutions to our challenges, which means we all have a role to play in reducing polarization.

There is no one cause of the divisiveness, but we can identify factors that likely contribute to it.

Navigating life is much more complex than when I was growing up. Population growth, globalization, and advances in technology have created changes in our environment that can be both uncomfortable and challenging for us. In 1972, when I cast my first vote in a presidential election, the total population of the United States was about 209 million people and today it is about 331 million people. During the same time period, we have seen significant growth in international business relationships. According to the World Bank, the total value of world merchandise exports (priced in current US dollars) in 1960 was $123 billion and had grown to more than $25 trillion by 2022.

Even positive changes can take us out of our comfort zone. We are also a more diverse population in the United States than in earlier times. And while diversity can lead to better decision-making and outcomes, research shows that increased ethnic and racial diversity can result in an initial loss of trust in our communities. But over time with sustained contact, racially diverse populations develop positive feelings and relationships toward one another.

A related challenge we face is that people have been "sorting themselves" into communities that share the same or similar beliefs. Red states are becoming redder and blue states are becoming bluer, and that creates a situation in which it becomes less likely that there will be opportunities for those who disagree to interact and get to know each other.

We humans have much more in common with one another than we realize. We want to live our lives to our full potential; we want to be able to provide for ourselves and our families; we want the freedoms guaranteed in our Constitution; and we want others to respect us and our right to make our own choices. We also want our country to continue to be a model of democracy and opportunity.

There is much more that unites us than divides us, and we must all do our best to work together and address those issues that challenge us as individuals, as communities, and as a nation.

While we know there is not just one single cause of polarization, we can identify variables that make it less likely for people to come together, collaborate, and find workable and balanced solutions to the problems we face.

I believe gerrymandering of congressional districts contributes to the polarization of the political process and our nation. While the research findings to date have not been conclusive, it seems likely that a congressional district whose voting population skews heavily to the political right or to the left would be more likely to elect a representative whose leanings are also skewed to the right or left. Conversely, it seems reasonable that a district whose voting population is more politically balanced would prefer a more moderate representative.

Many congressional districts are so politically skewed that in most of their congressional elections, it is the primary and not the general election that determines who will represent the district. In such circumstances there is not much incentive for collaboration, cooperation, or compromise.

I also believe that social media platforms are contributing to political polarization. In a study on the dissemination of truth and lies through social media, it was found that lies spread more quickly and broadly than truth. Specifically, researchers at the Massachusetts Institute of Technology used a data set to track the speed and breadth of dissemination of both factual and false information through X (formerly known as Twitter). They found that "falsehood diffused significantly farther, faster, deeper, and more broadly than the truth in all categories of information, and the effects were more pronounced for false political news" than for false news about other topics.

It is not clear why people are more likely to share falsehoods than facts. It may be that fabrications tend to be more unique and interesting than truths. But spreading false information can lead to further polarization and the undermining of our democracy.

Independent journalism is critical to the democratic process, and legitimate journalists adhere to a strong code of ethics with a commitment to accuracy, fairness, and integrity. Spreading falsehoods not only undermines good policy making, it also can contribute to polarization that more broadly undermines our democracy and our country.

Money in politics contributes to polarization. Research findings show that higher individual political contributions lead to more polarized state legislatures. Additionally, it has been found that super PACs in general support more polarized and polarizing candidates.

Clearly, there are a number of factors that contribute to political divisiveness. And while we do not have all the answers for resolving the challenges that polarization creates for democracy, we do know the underlying principles of a democratic process. Quite simply, if the process violates democratic principles, then we are undermining our democracy. In other words, in democracy, the process is as important as the outcome.

And it is important to not expect every compromise to lead to better public policy. There will be times when a compromise is reached because the overall result is better than doing nothing. It is very important to honestly evaluate the impact of not compromising and not addressing a problem versus supporting an imperfect compromise that is better than not addressing the problem at all.

Our Founding Fathers understood the important role that individuals, with their independent thinking, play in the democratic process. The First Amendment to the Constitution reflects the value America places on the right to hold one's own beliefs and speak one's own mind.

I believe that American history teaches us that working together in a bipartisan way has been essential to our becoming a political and economic world leader. And I also believe that collaboration, cooperation, and compromise are not possible without respect for one another.

BIPARTISAN SUCCESSES

Our national history is filled with successes built on bipartisanship and cooperation.

The Connecticut Compromise—I would argue that bipartisanship is in our country's DNA because it began at the Constitutional Convention. It was the Connecticut Compromise in 1787, now known as the Great Compromise, that created the structure of the United States Congress.

While the states were generally in agreement that the legislature should consist of two bodies, there was strong disagreement on the number of representatives for each state. There appeared to be no way to resolve the disagreement until the Convention delegates voted to establish a "compromise committee" to develop a compromise plan. As we all know, the plan included a bicameral legislature with the two bodies having different numbers: the US Senate with equal representation by state, and the US House with representation based on population count.

Equal representation in the Senate and proportional representation in the House reassured our Founders and early citizens that states' rights would be protected from imbalance of power in the Congress. The structure provides protection against the federal government becoming too powerful, while also ensuring that regardless of the population of the state in which one resides, the representation in Congress will have balance.

This structure ensures separation of powers, federalism, and individual rights. It also supports a process that, in general, requires thoughtful study of the issues before legislation is passed and signed into law. Because of a bipartisan effort, we have been able to build a great democracy and to develop into a principled world leader.

Senator Vandenberg's Foreign Policy—Senator Arthur Vandenberg of Michigan was known as an isolationist until early 1945 when he delivered a speech announcing he had become convinced that internationalism was in the best interest of the United States and the world. Technological advances of the twentieth century included greater geographic mobility that had changed individual countries, as well as the world. While increased mobility can provide new opportunities, it can also increase the potential for foreign nations to undermine and threaten the autonomy and security of other countries.

To not engage internationally would lessen a country's potential for shaping the international geopolitical climate, and that could severely undercut national security.

Two years after delivering the speech in the Senate chamber, Vandenberg became the chair of the Senate Foreign Relations Committee. He was a Republican who made the commitment to work in a bipartisan way and he stated we must stop "partisan politics at the water's edge." He followed those words with actions that included working with President Truman to build bipartisan support for the Truman Doctrine, the Marshall Plan, and NATO. His leadership in building bipartisan support for international engagement was instrumental in building US influence and democratic values around the world.

Civil Rights Act of 1964—In the US Senate, a bipartisan team led by Majority Whip Hubert Humphrey and Minority Whip Thomas Kuchel was created to develop a strategy for passing the Civil Rights Act of 1964. Democrats held the majority, and an important component of the strategy was a plan to stop a well-organized filibuster that was led by an opposing faction in the party.

Senator Everett Dirksen, a Republican from Illinois, was determined to carry forward the legacy of Abraham Lincoln. He worked diligently to develop numerous amendments for consideration, with the goal of using the legislative process to develop a civil rights bill that would gain the support needed to be passed and signed into law. The bill was debated on the floor of the US Senate for sixty days and was ultimately passed on June 19. The US House of Representatives voted to pass it on July 2, and President Lyndon Johnson signed the bill into law that evening.

This bipartisan effort protects voting rights and bans discrimination in public facilities, and it established equal employment opportunity as Federal law. We are a stronger and better nation because of the Civil Rights Act of 1964.

Title IX—"No person in the United States shall, on the basis of sex, be excluded from participation in, be denied the benefits of, or be subjected to discrimination under any education program or activity receiving Federal financial assistance." Inspired by his wife Marvella, Senator Birch Bayh of Indiana wrote these words and created Title IX of the Education Amendments of 1972. The senator and his work generated bipartisan support and the legislation was signed into law by President Richard Nixon.

I was an undergraduate student at the time the law was adopted, and even today I find myself reminded of how much we have changed for the better as a result of Title IX. By opening doors for girls and women to participate in varsity athletics, we have created opportunities for everyone to learn how to compete and to be accepted doing so. And that has opened minds on the myriad roles everyone can play, regardless of one's gender.

In 1970 when I graduated from high school and began my studies in college, I chose physical education for my major. As a competitive baton twirler, I thought it would be interesting to own and operate baton twirling and cheerleading camps located across the country. To run them successfully, I also thought it would be good to enroll in some business courses—accounting, finance, marketing, management—to gain knowledge in how to profitably operate the camps.

It quickly became clear to me that I was not particularly good at any sport, other than baton twirling, but I performed well in business courses. I changed my major to business and ultimately earned a BS in business, an MBA, and PhD in business. At the time, we women were very much in the minority in both undergraduate and graduate business programs. In the last half century that has changed and the enrollments are more gender-balanced.

I believe Title IX was instrumental in making that change possible, and we are better off as a nation and a world because of those changes. As stated earlier, companies that have gender diversity in their leadership are more likely to have profitability above the mean for their respective industries. When we are inclusive and diverse, our decision-making improves. Bipartisan support for Title IX of the Education Amendments of 1972 has allowed us, as a society, to perform at a higher level.

Americans with Disabilities Act—President George H. W. Bush and Senator Tom Harkin worked in a bipartisan way to pass the Americans with Disabilities Act, legislation that was long overdue. It officially became law in 1990, and is legislation that has been widely recognized as the most comprehensive civil rights legislation since the Civil Rights Act of 1964.

Today, some might wonder why it took so long to statutorily protect these rights. But at the time, there was strong opposition by some powerful forces, including the National Federation of Independent Business. President Bush and Senator Harkin, as well as many others, understood that disabilities do not stop people from making all kinds of contributions that strengthen our nation and world. Adopting this legislation was a demonstration of respect for millions of individuals and the contributions they make to a stronger America. Even more significantly, we are an economically and socially stronger nation today because of the value added by individuals whose talents are being utilized.

Personal Responsibility and Work Opportunity Reconciliation Act—The process of adopting a welfare reform bill was messy. President Bill Clinton had made reform of our welfare system a major issue in his campaign for the White House in 1992, but after being elected, he faced strong pushback from many Democrats in Congress. He vetoed two welfare reform bills before signing the Personal Responsibility and Work Opportunity Reconciliation Act in August 1996.

The reform was not perfect. Many challenges remained and new challenges have arisen. The legislation placed a focus on work requirements for those participating in the various programs. Prior to the adoption of the bill, the main goal had been on distribution of money. After the changes were adopted, states began to help families find work. A shortcoming has been an inability of some mothers to find and keep jobs. Additionally, with the growth in income disparity, many working parents do not earn enough to support themselves and their families.

The bipartisan effort led to more money for child care and an expansion of Medicaid coverage for children.

While there have been both improvements and shortcomings, adoption of the bill demonstrated it is possible to build bipartisan support and begin to address serious socioeconomic challenges.

WE ARE BETTER WORKING TOGETHER

Strong, effective leadership is essential to democracy. It is not easy, nor is it a random occurrence. The challenges we face today and the challenges we will face tomorrow can only be overcome if we respect our fellow Americans and recognize they have something of value to offer as well as a right to participate in the democratic process.

We must accept democracy as a shared responsibility in which we all commit ourselves to collaboration, cooperation, and compromise.

It is also important for us to recognize that even with collaboration and mutual respect, we will not always adopt the best policy. After all, we are a population of humans, and therefore, we are not perfect. But in the long run, if we work together and include the input of everyone, we will make better decisions.

One of America's great leaders, the late Honorable John Lewis said, "We all need to do our part, to push and pull together, to make a difference in our society. Democracy is not a state; it is an act. We must all stay in the continuing struggle to create a Beloved Community, a nation and a world society at peace with itself."

Having spent much of my life on a farm, I know what has to be done when a piece of equipment becomes stuck in the mud—we push and we pull until we are free of the mud.

To be a good leader, one must make every effort to stay clear of the mud. And we know it is easier to avoid the mud if we respect and seek the truth and if we are honest enough to admit that no one person or political party has all the answers. It is also easier to avoid the mud if we show genuine respect for others and we recognize their input is essential to finding and executing the best solutions for addressing our challenges. When we work in a bipartisan way, we push and pull together, and we do whatever is necessary to get us to our goal of solving a problem.

As the world becomes more complex, working together with mutual respect will become even more important to protecting our people, our democracy, and our world. No one person or political party can do it alone.

Bipartisanship is essential to our democracy.

JILL LONG THOMPSON *is a former Democratic member of the US House of Representatives, former Board Chair and CEO of the Farm Credit Administration, and a former Under Secretary for Rural Development at the US Department of Agriculture.*

For Indiana University Press

Anna Francis, Assistant Acquisitions Editor
Anna Garnai, Editorial Assistant
Gary Dunham, Acquisitions Editor and Director
Brenna Hosman, Production Coordinator
Katie Huggins, Production Manager
Darja Malcolm-Clarke, Project Manager/Editor
Dan Pyle, Online Publishing Manager
Michael Regoli, Director of Publishing Operations
Stephen Williams, Assistant Director of Marketing
Jennifer Witzke, Senior Artist and Book Designer